THE NATIONAL INSTITUTE OF
ECONOMIC AND SOCIAL RESEARCH

Occasional Papers

XVIII

THE COST OF THE NATIONAL HEALTH SERVICE IN ENGLAND AND WALES

The National Institute of Economic and Social Research is an independent, non-profit-making body founded in 1938. It has as its aim the promotion of realistic research, particularly in the field of economics. It conducts research by its own research staff and in co-operation with the Universities and other academic bodies. The results of the work done under the Institute's auspices are published in several series, and a list of its publications up to the present time will be found at the end of this book.

THE COST OF THE NATIONAL HEALTH SERVICE

IN ENGLAND AND WALES

BY

BRIAN ABEL-SMITH

AND

RICHARD M. TITMUSS

CAMBRIDGE
AT THE UNIVERSITY PRESS
1956

CAMBRIDGE
UNIVERSITY PRESS

University Printing House, Cambridge CB2 8BS, United Kingdom

Cambridge University Press is part of the University of Cambridge.

It furthers the University's mission by disseminating knowledge in the pursuit of education, learning and research at the highest international levels of excellence.

www.cambridge.org
Information on this title: www.cambridge.org/9781316606889

First published 1956
First paperback edition 2016

A catalogue record for this publication is available from the British Library

ISBN 978-1-316-60688-9 Paperback

CONTENTS

LIST OF TABLES

LIST OF FIGURES

FOREWORD

The Director of the National Institute for Economic and Social Research, Mr W. A. B. Hopkin, has explained in his Introduction to this volume the circumstances in which Mr Abel-Smith and Professor Titmuss were asked to investigate the costs of the National Health Service.

The two authors have accomplished their task with conspicuous thoroughness and skill; and the results of their labours constitute a valuable piece of pioneer work in this field. For the first time the modern technique of social accounting has been applied in an expert manner to one of the major sectors of the social services. By these means it has been possible to trace for the National Health Service as a whole in England and Wales, and for each of its main branches, the changes in the factor cost and in the amount of resources absorbed since the Service was established. Thus it is likely to come as a surprise to many that, although the gross cost (i.e. before deduction of charges) of the National Health Service in England and Wales was £77 million larger in 1953/4 than in 1949/50, the additional volume of resources when measured at constant (1948/9) prices was £32 million, which represented an increase of less than 9 per cent.

The analysis of the costs of the Service undertaken by Mr Abel-Smith and Professor Titmuss has been of great value to the Committee set up by the Minister of Health and the Secretary of State for Scotland to inquire into the National Health Service in this country; and we have based most of Part I of our Report on the facts and findings which are set out in full in the present volume.

The fact that this study has had to be confined to England and Wales and does not also cover Scotland is a matter of regret, but it was unavoidable in view of the complexity of the work involved and the limited time available: there is however no reason to think that the inclusion of the data for the Service in Scotland would have altered the main conclusions of the study.

In my opinion the authors of this study have made a real contribution in the sphere of social accounting, and it is my hope that it may lead to similar investigations being carried out on other social services.

C. W. GUILLEBAUD

CAMBRIDGE
October 1955

INTRODUCTION

This book originated in a suggestion made by Mr Claude Guillebaud, the Chairman of the Departmental Committee on the Cost of the National Health Service. Soon after the Committee was set up he asked the Institute whether it would sponsor the preparation, for the information of his committee, of a memorandum presenting an economic analysis of the costs of the National Health Service. The memorandum he envisaged would relate these costs to the size of the national income; would analyse the causes of the trends so revealed, separating, for example, the effects of price changes from the effect of changes in the quantity of productive resources absorbed by the service; would distinguish between different kinds of resources—personnel of various grades, medical and other supplies bought from outside suppliers; would distinguish between capital and current expenditures; and would attempt to assess the importance, for the cost of the service past and future, of changes in the numbers, age and sex distribution of the population. The Institute was glad to undertake the task and entrusted the preparation of the report to Mr Brian Abel-Smith, with Professor Richard Titmuss of the London School of Economics as Consultant. Their report was presented to the Guillebaud Committee as a memorandum of evidence in February 1955, and after some further revision and amplification reached the form in which it is now published.

Mr Guillebaud, in asking the Institute to undertake this work, and the Institute itself in agreeing to do so, were both proceeding on the assumption that the preparation of an economic analysis of the costs of the National Health Service was a task for research. It would not, that is to say, emerge ready-made from the Appropriation Accounts or other official records of the expenditures on the service. It may seem strange that information of a kind which would seem essential to an informed public discussion of the Health Service expenditures—a matter which has not lacked public discussion—should not have been available before. The fact is that the existing system of government accounts is not, in general, well designed to form a background for discussions of major policy issues. This does not apply only to the accounts of expenditure on the National Health Service; indeed, those accounts are in some respects above the average of government expenditure accounting. It is a general difficulty, and it appears to arise from the complete dominance which has been exercised on the design of government accounts by considerations of accountability. Such considerations are of course vital; but it may be questioned whether their importance necessarily makes it impossible to organize—possibly as a separate operation—a set of records more satisfactory for the presentation and analysis of the real issues of expenditure policy. The reader may judge for himself whether the process of elaboration, adjustment, reclassification and analysis of the official records which has been undertaken by Mr Abel-Smith and Professor Titmuss has helped to clarify the background against which policy decisions have to be taken. If such analysis is thought to be useful, it arises for consideration whether the Government might not in future include something of the sort as a normal part of its accounting procedures. Nor, indeed, is the scope for reform on these lines confined to the National Health Service.

Allied to the problem of the accounts of the National Health Service is that of its statistical intelligence. It will appear at a number of points in the study by Mr Abel-Smith and Professor Titmuss that there is a need for better statistical records of the operation of the Service, and in particular for fuller and more scientifically organized information on the kinds of people who use it and the purposes for which they use it. It would go beyond the scope of this introduction to suggest in detail how this need should be met, but it seems probable that changes would be required both in the attitudes and in the organization of the departments administering the Service.

The conduct of this study has been made possible by the support and co-operation of a very large number of bodies, official and other, outside the Institute. For the first of the two years over which the work extended the Institute received financial support from the Nuffield Foundation, and I should like to put on record our gratitude for this most practical encouragement to the research.

Help of another, equally essential, kind has come from government departments and above all from the Ministry of Health. The preparation of a useful report depended entirely on full access to the detailed accounting and other records in the possession of the Ministry. This has been most generously accorded, and many of the officials of the Ministry have devoted time to answering our frequent and persistent requests for further information. Without such assistance it is hardly an exaggeration to say that the study would have been impossible, and our appreciation of the Ministry's help is correspondingly great. In all our dealings with the Ministry we have been able to rely on the good offices of Mr Halliday, the Secretary to the Guillebaud Committee, as well of course as on those of Mr Guillebaud himself.

We have also received important assistance from the Registrar General for England and Wales. At our suggestion he undertook a special tabulation of the 1951 Census material to obtain data on the demographic characteristics of the hospital population. This information has been basic to the work done by Mr Abel-Smith and Professor Titmuss on the prospective effect on the Health Service of future population changes. It has also provided, for the first time, much-needed information about demand for hospital care and, in so doing, has helped the authors to extend their studies into some of the more important social aspects of the work of the health services. We are, therefore, extremely grateful to the Registrar General and his staff for undertaking these tabulations and making the results available to us. We also owe him a debt of gratitude for the comments and criticism of our drafts which we have received from his office.

Another institution on which we have relied heavily for information and help is the South West Metropolitan Regional Hospital Board. On a number of important points not covered in the records held centrally at the Ministry they were able to give us information for their area. In this way they have enabled us to deal in an informed way with important topics which otherwise could have been given only cursory attention.

These are our major obligations of gratitude. In lesser degree we are indebted to a number of other institutions. Official bodies which have given us information on particular points are:

The Board of Trade
The Central Statistical Office
The General Register Office
The Government Actuary's Department
Her Majesty's Stationery Office
The Ministry of Agriculture and Fisheries
The Ministry of Pensions and National Insurance
The Ministry of Supply
The Ministry of Works
The National Assistance Board
The North West Metropolitan Regional Hospital Board
The Paddington Group Hospital Management Committee
The Scottish Statistical Office
The Social Survey
The Treasury
The Whitley Councils for the Health Services

Non-government organizations which have helped us are:

The Acton Society Trust
The Association of British Pharmaceutical Industry
The Association of Wholesale and Manufacturing Opticians
The British Federation of Master Printers
The Central Midwives Board
The Department of Applied Economics (Cambridge)
The Institute of British Launderers
The Institute of Hospital Administrators
The Institute of Municipal Treasurers and Accountants
King Edward's Hospital Fund for London
The London County Council
The National Coal Board
The Nuffield Foundation

To all of these, official and non-official alike, I wish to express the sincere thanks of the authors and of the Institute.

W. A. B. HOPKIN
Director, National Institute of Economic and Social Research

LONDON
June 1955

CHAPTER I

THE BACKGROUND OF THE STUDY

The one aspect of the National Health Service which, since its inception in 1948, has given rise to more critical discussion and controversy than any other single issue has been its cost. This interest in the public cost of the Service has not been confined to Britain. In many countries, governments, professional associations and public opinion generally have followed with deep interest the changing fortunes of this experiment in the organization of medical care. Perhaps no other development in social policy in any country has evoked so much international interest in recent times as the National Health Service and its economic implications. One reason for this has undoubtedly been the common experience of the rising costs of medical care; in part a consequence of the scientific and technical changes which have universally invaded medicine during the last decade or so.

It is not our purpose to discuss these broader issues. In the search for an appropriate title for this book we hope, therefore, that we have not claimed too much in the ascription we use. For our aim is limited to showing what the Service has cost in England and Wales between July 1948 and March 1954 and to identifying some of the more important factors which have determined costs during this period. Before turning to this task, which must necessarily begin with a detailed explanation of definition and method, we attempt a brief historical sketch of policy and opinion as they relate solely to the question of cost. This background of concern serves to illuminate the Government's decision to appoint the Guillebaud Committee in 1953; it also sets the stage for the present study.

In the following chapters we shall show that the Government's Appropriation Accounts have failed to indicate the cost of the National Health Service in any economically useful sense. Nor have they proved a reliable measure of secular trends. Nevertheless, it is these accounts which have in the main influenced the trend of public opinion about costs, and which have been used by Parliament and the executive to form judgements and decide future policy. It would not be possible to explain the changing climate of opinion about the cost of the Service without an understanding of the particular role played by these accounts. As explained later, we have preferred to use a different cost concept; for comparative purposes we set the figures so derived against those taken directly from the Appropriation Accounts. For the moment, however, in describing the development of public discussion since 1948, we must employ the conventional figures of government accounting, in terms of which that discussion was conducted.

When, in 1946, the National Health Service Bill was presented to Parliament it was estimated in the accompanying financial memorandum that the net annual additional expenditure falling on the Exchequer would be £95 million for England and Wales.[1] The Service would also replace existing Exchequer expenditure of £15 million. Therefore, the total net cost of the Service to the Exchequer would be £110 million a year. The estimate appears to have been the same as the 'rough' calculation used in the Beveridge Report in 1942.[2] It is now clear that this was a gross under-estimate of the prevailing costs of medical care; an under-estimate due in part to the extreme paucity of data before 1948 and to the use of unrealistic concepts of cost. The estimate made at the end of 1947 for the period between 5 July 1948 and 31 March 1949 was at an annual (net) rate of £179 million. At the beginning of 1949 a supplementary estimate was added at the rate of £71 million. In Parliament, the Leader of the Opposition (Mr Churchill) described this supplementary estimate as 'the most wild miscalculation'.[3] In the course of the debate one Opposition member asked 'Where is this going to end?'[4] The net cost for 1948/9 eventually turned out to be at an annual rate of £242 million.

The estimate of the net cost for the financial year 1949/50, made at the end of 1948, was over £228 million. To this was added, in early 1950, a supplementary estimate of over £89 million, making £318 million in all. The net cost actually came to £305 million. The supplementary estimates were debated in Parliament on an Opposition amendment in the following terms: 'This house... deplores the failure of the Chancellor of the Exchequer to enforce his own instructions to Departments not to overspend so extensively their Estimates for the current year.'[5] In the course of the debate the Chancellor of the Exchequer, Sir Stafford Cripps, announced that a ceiling was to be imposed on expenditure for the following year[6] which was estimated to be £352 million (net). Net expenditure from the vote was £337 million in 1950/1 and £348 million in 1951/2.

[1] Ministry of Health, *National Health Service Bill: Summary of the Proposed New Service*, Cmd. 6761 (H.M.S.O. 1946) and *National Health Service Bill, 1946, Financial Memorandum* [Bill 94].

[2] *Social Insurance and Allied Services*, Report by Sir William Beveridge, Cmd. 6404 (H.M.S.O. 1942), p. 201.

[3] *House of Commons Debates*, 10 February 1949, col. 536.

[4] Mr David Eccles, *H.C. Deb.* 17 February 1949, col. 1432.

[5] *H.C. Deb.* 14 March 1950, col. 916.

[6] 'I believe it is necessary to call a halt to further development of these services. We must, therefore, regard the Estimates for the forthcoming year as a ceiling beyond which we must not be carried by new developments or extensions of existing services which cannot be provided out of ascertained economies in other directions.' *H.C. Deb.* 14 March 1950, col. 937.

As part of the policy of applying a ceiling to expenditure, charges for dentures and spectacles were introduced in May 1951.[1] After the general election in the same year the new Chancellor of the Exchequer stated in January 1952 that the cost of the Service would be kept within the same bounds as laid down by Sir Stafford Cripps two years earlier.[2] To this end, further and more extensive charges were introduced in June 1952 (including a prescription charge).[3] The aim of these new charges, said the Chancellor, was 'to preserve the scope and purpose of the various measures, while correcting or avoiding abuse or faulty emphasis. The real danger to the social services...comes from the threat of bankruptcy.'[4]

However, the final settlement of the remuneration of general practitioners[5] in March 1952 made it impossible for the Government to maintain the ceiling on expenditure, and the net cost of the Service rose to £384 million in 1952/3. Concern about the rising figures of expenditure continued to manifest itself in various administrative measures and, ultimately, the Government decided to refer the question for study by an independent committee. On 1 April 1953 the Minister of Health announced the appointment of the committee under the chairmanship of Mr C. W. Guillebaud with the following terms of reference:

'To review the present and prospective cost of the National Health Service; to suggest means, whether by modifications in organization or otherwise, of ensuring the most effective control and efficient use of such Exchequer funds as may be made available; to advise how, in view of the burdens on the Exchequer, a rising charge upon it can be avoided, while providing for the maintenance of an adequate Service; and to make recommendations.'[6]

The announcement was not well received by the Opposition. The Minister was accused of 'seeking another instrument by which he might mutilate the National Health Service'.[7] In the debate seven weeks later, the preceding (Labour) Minister of Health spoke of 'the inevitably rising expenditure on the National Health Service'.[8]

In many debates and discussions on this subject during these years one matter which was given increasing prominence was the effect on the cost of the Service of a growing proportion of elderly people in the population. Mr Iain Macleod, later to become Minister of Health,

[1] *National Health Service Act, 1951*, 14 & 15 Geo. 6, ch. 31.

[2] A gross figure of £400 million (*H.C. Deb.* 29 January 1952, col. 54).

[3] *National Health Service Act, 1952*, 15 & 16 Geo. 6 & 1 Eliz. 2, ch. 25 and *National Health Service (Amendment) Act, 1949*, 12, 13 & 14 Geo. 6, ch. 93.

[4] *H.C. Deb.* 22 January 1952, col. 55.

[5] Mr Justice Danckwerts, acting as adjudicator, awarded higher remuneration to general practitioners.

[6] *H.C. Deb.* 1 April 1953, col. 1229.

[7] Mr A. Bevan, *H.C. Deb.* 1 April 1953, col. 1230.

[8] Mr H. Marquand, *H.C. Deb.* 18 May 1953, col. 1822.

made this point in his maiden speech in the House of Commons in 1950: 'In the absence of drastic action, the cost of this scheme will inevitably increase for...we are an ageing population, and for the next generation, in the absence of dramatic scientific or medical discoveries, the demands of sickness will inevitably increase.'[1] Mr Blenkinsop, who had been Parliamentary Private Secretary to the Ministry of Health under the Labour Government, spoke in similar terms in a debate in 1954.[2] The connexion between an ageing population and the cost of the Service was particularly stressed in a book by Dr Ffrangcon Roberts[3] published in 1952 which received considerable publicity. There seemed to be a growing conviction that 'an ageing population' might lead to a situation in which the cost of the Service would get out of control. This view of a possible future was, to some extent, a natural extension in the interpretation of past trends in expenditure figures for, as we have seen, to set out in sequence the estimates and actual expenditures (beginning with the extraordinarily low estimate in the Beveridge Report) could only leave an impression of a great and continuing rise in the cost of the Service.

This brief resume of some of the salient facts in the story of financial development provides a general explanation for the particular approach adopted in this book. As explained in the Introduction, the study originated as a memorandum of evidence which was eventually submitted to the Guillebaud Committee in January 1955. In large measure this has determined its scope and content. In making what proved to be difficult decisions about possible fields of study we have continuously had to ask ourselves what would be the most useful evidence to present to the Committee to accord with its particular terms of reference. At one stage, for example, we contemplated a comparative study of expenditure on medical care under the National Health Service with expenditure immediately before the Service was introduced and with a period prior to the Second World War. Preliminary investigations showed, however, that such a study would have absorbed a disproportionate part of our limited time and resources. The task would have been a very heavy one and so we abandoned it with regret. At another stage we considered extending our study to cover the whole of Great Britain, but this, again, we realized was beyond our resources. There are some extremely complicated problems of comparability to be resolved here, and we decided, therefore, that a more intensive study of expenditures in England and Wales was preferable to a less intensive study covering the whole of Great Britain.

Though attracted from time to time to an examination of various special aspects of the operational running of the Service we have, in

[1] *H.C. Deb.* 14 March 1950, col. 961. [2] *H.C. Deb.* 10 May 1954, col. 861.

[3] F. Roberts, *The Cost of Health* (London, 1952).

general, had to restrict the aims of the inquiry within severely narrow limits. The resources at our disposal have not permitted more than a very limited amount of field work. What we present, therefore, is an analysis of existing material brought together from many different sources; much of it has not hitherto been published. Broadly defined, our purpose is to show what the National Health Service in England and Wales has cost each year between 5 July 1948 and 31 March 1954 in a sense which may usefully and realistically be related to the national economy. The primary emphasis throughout is on *trends* in cost. We therefore consider the effect on cost of changing prices and the operation of charges paid by the public for services provided. We relate current expenditure to the national income and capital expenditure to total capital expenditure in the economy. We take account of changes in the population liable to use the Service. These are the main elements in the following chapters. In the course of our work, however, various problems were more clearly identified and were seen to be of sufficient importance to justify more detailed study. Several such problems were investigated further and the results are contained in the appendices to this book. Some of these appendices are necessarily complicated and technical; others we believe are of more general interest.

The arrangement of this book, like its content, has been strongly influenced by its origin in a technical memorandum for the Guillebaud Committee. Had we been writing from the start for the general reader we should have presented the material in a different form. To have attempted, however, at a late stage a thorough reorganization of the material would have delayed publication until long after the Guillebaud Committee had reported. Accordingly, we decided to publish this study substantially in the form in which it was presented to the Committee. This decision also meant assuming on the part of our readers a fair knowledge of the organization and development of the National Health Service. It further meant that we had to leave many gaps in the story; many unanswered questions and ill-defined problems.

To mitigate some of the difficulties of arrangement we now describe the content of the different chapters and appendices.

Chapter II deals with concepts and definitions. We explain that we are trying to measure the productive resources used on the Service each year. We describe the different break-downs which we employ and indicate their limitations.

Chapter III explains the sources of our material and attempts to assess within broad limits the accuracy of our results.

In Chapter IV we start on the main story. We show the cost as we have defined it; compare it with the cost as shown in the Appropriation Accounts and apportion the current cost between the three major branches of the Service—the hospital service, the executive council services and the services administered by local authorities. We analyse each branch in turn, showing the effects of charges and changing prices.

Chapter v is devoted to the capital cost. We show the role of stocks and new fixed assets and relate the latter to total capital expenditure in the economy. We then present a break-down of capital expenditure and compare capital expenditure on hospital buildings with expenditure before the war and with recent expenditure on hospitals in the United States. Lastly, we discuss the level of capital expenditure required in the future to maintain the service at its present level in view of the need to replace old buildings and to take account of population changes.

Chapter vi falls into two parts. The first part brings together from Chapter iv the main facts about the current cost of the Service, and relates this cost to the national income and to the population at risk. Changes in the use of resources by the Service are analysed by certain types of resources. The second part discusses various social and demographic factors which are thought likely to play an important part in determining future costs. Finally, we draw attention to the need for future research into contemporary problems of medical care and its administration.

Appendix A, we readily admit, is of a somewhat specialized interest. Its purpose is to explain in some detail how we have derived our concept of cost and its relation to cost as measured by the Appropriation Accounts. The conceptual problems we discuss should be of interest to those acquainted with the principles of social accounting, but the appendix is also intended to explain to those familiar with the accounting system of the Service the limitations of that system and the use we have made of it. The Ministry of Health has checked our calculations. To have explained them in sufficient detail to enable the reader to check every one or make similar calculations in future years would have made the appendix intolerably long.

Appendix B is also a technical appendix showing how we have rearranged the material that emerged at the end of Appendix A and how we have represented the cost of the Service in constant prices. One of its purposes is to enable the specialist reader to assess the reliability of the index numbers we have applied.

Appendix C is of more general interest than perhaps its title would imply. Most of it is concerned with payments made by the staff of hospitals for board and lodging. We show how the proportion of resident staff varies between different types of hospitals, and draw attention to the fact that, as a whole, hospital staffs are provided with board and lodging substantially below cost.

Appendix D analyses in financial terms the controversial problem of the role of part-time and whole-time medical and dental staff. Costs of part-time and whole-time service are compared and a study is made of relative increases in part-time and whole-time staff. As part of this study, we review the growth of the domiciliary specialist service.

Appendix E explains the methods used in estimating the role of different factors responsible for the increase in the cost of the pharmaceutical service.

Appendix F illustrates from evidence provided by the South West Metropolitan Regional Hospital Board the opportunities for capital expenditure designed to reduce current expenditure.

Appendix G, like Appendix E, provides the evidence from which conclusions are drawn in the text of the book. In this case we give details of hospital capital expenditure in 1938/9 and 1952/3.

Appendix H on the hospital population provides, we believe, some interesting new material bearing on the important question of demand for hospital in-patient care. The study is primarily based on a special tabulation by the General Register Office of the 1951 Census schedules for all hospitals in England and Wales, and shows the demands made upon the hospitals by different age and social groups in the population.

Appendix I examines very tentatively the possible effects of projected changes to 1971 in the size and age structure of the population of England and Wales on the current cost of the National Health Service.

CHAPTER II

EXPENDITURE ON HEALTH: CONCEPTS AND DEFINITIONS

1. THE ROLE OF THE NATIONAL HEALTH SERVICE

Health is not an element in national expenditure which lends itself easily to statistical treatment. In the widest sense all individual and collective expenditure which contributes to the maintenance of health and the prevention and cure of disease must be called into account. What is spent on food, clothing, housing and the physical environment of man plays a major role in health and disease. Each culture and each age have, too, their own concepts of health and disease—psychological and physical. And, within limits, each country decides its own sickness rate by the ways in which it allocates its resources and orders its affairs.

We are not here concerned with these fundamental questions. Their relevance to expenditure on medical care has been made clear by Sigerist in his studies of civilization and disease, by the medical historian Charles Singer and by other writers. Our primary concern is the role of the National Health Service within the total national expenditure on health and disease, though even here, as the study proceeded, we were increasingly impressed by the difficulties of distinguishing between the three major fields of expenditure: the National Health Service sector, other public expenditure, and the private sector.

In delimiting our field of study the first point to make clear is that public expenditure on environmental services is ruled out.[1] We therefore restrict this study to such expenditures as are concerned with the health and medical care of the individual (including, of course, as they fall within the scope of the Service, the costs of confinement, child welfare and other 'health' activities).[2] Broadly, these may be said to fall into five categories:

(*a*) Private expenditure by individuals on doctors, dentists, drugs, nursing homes and other goods and services.

(*b*) Collective private expenditure, such as industrial health services and other organized systems of individual medical care.

[1] Nevertheless, there is some element of cost for environmental services carried by the National Health Service which we cannot eliminate, e.g. bacteriological and other 'public health' services.

[2] One difficulty in applying this distinction arises with the treatment of what have been called 'hotel' expenses. Strictly speaking, only the increase in expenditure on food, accommodation, and the like over what is 'normally' made falls within our definition. The material on which our study is based does not, however, permit us to make such a distinction.

(*c*) Collective public expenditure outside the statutory terms of the National Health Service attributable to certain functions of the Ministries of Education, Labour, Health, Pensions and National Insurance, the Home Office, the University Grants Committee, the Defence Departments and so forth.

(*d*) Expenditure on goods and services supplied by or administered through the National Health Service and privately paid for in whole or in part by the individual. This includes the two types of charges—those that are intended to meet the full cost of providing a service, for example private hospital beds, and those which represent standard part payments towards the cost of goods and services, for example the 1*s*. charge on prescriptions.

(*e*) The cost of the National Health Service to public funds (central and local).

While it is relatively easy to establish these five categories it is in practice extremely difficult to determine, in studying changes over time, how much expenditure is transferred and re-transferred between one and another of these five categories, and for what purposes.

In this study we are only concerned with categories (*d*) and (*e*)—individual health expenditure falling within the present scope of the National Health Service for England and Wales. Any use of food, accommodation and other services provided in hospital for patients and staff is included in this definition of expenditure. What the order of magnitude is of expenditure within the other categories—particularly (*a*) and (*b*)—it is extremely difficult to estimate. In broad terms, however, it seems reasonable to say that the cost of the National Health Service (as defined below) is some indication of the total national expenditure on medical care. Nevertheless, the relationship between the two may change from year to year as expenditure is switched from sector to sector. These complex processes and the parallel switching of demand from sector to sector merit detailed research. For purposes of illustration we may cite the fact of transferences of work from the school health service to the National Health Service at various times since 1948, and of a re-transference of dental work to the former service after charges were imposed in the National Health Service. There has, too, been some switching of work between the National Health Service and the medical services organized for the Defence Forces, but as there is no cross-accounting between these two services it is difficult to estimate with any accuracy the costs involved. An estimate worked out in 1952 by the departments concerned indicated that the annual amount involved was unlikely to exceed £100,000. Similar transferences of costs have taken place during the period under review between the National Health Service and the Ministry of Pensions (particularly in respect to hospital cases) and between the former and local welfare authorities responsible for providing accommodation under Part III of the National Assistance Act (particularly elderly 'mental' cases transferred from 'welfare' to 'hospital' services).

What is also important in considering this problem of shifting responsibilities is that there has probably occurred a substantial switch in costs from category (*b*) to the National Health Service (particularly in the form of services falling under the heading of 'industrial health', for example, the treatment of industrial accidents, use of ambulance services and so forth). In another sphere of costs it is necessary to bear in mind that the functions of the National Health Service include the training of doctors, nurses and other professional staff, all of which involves heavy expenditure. If all these persons were later employed in the National Health Service this expenditure would be appropriately included as part of its cost and regarded as a form of investment. This, however, is far from being the case. A substantial part of this training expenditure might be more appropriately allotted to the Ministry of Education, the University Grants Committee, the Defence Departments, the Colonial Office and other government departments, to private industry and the private sector in general. In addition to its absolute size in any given year, this type of expenditure probably increased during the first six years of the National Health Service.

Without much additional research, the evidence available to us on all these transfer questions is insufficient to permit even a global estimate to be given. It is, for instance, impossible to gauge the size of the shift from the National Health Service to the private sector—particularly in dentistry after the imposition of charges. Apart from this type of transference, it would seem that the net effect of other movements has been a gradual shifting from year to year of work and functions to the National Health Service. This, of course, has the effect of increasing the cost of the Service to public funds, but it does not necessarily follow that the total national expenditure on individual health is correspondingly increased. This factor should be borne in mind in appraising the results of this study, for we have not been able to make any allowance in our estimates for the costs of these new, expanded or training activities of the Service.

In analysing cost we consider two concepts:

The gross cost of the National Health Service. This is the sum of categories (*d*) and (*e*)—all current productive resources administered by the Service and paid for publicly and privately.[1]

The cost of the National Health Service to public funds (*the net cost*). This is category (*e*) and relates to current productive resources used at public cost. It is a concept of cost which is liable to be misunderstood, for it is not (as is sometimes supposed) a reliable guide to the incidence of taxation caused by the existence of the Service. There are several reasons for

[1] The term 'gross' is used throughout in this sense.

this. First, if we were concerned with measuring the National Health Service tax 'burden' we should need a different cost concept. Secondly, we should in consequence have to take into account the tax treatment of those working in the Service, for example, the practice expenses and special tax allowances of general practitioners[1] and consultants. Thirdly, to arrive at an estimate of the present tax 'burden', we should need to assess the revenue position in an imaginary situation of no public provision in this field of individual health services. To do so would also involve assumptions both about the alternative employment and remuneration of certain of the resources at present used in the Service and about the consequent effects on the size of the national income. There is obviously no practical value in attempting an assessment of the National Health Service tax 'burden'.

2. THE DEFINITION OF COST AND OF THE NATIONAL HEALTH SERVICE

We must now make clear what we mean by 'cost', and by 'National Health Service'. 'Cost' in this particular context may be defined in a number of different ways, and in choosing the most appropriate one for our purposes certain factors have to be considered. Some costs, for example, were inherited from the past and have to be currently met, although no current benefits accrue to the National Health Service. Such costs include the payment of debts of voluntary hospitals that were outstanding on the 'appointed day', payments to local authorities for stores handed over on the appointed day, compensation to general practitioners for the right to sell their practices, and to others for loss of office. Costs to the Exchequer of a different kind are increases in hospital cash balances involving a transfer of cash but no use of current productive resources.

This study attempts to classify these and other types of cost and to arrive at a definition appropriate to the purposes in hand. Detailed classifications are given in Appendix A which attempts a classified reconciliation between the cost of the National Health Service to public funds in productive resources and the Appropriation Accounts. For most of this study we will be concerned only with the current consumption of resources (goods and services) which could be of benefit to the community in alternative uses. This means that the transfer of money without any use of goods and services is excluded from our definition of cost. Similarly, expenditure in settlement of liabilities inherited from

[1] In considering the gross rates of remuneration paid to general practitioners, dentists and others the level of practice expenses and allowances is an important factor. To give the doctor or dentist the same disposable income these expenses and allowances could be increased and the rate of remuneration lowered by an equivalent amount.

the past is omitted, for we are concerned only with resources used to provide the National Health Service now and in the future. Such adjustments are essential if fair comparisons are to be made from one year to another. When existing assets, for example hospital buildings, are purchased for use in the Service this does not involve any use of current productive resources when these assets were used for the same purpose before they were taken over. The purchase of such assets does not therefore enter into our classification of cost. Where the word 'cost' is used hereafter it should be read as an abbreviation for the cost in terms of the use of current productive resources.

The cash used to finance the Service comes from a number of different public sources—central and local government, the National Insurance Fund[1] and the Hospital Endowments Fund. There are also grants from the central government to local authorities for use on the Service. In measuring the cost to public funds, we are treating all these accounts as if they were consolidated; that is, as if they were a single spending unit.

In defining the National Health Service there are certain public responsibilities which, according to different views, may or may not be thought to lie within its field of activity. It is important, however, to ensure that the same definition of scope and content is used for each year. Accordingly, we decided to define the National Health Service by its scope and content in the year 1951/2.[2]

As regards other cost questions, we have brought into account expenditure from non-Exchequer funds,[3] and we have also included in our classification of costs the remitted charges met by the National Assistance Board. Throughout, we have attempted to include all the costs of administering the Service, although some are not charged to the National Health Service vote. In this process of classifying functions and costs we decided to restrict our study to the peace-time role of the Service. Expenditures on civil defence and stock piling are therefore omitted, although it should be borne in mind that but for the existence of the Service in its present form substantial expenditure from public

[1] The National Insurance Fund is built up in part from employers' and employees' contributions. These contributions are compulsory and therefore analogous more to taxes than to private insurance premiums. Payments from the Fund are therefore treated as a form of national expenditure.

[2] The cost of Broadmoor, for example, has been included for the whole period, although, administratively, it was excluded from the National Health Service for the first year of the Service.

[3] These funds are partly the result of endowments (plus interest on accumulated sums) after the appointed day. Expenditure from these funds would appear to fall within the field of expenditure on individual health, and as they are controlled by statutory authorities they would seem to be part of public rather than private expenditure, even though the Minister cannot use these endowment funds to meet the ordinary running costs of the National Health Service.

funds would have been necessary for civil defence hospitals and other services.

In valuing the resources consumed we include superannuation contributions paid by the employing authority as part of current costs, i.e. we treat them as part of the salary or wage. Although the benefit is not paid out concurrently, its value is one of the factors influencing the decision to take employment or accept contracts of service with the National Health Service.

3. THE DISTINCTION BETWEEN CAPITAL AND CURRENT COSTS

The distinction between capital and current expenditure is important. The general principle of the distinction is that current costs are incurred for benefits immediately obtained, while capital costs are for benefits which go on accruing after the end of the accounting period. Capital expenditure is often, though not always, liable to fluctuations and is affected by special influences which do not apply (or at least not to the same extent) to current expenditure. It is for these reasons that it is necessary to separate them for the purposes of this study.

It is not practicable, however, to classify *all* purchases that provided benefits after the end of the accounting period as capital. It is normal accounting practice in the National Health Service in England and Wales to treat as current expenditure such items as crockery, linen and consumer durables. Our definition, determined partly by the nature of the accounts, does not correspond to any neat theoretical concept. In the hospital field capital is defined as 'expenditure on works of construction, reconstruction or alteration, and associated purchases of furniture and equipment'.[1] This extremely broad definition has not been interpreted consistently from year to year by different hospital boards and management committees. In the earlier years some items were charged to building maintenance which, later, were charged to capital. Corrections have been made where possible, and to the resulting capital figures we have added expenditure on X-ray equipment,[2] mass radiography units, blood-drying units, capital expenditure on the public health laboratory service, and work on adaptations and conversions carried out by the Ministry of Works. We have also treated changes in the value of stocks as capital expenditure. Purchases of goods added to stocks benefit later years and not the activities of the current accounting period in which the increases take place.

In the executive council services we have included as 'capital' only

[1] *The National Health Service (Hospital Accounts and Financial Provisions) Regulations, 1948*, Statutory Instruments 1948, no. 1414, p. 6.

[2] X-ray equipment bought for replacement. Other purchases of X-ray equipment are already included in the capital expenditure figures.

expenditure on the purchase, construction and adaptation of premises for the dental estimates board, joint pricing committees and the executive councils themselves.

In the local authority services the capital figures come from the capital payments return made to the Ministry of Housing and Local Government. This return is, for our purposes, preferable to the figures of expenditure on capital account in the Local Government Financial Statistics, because the latter represents a classification based on the account to which the expenditure was charged rather than on whether the expenditure itself was of a capital or current nature. The figures which we have used are not, however, ideally suited for our purposes because they are figures of payments rather than of expenditures during a particular accounting period.

It is evident therefore that the break-down we have used between capital and current is somewhat arbitrary and the results must accordingly be interpreted with caution.

4. THE BREAK-DOWN INTO SERVICES

The National Health Service as a whole provides an immense range of different types of service, each of which makes different demands on current productive resources. Moreover, measured in terms of cost, as defined above, these different services show substantial differences in trends since 1948. To understand the nature of these trends in costs it is necessary to apply some form of break-down. Theoretically, it would for our purposes be more rewarding to conduct this analysis in terms of either (i) types of individual need as expressed by the demands met or (ii) types of resources consumed. In practice, however, the first is not possible while the second can only be crudely attempted because of the form in which the statistics are collected and presented. This means that, by and large, the main break-down we use in this study follows the organizational structure of the Service.

As arranged for administrative purposes, the Service is divided into three main streams—hospital, executive council and local authority services. We can divide the hospital service into (i) hospital management committees and board of governors and (ii) the remainder, and further subdivide group (i) by type of hospital. These are the break-downs we use for the hospital service, but the extent to which we can show what money was spent on what resources is seriously limited by the form of accounts.

The executive council services are divided into five groups: administration, general medical, dental, pharmaceutical and ophthalmic. For the local authority services we have adopted a broad division into four groups:

(*a*) Child health and maternity: care of mothers and children, health visiting, domiciliary midwifery.

(*b*) Ambulance service.

(*c*) Domestic help service.

(*d*) Other: health centres, home nursing, vaccination and immunization, prevention and after-care services, mental care services.

We have already referred to the difficulties of estimating the year-by-year switches in cost as between the total National Health Service sector and other, non-National Health Service, sectors. Similar difficulties arise in all these internal break-downs. Some part of the cost of medical care by general practitioners has been switched to hospital diagnostic services. This may also relieve expenditure otherwise falling on practice expenses. The number of X-rays directly referred from general practitioners rose from 665,000 in 1951 to 741,000 in 1952. Pathological laboratories examined 456,000 specimens from general practitioners in 1951 and 554,000 in 1952. This upward trend, though undocumented before 1951, was undoubtedly at work from 1948 onwards. The rise in road accidents, greater use for minor treatments by industry for its workers, and other factors have also led to more cost transfers from the general medical and other services to the hospital service.

Bearing in mind these and other changes which have been in progress since 1948 it is not, therefore, safe to assume that the cost of the general medical service represents the total cost of general medical attention for those not in hospital. Nor can valid comparisons be made with any certainty from year to year. Similarly, the cost of the pharmaceutical service does not represent the whole of the cost of pharmaceuticals for those who are not hospital patients. There has probably been an increase in the use of hospital dispensaries for out-patients—particularly road and industrial accident casualties. The cost of the ophthalmic service does not represent the total cost of sight testing and the supply of spectacles within the National Health Service. The hospital share of this work has probably been increasing since 1948. Similarly, the cost of the dental service does not represent the whole cost of dentistry under the National Health Service. Dental care is provided in hospital and for the priority classes of mothers and children in the local authority services. Lastly, it should be remembered that there are a great many possibilities of substantial switches in costs as between the local authority and hospital services. By sending patients home early the hospital may cause a rise in demand for home nursing. By failing to provide the necessary 'welfare' services the local authority may transfer costs of caring for the elderly and infirm to the hospital. The volume of switching which may go on from year to year in respect of the costs of confinement as between the three main streams of the National Health Service is also likely to be very considerable. These are but a few examples of the many reasons which make it difficult to be at all precise about the differential costs of the component parts of the Service.

So far as the costs of administration are concerned, it would have been useful to have given some measure of what is involved under this broad heading. But this is not possible for a number of reasons. In the first place it is extremely difficult to devise any meaningful definition of administrative expenditure and, in the second place, the form of the accounts does not permit reliable estimates to be made of the cost of administrative and clerical staff. Such figures as do exist are misleading. It is impossible to determine who does what and who has done what in any administrative service as between the three main branches of the Service. Nor do we know how much administrative work is done by nursing staff, professional and technical grades and what changes have been in progress since 1948.

5. THE BREAK-DOWN INTO 'MEDICAL' AND 'OTHER'

We attempt this kind of break-down of the National Health Service so as to throw some light on the use of different types of resources. Obviously, opinion will differ about what should appropriately be put under these two categories. The fact, for example, that ward orderlies are not included in the 'medical' category must not be taken to mean that in our view ward orderlies have no medical functions. The following list shows the broad headings under these two categories:

Medical

The hospital service

Doctors and dentists
Nurses and midwives
Almoners, physiotherapists, laboratory technicians and other professional and technical workers[1]
Drugs and dressings, medical and surgical appliances

The executive council service

All except administration

The local authority service

Doctors, nurses, health visitors and similar grades
Drugs and dressings

Other

The remainder—certain administrative costs, ambulance and transport services, and a large group of non-medical professional, technical and ancillary workers such as ward orderlies, engineers, gardeners, porters, cleaners, etc.

[1] All those classified as 'professional and technical' except chaplains and those concerned with catering, engineering, building and farming.

6. THE BREAK-DOWN BY FACTORS

In this break-down we attempt a further analysis of the use of resources by applying a classification of 'goods and contracts' and 'services'. It is not, however, possible to do so as accurately as we should like owing to the form in which the accounts are presented. For example, where a group of hospitals share a laundry—the labour being directly employed by the National Health Service—the cost is shown in the accounts under 'laundry' without any break-down into staff and materials. Accordingly, we have had to allocate this item to 'goods and contracts'.

The general medical, dental and ophthalmic services do not fit happily into this twofold classification. For instance, the general practitioner is not directly employed by the National Health Service; he contracts for a fee. Rather than put these three services, therefore, under 'goods and contracts' we introduce a third category, 'contracted services', to cover the general medical, dental and sight testing services. The supply of spectacles seemed to be too akin to the pharmaceutical service to be treated in this way. It has therefore been placed along with the latter under 'goods and contracts'.

CHAPTER III

SOURCES AND METHODS

1. THE MATERIAL

When applied to the statistical material the concepts of cost as defined in Chapter II produce substantially different results from those shown in the Appropriation Accounts. These accounts record the amount of cash supplied by the Treasury for the National Health Service under its vote for the particular financial year. Thus, they fail to distinguish between cash issued and payments actually made; they do not show what has been spent on current services as distinct from past services,[1] and they are quite uninformative about different types of resources and costs.

These accounts are supplemented by an additional set of accounts for the hospital and executive council services prepared in accordance with Section 55 of the National Health Service Act, 1946. They record expenditure on current consumption of goods and services and they attempt a reconciliation of such expenditure statistics with payment statistics. Nevertheless, they are in many respects unsatisfactory. In structure, they are extremely complex; many items are liable to misinterpretation, for there are insufficient or no notes of explanation, and the summary tables are inadequate. Moreover, expenditure on trading activities is not distinguishable from other expenditure and numerous items are not comparable from year to year. As to this last point, it must, of course, be readily admitted that the lack of comparability is part of the price that has to be paid for improvements in the quality of the material. In general, however, the basic defect in these accounts is their failure to indicate the cost of the National Health Service in terms of the use of productive resources.

In consequence, we have had, so to speak, to examine under a microscope a great many items of expenditure; to collect much additional information from various sources, and to make numerous estimates—often little more than guesses—in order to fill gaps and check other data.

All this has been a necessary preliminary to a resetting of the accounts for the hospital and executive council services to accord with our concepts of cost.

Similar difficulties have arisen in presenting the accounts for the local authority services. The material here on which we had to work

[1] For example, over a large part of National Health Service expenditure there is often a substantial delay between the use of resources and payment for such resources. Moreover, the extent of the delay has varied markedly each year since 1948. The effects of this time-lag are further discussed in Appendix A.

consisted of the grant claims submitted to the Ministry of Health, supplemented by the returns published by the Institute of Municipal Treasurers and Accountants. These two returns are not, however, identical, partly because the Institute uses a different system of classification (for example, administrative expenses are excluded), and partly because it is several years after the end of the accounting period before the grant claims attain their final form, whereas the Institute's returns are based on provisional figures.

Many of the revised estimates presented in this study have been worked out with the Ministry of Health. We have also drawn on the South West Metropolitan Regional Hospital Board for additional information which was not available in the Ministry. Had time and resources permitted, we would have liked to consult other Regional Boards to ascertain whether the experience of this, the largest region, is typical of England and Wales as a whole.[1]

As acknowledged in the Introduction, we have had the most generous help from all those we have consulted. Despite all this help, we are very conscious of the inadequacies in the data we present. Basically, these derive from the defects in the material to which we have drawn attention, though we ourselves, in resetting the accounts and making numerous estimates in the absence of precise information, have probably contributed to them. We accept full responsibility for the results.

2. THE RELIABILITY OF THE RESULTS

In Appendix A we have classified the different types of cost (Table 45) and have shown in detail the adjustments which need to be made to the vote figures to arrive at an estimate of cost as defined in Chapter 1. Current cost is shown in Table 46 and capital cost in Table 47.

It will be clear from our discussion of the material that the estimates we present are subject to a degree of error which, moreover, varies from year to year. In general, however, our view is that, from the experience gained in working over all this material, the later the year the more reliable the estimate. This is particularly true of the hospital, dental and ophthalmic services, the figures for which are especially uncertain in respect to the first year and to a lesser extent in the second year. The task of taking over the hospitals in 1948 was an immensely complicated one for the accounting officers of the Ministry of Health. Inevitably, therefore, some items of expenditure were charged to 1949/50 which should have been charged to the first nine months. Similar discrepancies arose—and to some extent still arise—in the dental and ophthalmic

[1] It is not typical in one respect, for the region controls an abnormally large complement of mental hospital beds.

services. Estimates have had to be made on inadequate data about work in progress at the end of each accounting period.

We have made as many corrections as possible to reduce the range and amount of error. Nevertheless, we have probably not eliminated altogether the tendency for the hospital service estimates to be understated for 1948/9 and overstated for 1949/50. Broadly, we believe that the maximum possible error in the figures for the National Health Service as a whole is in the neighbourhood of £5 million for 1948/9 and not more than £4 million for 1949/50. For later years we are reasonably confident in saying that the maximum possible error is not likely to be more than £1–2 million. Whatever the figure may be, however, we are quite confident that—if our concept of cost is accepted—the picture we give of the economy of the National Health Service is a more faithful and realistic one than that drawn by the conventional accounts presented to Parliament.

There is an error of a quite different kind in the figures for the current cost of the hospital service. In the previous chapter we distinguished between capital and current costs and pointed out that the latter are for benefits immediately obtained. But to obtain these benefits at once—that is to say, in a defined accounting period—not only are resources of a transient nature (for example, food) consumed but use is also made of resources of a more lasting nature (for example, buildings). The use of such capital resources is part of current cost. It may be distinguished from the use of resources for the creation of new lasting assets (for example, new buildings). This 'capital charge' element of current cost is included in our current cost figures for the local authority service for the simple reason that the grant claims of these authorities on the Ministry of Health include loan charges. No such element is included in our figures for the executive council services. The amount involved, however, is much too small to justify the trouble of providing an estimate. Our principal difficulty thus relates to the hospital services.

Theoretically, hospital capital charges should include both rent for the land used and interest and depreciation on buildings and equipment. It is, however, extremely difficult to make even rough estimates, quite apart from the problem of deciding on the most appropriate basis. Strictly, rent should be charged on the value of the land in its most lucrative alternative use, while the interest and depreciation charges should be related to the current cost of replacing the capital assets and to their expected length of life. Even if it were possible to make estimates on these bases it would have to be borne in mind that they would be unrealistically high compared with capital charges calculated on the basis of the historical cost of the assets. Differences between historical and replacement cost arise, of course, from changes in the price level, and this is an important matter where hospitals are concerned, for, in general, they are considerably older than most other capital assets in the economy. Any estimate for hospitals based on historical cost would, for these reasons, have little economic significance.

From this brief discussion it will be evident that the difficulties are too great to allow any estimate of this capital charge element to be included in our current cost figures for the hospital service. Nevertheless, it is necessary to remember that its omission is likely to make only a negligible difference in assessing the *trend* of the National Health Service costs over a short period of years. The omission does mean, however, that our figures cannot be used for such purposes as international comparisons without some adjustment.

3. PRICE DEFLATION

In attempting to answer the question whether the National Health Service absorbed more or less resources in the different years covered by this study, one essential step is to eliminate the effects of changing prices. We discuss in some detail in Appendix B the difficulties we have encountered in undertaking this task, and, in particular, the hazardous calculations made necessary by the defects in the government accounts. To overcome these handicaps we have had to devise and apply special price indices for certain categories of resources. These, it should be emphasized, are not based on any extensive field work and we have no doubt that with more study they could be improved. So far as possible, however, care has been taken in the more important cases to ascertain from various spending authorities the composition and market of purchase of particular categories of goods and services. In many cases we have used and adapted existing indices, in others we have constructed special ones. For wages and salaries, which play a dominating role in the total of costs, we have used weighted indices in the more important cases; in others, we have traced the trend of remuneration for a large grade in the middle of the salary scale.

The results, given in detail in Appendix B, of this attempt to eliminate the effects of price changes between 1948/9 and 1953/4 must be accepted with caution. The magnitude of the error involved (allowing for other kinds of error in the material to which reference has already been made) is probably in the region of plus or minus £5 million in estimating the amount of change in the total of resources used between 1949/50 and 1953/4.

4. TRADING ACTIVITIES

As part of the process of resetting the National Health Service accounts we have attempted, in Appendix C, to eliminate the effects of certain activities which we group together under the broad heading of 'trading activities'. In the main, these include (*a*) the provision of medical services at full cost, for example, private hospital beds; (*b*) the provision of certain patient and staff services at full cost, for example, canteens and shops; (*c*) the provision of farms and gardens partly as a means of obtaining goods and partly as a form of occupational therapy; and (*d*) the provision at full or part cost of board and accommodation for hospital staff. It is important to disentangle the effects of these 'trading activities' (involving a turnover of more than £20 million in 1953/4) if we are to analyse the resources used in the National Health Service in terms of the categories described in Chapter 1.

The principal difficulty in doing so, however, is that the accounts show certain receipts under various headings, but they do not tell us what expenditure was incurred to earn these receipts. As the accounts stand it is not possible, for instance, to distinguish in respect to (*d*) between the cost of the staff and the cost of the patients. Similar difficulties of breaking down costs into salaries and wages on the one hand, and goods and contracts on the other, arise in analysing other forms of trading activities.

In constructing a trading account in Appendix C we have therefore had to make certain assumptions. In estimating the extent to which the receipts shown truly represent the full cost of the trading activity we have assumed on the basis of evidence specially obtained that expenditure on farms and gardens and canteens and shops has been covered by the receipts. No such assumption can, however, be made for staff payments. There is a great deal of evidence which suggests that goods and services have been provided for staff at well below cost.

It is clear from such data as we have been able to collect that the scope for such concealed subsidies is substantial and includes meals, laundry, lodging, clothing, transport, secretarial assistance to specialists and consultants for their private work and other benefits. Moreover, a large proportion of the staff of hospitals is involved; a special analysis made for us by the General Register Office shows that the ratio of resident staff to the 'inmate' population ranges from 6 % for mental deficiency institutions to over 50 % in teaching hospitals. In all, it was at least 22 % in 1951.

The importance of this matter is such that we have had to make some assumption about the total amount of subsidy involved. On the basis of certain evidence (given in Appendix C) we have selected a figure of 40 % and applied it to each of the years under review. In effect, this means we are assuming that the cost of providing these particular goods and services was 40 % higher than the payments made by the staff for them. In estimating the value of the goods and services we have chosen to work from what we may call a 'reasonable subsistence minimum' and have disregarded higher standards of amenity enjoyed by certain categories of staff.

5. THE CHOICE OF A BASE YEAR

We have commented earlier on the possibilities of error in the estimates of the cost of the National Health Service during the first nine months of its operation. In the main, these are attributable to the inevitable accounting difficulties associated with inaugurating the Service. During this period the switch from private medical care to public service was still in progress; many doctors and dentists did not take part until well after the appointed day; the transfer of administrative costs of the hospitals took months to complete, and so forth.

Adjustments have been made wherever possible, but, nevertheless, the figures for 1948/9 still remain more unsatisfactory than those for later years. In converting, for comparative purposes, the figures for the 270 days of the financial year 1948/9 into a full year the error is naturally increased. Although the converted figures are included in our tables we decided to treat 1949/50 as our base year in representing trends.

CHAPTER IV

TRENDS IN COST, 1948–1954

This chapter examines the trends in cost of the National Health Service as a whole and each of its three main branches. The principal results of these analyses are brought together and summed up in Chapter VI.

We begin by drawing attention to the differences in the total figures which result from the application of our concept of cost as compared with those derived from the Appropriation Accounts.

1. COMPARISON WITH THE APPROPRIATION ACCOUNTS

Table 1 shows the gross total of the vote and net total of the vote from the Appropriation Accounts. These totals are compared with our estimate of the cost of the National Health Service to public funds (capital plus current).

Table 1. *The net cost to public funds of the National Health Service (capital plus current) compared with the Appropriation Account totals (England and Wales, 1948/9–1953/4)*

(£m. in actual prices)

	5 July 1948/9	Annual rate 1948/9*	1949/50†	1950/1	1951/2	1952/3	1953/4
The net cost‡ of the National Health Service to public funds (capital plus current)	251·2	339·6	385·3	405·8	418·6	426·7	439·1
Gross total of the vote	241·4	326·3	387·6	398·3	410·7	450·8	432·7
Net total of the vote	179·3	242·4	305·3	336·6	348·5	384·2	367·9

* Interpolated from the 270 days for which the National Health Service operated.
† 1949/50, etc., indicates the financial year (from 1 April 1949 to 31 March 1950).
‡ See Chapter II for definition of cost (p. 11).

The same information is presented in Fig. 1. It is apparent that our measure of the cost shows a steadier and less sharply rising trend than that shown in the Appropriation Accounts. The divergence from the gross total of the vote is most striking in comparing 1951/2 with 1952/3. The gross total of the vote rises by £40 million between these years compared with a rise of only £8 million in our measure of cost. One important factor accounting for this difference is the Danckwerts award under which general practitioners were paid £24 million in 1952/3 for services rendered in earlier years. It is apparent that neither the gross total of the vote nor the net total of the vote give a correct indication of the real cost of the Service.

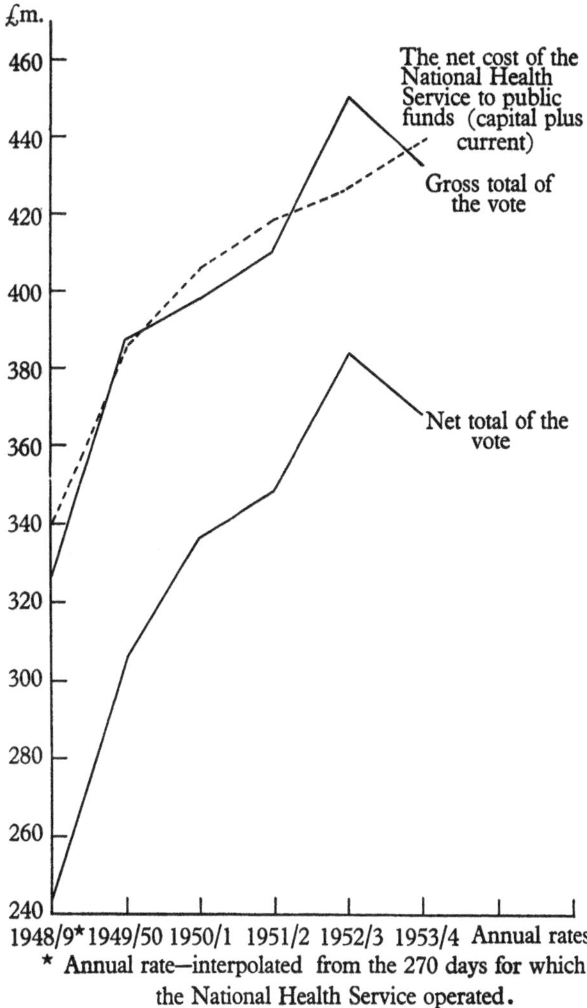

Fig. 1. The net cost to public funds of the National Health Service (capital plus current) compared with the Appropriation Account totals.

2. THE CAPITAL AND CURRENT COSTS OF THE NATIONAL HEALTH SERVICE TO PUBLIC FUNDS

Table 2 shows the capital and current costs of the Service to public funds.[1]

The capital cost has represented less than 5 % of total cost each year. It showed a rise up to 1951/2 and then fell from £16·5 million to £8·8 million in 1953/4. This fall was largely accounted for by changes in

[1] For definition of capital and current see Chapter II, p. 13.

the value of stocks in the hospital service. Up to and including 1951/2 there had been a steady rise; in that year the increase amounted to £4 million. In both 1952/3 and 1953/4 there were, however, decreases in stock values of over £2 million.

Table 2. *The capital and current net costs to public funds of the National Health Service (England and Wales, 1948/9–1953/4)*

(£m. in actual prices)

	5 July 1948/9	Annual rate 1948/9*	1949/50	1950/1	1951/2	1952/3	1953/4
Capital cost (real asset expenditure)	8·8	11·8	13·7	15·3	16·5	9·8	8·8
Current cost to public funds	242·5	327·8	371·6	390·5	402·1	416·9	430·3
Total†	251·2	339·6	385·3	405·8	418·6	426·7	439·1

* Interpolated from the 270 days for which the National Health Service operated.

† Throughout this study, totals do not necessarily add up owing to rounding.

The trend of current costs shows a generally even and relatively low rate of increase between 1949/50 and 1953/4, roughly £15 million per year. The figures in this table point to the importance of separating capital and current costs, for year by year fluctuations in capital expenditure can largely obscure the trend of current cost.

3. THE BREAK-DOWN INTO SERVICES

The first step in analysing and explaining these trends is to break down the current cost to public funds into the three administrative branches of the Service. This is done in Table 3.

Table 3. *The current net cost to public funds of the National Health Service by services (England and Wales, 1948/9–1953/4)*

(£m. in actual prices)

Service	1948/9*	1949/50	1950/1	1951/2	1952/3	1953/4
Central and miscellaneous†	2·4	2·5	2·9	3·1	3·3	3·6
Hospital	166·3	192·4	207·9	228·9	250·3	263·2
Executive council	133·4	147·2	146·5	134·9	124·2	123·1
Local authority	25·6	29·4	33·2	35·1	39·2	40·4
Total	327·8	371·6	390·5	402·1	416·9	430·3

* Annual rate—interpolated from the 270 days for which the National Health Service operated.

† Central and miscellaneous covers those items which cannot be conveniently allocated to any of the three main branches, such as the costs of the Ministry of Health, and of Rampton, Moss Side and Broadmoor institutions.

Between 1949/50 and 1953/4 the current cost of the hospital service rose fairly steadily. It also absorbed an increasing proportion of the total—52 % in 1949/50 and 61 % in 1953/4.[1] The cost of the executive council service was at its peak in 1949/50; thereafter it fell, particularly between 1950/1 and 1952/3. Its share of the total fell from 40 % in 1949/50 to 29 % in 1953/4. The cost of the local authority services has risen steadily though on a much smaller scale. Its share of the total has increased from 8 % in 1949/50 to over 9 % in 1953/4.

In absolute terms, the total rise in current cost between 1949/50 and 1953/4 was £59 million. The hospital service rose by £71 million, and the local authority service by £11 million. These rises were offset by a fall of £24 million in the executive council services. It is clear that the rise in the cost of the hospital service by 37 % since 1949/50 has been largely responsible for the rise in the cost of the National Health Service in actual prices.

We now turn to analyse in detail each of the three branches of the Service.

4. THE HOSPITAL SERVICE

Table 4 shows the current cost of the hospital service including and excluding charges.

Table 4. *The current cost of the hospital service including and excluding charges (England and Wales, 1948/9–1953/4)*

(£m. in actual prices)

	1948/9*	1949/50	1950/1	1951/2	1952/3	1953/4
Gross cost of the hospital service	169·2	195·1	210·5	231·6	253·2	266·4
Less charges:						
(*a*) From patients:						
Section 4 beds	−0·1	−0·1	−0·2	−0·2	−0·3	−0·3
Section 5 beds	−2·6	−2·3	−2·2	−2·2	−2·2	−2·2
Supply and repair of appliances, drugs and medicines	—†	—†	—†	−0·1	−0·3	−0·5
(*b*) From Road Traffic Acts	−0·1	−0·1	−0·1	−0·2	−0·2	−0·2
Total charges	−2·8	−2·6	−2·6	−2·6	−3·0	−3·2
Net cost of the hospital service	166·3	192·4	207·9	228·9	250·3	263·2

* Annual rate—interpolated from the 270 days for which the National Health Service operated. † Under £50,000.

This table shows that charges have always represented a very small part of the gross cost of the hospital service; little more than 1 % in fact. In terms of revenue, there has been no noticeable tendency for the demand for hospital treatment at private cost to increase.[2] Amenity

[1] These comparisons of trends in cost as between the different services are, of course, subject to the qualifications (discussed in Chapter II) concerning the transfer of work and functions from service to service.

[2] To some extent the figures of revenue from charges may not show the real movement in demand because the charges made have changed during the six years for reasons other than price changes. The aim of recovering 'full costs' has been difficult to interpret in practice.

beds (Section 4 beds) have become more popular, but for various reasons they do not bring in much revenue. The revenue which the hospital service obtained from the charges introduced in 1952 amounted to only a few hundred thousand pounds.

Over 90 % of the cost of the hospital service goes on the hospitals themselves (counting the specialists as part of hospital costs). The remainder goes on the boards and committees that run them, the cost of appliances issued through the hospitals, payments to hospitals not vested in the Minister, and such other services as blood transfusion, bacteriology, etc. Table 5 gives a break-down of hospital expenditures by four broad types of hospital.

Table 5. *The current net expenditure in respect of different types of hospital (extracted from Section 55 accounts) (England and Wales, 1950/1–1953/4)*

(£m. in actual prices)

Type of hospital	1950/1	1951/2	1952/3	1953/4
I. Teaching (general and maternity)	22·5	22·2	23·0	23·6
II. Non-teaching (general and maternity)	78·5	84·8	91·6	95·5
III. Tuberculosis, convalescent, isolation and other	45·4	50·6	56·2	60·0
IV. Mental and mental deficiency	35·0	37·4	41·9	44·7

This table, it should be emphasized, is on a quite different basis from all other tables in this study. The figures in it are taken direct from the Section 55 accounts. The cost of specialists is excluded here as it is not possible to allocate the total (approximately £17 million in 1952/3) between different types of hospital. Also, certain adjustments made to various items of maintenance expenditure cannot be similarly divided. Nevertheless, the figures do serve to show very roughly the proportion of expenditure devoted to different types of hospital. The classification of types of hospital is not strictly comparable between 1952/3 and earlier years.[1] We have not shown any figures before 1950/1, as changes in the classification of hospitals were too great to justify comparisons.

In 1953/4 53 % of the cost of maintaining the hospitals was devoted to general and maternity work (10 % teaching, 43 % other). It is significant that the mental and mental deficiency hospitals which cared for over 40 % of the in-patients absorbed only 20 % of the cost of the hospitals and little more than 10 % of the cost to public funds of the National Health Service.

Table 5 also shows that the cost of the teaching hospitals has risen little since 1950/1, while the cost of the other hospitals has risen substantially. To what extent this trend would be changed if we could have

[1] For example, 30,000 beds in non-teaching general hospitals (group II) were reclassified into group III from 1952/3.

allocated the cost of consultants and specialists (including merit awards) it is impossible to say.

A major factor accounting for the increased cost of the hospital service has been the rise in prices.[1] Table 6 shows the gross cost of the service in actual and constant prices and the implied rise in hospital prices.

Table 6. *The current gross cost of the hospital service (i.e. before deduction of charges) in actual and in 1948/9 prices (England and Wales, 1948/9–1953/4)*

(£m.)

	1948/9	1949/50	1950/1	1951/2	1952/3	1953/4
Gross cost of the hospital service in						
actual prices	169·2	195·1	210·5	231·6	253·2	266·4
in 1948/9 prices	169·2	186·0	196·7	201·5	209·0	215·6
Implied price index*	100	104·9	107·0	114·9	121·1	123·5

* See Appendix B.

Between 1948/9 and 1953/4 prices in the hospital service rose by 23½ %. This may be compared with a rise of 29 % in the retail price index over the same period. A major reason why hospital prices rose in this period less than other prices is the fact that medical salaries were not revised until the beginning of 1954/5. They went up substantially at the beginning of the National Health Service and again in 1954/5.

Expressing the cost in constant prices reduces the rise between 1949/50 and 1953/4 from £71 million to £29½ million, from a rise of 37 % to only 16 %. Our figures in constant prices also show that this smaller rate of increase slowed down over the period in question.

This increase of £29½ million between 1949/50 and 1953/4 in the gross cost of the hospital service in 1948/9 prices can be broken down in a number of ways. Table 7 shows a break-down into 'medical' and 'other'.[2]

Table 7. *Break-down of the current gross cost of the hospital service (i.e. before deduction of charges) into 'medical' and 'other' (England and Wales, 1949/50 and 1953/4)*

(£m. in 1948/9 prices)

	1949/50	1953/4	Increase 1949/50–1953/4
Medical	87	104½	17½
Other	99	111	12
Total	186	215½	29½

The major increase is attributable to 'medical' costs which account for £17½ million of the £29½ million. This is an increase of 20 % com-

[1] The word 'price' is used to include both the prices of goods and the prices at which services are purchased (salaries and wages).

[2] For definitions see Chapter II, p. 16.

pared with an increase of 12% in the cost of other resources. This increase of £17½ million of 'medical' costs is mainly the result of an additional £13 million for medical staff, of which about £7 million falls under the heading of nursing staff. The remaining £4½ million increase in 'medical' costs can be subdivided into £3 million for drugs, equipment, etc., provided by the hospitals, and £1½ million for appliances, etc., provided by the Ministry of Pensions.

The increase of £12 million in other, 'non-medical', costs has also been primarily due to increases in staff. These account for £8½ million of the total. 'Non-medical' goods and contracts have increased by only £4 million (7%), although they account for about half of the 'non-medical' costs of the hospital service. This increase of 7% was about the same as the increase in average daily occupied beds over the same period.[1] One further point needs to be made in considering the significance of this increase of £29½ million at constant prices in the cost of the hospital service. Some part of it was attributable to the fact that the hospitals did more work—in-patient and out-patient.[2] Between the calendar years 1949 and 1953 the increase in average daily occupied beds was 26,500. Out-patient work increased much more markedly. Apart, however, from the fact that more services were provided for a larger national population it has to be borne in mind that some part of the additional resources consumed by hospital in-patients would have been consumed in other ways by these patients if they had not been in hospital. We may tentatively estimate these additional 'transferred costs' (food, clothing, accommodation and so forth) at about £2 million.[3]

We now turn to a more detailed examination of changing expenditure on 'non-medical' goods and services. This further analysis is conducted in gross terms, i.e. before trading receipts are subtracted, because while it is justifiable to allocate estimated trading expenditure between broad groups it is not reasonable to do so in any detail.

There are substantial variations in the trends of gross expenditure under different categories of goods and services. The details are given in

[1] The increase in average daily occupied beds between the calendar years 1949 and 1953 was 6·7%.

[2] See *Report of the Ministry of Health for the year ended 31st March, 1949*, Cmd. 7910 (H.M.S.O. 1950); *Report of the Ministry of Health, 1950, Part I*, Cmd. 8342 (1951); *Report of the Ministry of Health covering the period 1st April, 1950 to 31st December, 1951, Part I*, Cmd. 8655 (1952); *Report of the Ministry of Health for the year ended 31st December, 1952, Part I*, Cmd. 8933 (1953); *Report of the Ministry of Health, 1953, Part I*, Cmd. 9321 (1954).

[3] We have assumed that the transferred expenditure of ordinary living costs was on the average 30*s*. a week in 1948/9 prices for the additional patients. A pound a week was the payment made in 1948 by the National Assistance Board for the expenses, excluding rent, of an additional adult living in a household (*The National Assistance (Determination of Need) Regulations, 1948*, Statutory Instruments 1948, no. 1334, p. 3). To this £1 we have added 10*s*. for rent.

Appendix B (the following references in brackets refer to the itemized categories in the tables attached to this appendix). Expenditure on provisions (item 7) increased in real terms by only 4 % between 1949/50 and 1953/4. This, on the face of it, is surprising. To interpret this change we need to know the number of day-meals served[1] in the hospitals each year. This information is not, however, collected. Average daily occupied beds increased by nearly 7 % between 1949 and 1953. What we do not know is the number of meals taken by the staff during this period. The Treasurer of the South West Metropolitan Regional Hospital Board has kindly assembled for us figures for the financial years 1950/1 to 1952/3 for all the hospitals in this region making complete returns throughout the period.[2]

The results are summarized in Table 8.

Table 8. *Day-meals provided in hospitals in South West Metropolitan Region making complete returns between 1950/1 and 1952/3*

	1950/1	1951/2	1952/3	Increase 1950/1–1952/3 Number of meals	Increase 1950/1–1952/3 % of 1950/1
Staff:					
Resident	11,794	11,308	11,011	−783	−6·7
Non-resident	5,371	5,691	5,713	342	+6·4
Total staff	17,165	16,999	16,724	−441	−2·7
Patients	51,042	51,531	52,310	1,268	+2·5
Total	68,207	68,530	69,034	827	+1·2

It emerges from this table that about 20 % of all meals consumed in hospitals are taken by the staff. However, it is not possible to say for the country as a whole that the additional cost of more in-patients was, during this period, offset by a decline in the number and proportion of meals taken by hospital staffs. Changes in quality and type of meal for both patients and staff are factors which cannot be measured.

An increase of 33 % in the cost in constant prices of staff uniforms and clothing (item 8) since 1949/50 has added £½ million to the cost of the hospital service. Total staff has increased about 13 %, and there have also been increases in the proportion of the staff provided with uniform and in the range of uniforms supplied. For example, the proportion of the staff issued with white coats has increased to cover mental nurses and other categories of staff who come in contact with patients. There

[1] A day-meal means the food demands for one person in a twenty-four-hour period. Food consumed by part-time staff is included in the total of day-meals.

[2] The information covers more than three-quarters of the beds in the region and about a tenth of all beds in England and Wales.

are still very wide variations in the cost of uniforms issued in different hospitals.[1] The cost of fuel, light and power (item 12) has increased 13 %, adding £1¼ million to the cost of the Service. Laundry (item 13) shows a 54 % increase at a cost of nearly £1 million. In the absence of information about what proportion of laundry work was contracted and so charged to this heading in each year, and the proportion which was spread among other subheads, the increase shown under this item may not represent the true total increase of the cost of laundry. It is clear, however, that the cost of laundry work has been increasing. One factor has been the increase in the number of in-patients of about 7 %. But in one large hospital laundry, over half the cost of laundry is attributable to washing for the staff. The increase in nursing staff of 16 % and the increase in the use of uniforms have been the most important influences on cost.[2]

The cost of maintaining the buildings (item 14) has varied considerably from year to year. The rise since 1949/50 has been about £1½ million. Domestic repairs (item 15) cost about the same in real terms at the beginning and the end of the period. The heavier buying which took place in 1948/9 under these and other items can be attributed to a number of factors. Hospital equipment had been run down seriously before the Health Service took over. Part of this was deliberate policy in anticipation of the transfer, but other influences were undoubtedly the financial straits of many voluntary hospitals before nationalization and the difficulty of getting supplies in the early post-war period. Printing and stationery (item 17) in 1953/4 was under half the cost of 1949/50—a saving of over £1½ million in real terms. The transfer made it necessary to replace a certain amount of stationery, while modern accounting systems and medical records were instituted and developed for the first time in many hospitals. The later years show a fall in purchases as more supplies were provided through the Stationery Office.

These break-downs (given in more detail in Appendix B) show the allocation of expenditure under various headings. The same information can be alternatively represented in a form which indicates the type of resources used in the hospital service. For this purpose Table 9 shows a break-down into wages and salaries on the one hand, and goods and contracts on the other.

Salaries and wages accounted for 61·8 % of the cost of the hospital service in 1949/50 and 63·1 % in 1953/4. They were responsible for

[1] The cost of a dress issued to an assistant matron varies from 21*s.* in one hospital in Epsom to 115*s.* 5*d.* in one hospital in Kensington. In one hospital at Farnham nurses are issued with aprons at 13*s.* each, in another at Cane Hill aprons cost 5*s.* 6*d.* Belts vary from 7*d.* to 4*s.* 6*d.*

[2] In one large hospital laundry the number of white coats laundered per week has increased over four years from 4000 to 12,000.

£21 million of the total increase of £29½ million. Over half of the increase in goods and contracts was for medical goods.

Thus, the predominant cause of the increased cost of the hospital service arises from the increased number—and increased pay—of hospital staffs. It is therefore interesting to examine changes in staff in different categories between 1949 and 1953. These are set out in Table 10.

Table 9. *Break-down of the current gross cost of the hospital service (i.e. before deduction of charges) into salaries and wages, and goods and contracts (England and Wales, 1949/50 and 1953/4)*

(£m. in 1948/9 prices)

	1949/50	1953/4	Increase 1949/50–1953/4
Salaries and wages	115	136	21
Goods and contracts	71	79½	8½
Total	186	215½	29½

Table 10. *Hospital staff 31 December 1949 and 31 December 1953 in whole-time equivalents**

	1949	1953	Increase of 1953 over 1949	Percentage increase of 1953 over 1949
Medical and dental	12,693	15,039	2,346	19
Nurses and midwives	137,282	158,960	21,678	16
Administrative and clerical	25,667	29,306	3,639	14
Domestic, maintenance and transport	140,990	153,135	12,145	9
Professional, technical, etc.	22,341	24,989	2,648	12
Total	338,973	381,429	42,456	13

* For medical and dental staff, thirty-five hours of hospital work has been taken to represent one whole-time equivalent (see Appendix D). For other categories, a part-timer is treated as equivalent to half a whole-timer.

Over three-quarters of the total increase of 42,500 in staff is accounted for by more nurses and midwives (21,700) and more hospital domestic and other workers (12,000). The percentage increase in both categories between 1949 and 1953 is substantially in excess of the percentage increase in the number of occupied beds.

From the point of view of the national economy as a whole (and, in particular, the demand for young women in a variety of employments) it is necessary to remember that not all these additional hospital workers would have been employed elsewhere if they had not been employed in hospitals. Some indication of this emerges from Table 11.

Of the total increase of 31,500, part-time workers accounted for nearly 9,000. Moreover, a large proportion of these workers were in hospitals in isolated areas (mental hospitals and tuberculosis sanatoria) where the possibilities of alternative employment are very limited. It may well be, therefore, that a majority of these part-time workers would not have found employment elsewhere. This may also be true of the employment of older, married women as whole-time domestic workers.[1] These considerations mean, in effect, a lesser burden on the national economy brought about by the employment of additional staff than, on the face of it, the figures would suggest.

Table 11. *Increase in nursing and domestic staff in the hospital service between 31 December 1949 and 31 December 1953 broken down by sex, and whole-time and part-time*

(Whole-time equivalents)

	Whole-time	Part-time	Total
Male	5,031	39	5,070
Female	17,610	8,846	26,456
Total	22,641	8,885	31,526

The increase of 2,350 medical and dental staff in whole-time equivalents (amounting to 19 % between 1949 and 1953) shown in Table 10 is discussed in detail in Appendix D. The cost at constant prices rose by 17 % or by £4 million between 1949/50 and 1953/4. It is suggested in Appendix D that the development of the domiciliary specialist service may have contributed about £300,000 to the increase of £4 million.

Summary

The cost of the hospital service increased between 1949/50 and 1953/4 by £29½ million in 1948/9 prices. This was largely attributable to increases in the number of staff and, to a lesser extent, to increases in the supply of medical goods. From the point of view of resources which could have been consumed in alternative uses, and allowing for 'transferred costs', the lack of alternative employment for certain workers and other factors, the additional cost in the use of productive resources was probably about £25 million.

Against this have to be set the quantitative facts that the hospitals did more work for a larger national population; more confinements took place in hospital; more services were rendered to general practitioners (in part a switch from the doctor's private practice expenses to the hospital service); more road accidents were treated; more provision was made for industrial accidents which would otherwise have called for an expansion of industrial health services; more people were trained as doctors, nurses, almoners, physiotherapists and other categories of workers later to engage in private practice or other employment at home and overseas; more research was undertaken and completed, as indi-

[1] Unfortunately, no data exist which would allow an analysis by age and marital status or of the extent to which Irish and other immigrant workers have contributed to the total increase of 22,641 whole-time workers.

cated by a striking rise in the flow of articles to scientific and medical journals since 1948. All these are quantitative indices of activity; what cannot be assessed is the changing work of the hospital as an agent of humanity.

5. THE EXECUTIVE COUNCIL SERVICES

We now turn to examine by the same methods the trends in cost of the executive council services; namely, the general medical services, the pharmaceutical service, the dental service and the ophthalmic service.

Table 12 shows the cost (including and excluding charges) of all these services.

Table 12. *The current cost of the executive council services including and excluding charges (England and Wales, 1948/9–1953/4)*

(£ m. in actual prices)

	1948/9*	1949/50	1950/1	1951/2	1952/3	1953/4
Gross cost of the executive council services	133·4	147·2	146·5	138·9	137·7	139·7
Less charges	—	—	—	−4·0	−13·5	−16·6
Net cost of the executive council services	133·4	147·2	146·5	134·9	124·2	123·1

* Annual rate—interpolated from the 270 days for which the National Health Service operated.

Table 13 shows a break-down of the net cost (or cost to public funds) of the different services.

Table 13. *The current net cost to public funds of the executive council services (England and Wales, 1948/9–1953/4)*

(£ m. in actual prices)

	1948/9*	1949/50	1950/1	1951/2	1952/3	1953/4
Central administration	2·1	1·9	1·9	2·5	2·3	2·3
General medical services	44·2	45·7	49·9	50·5	52·0	51·9
Pharmaceutical service	27·7	33·2	38·5	44·1	42·5	39·5
Dental service	39·0	46·4	37·7	29·9	21·1	22·3
Ophthalmic service	20·4	20·1	18·4	7·9	6·3	7·1
Total	133·4	147·2	146·5	134·9	124·2	123·1

* Annual rate—interpolated from the 270 days for which the National Health Service operated.

The differences in the trend of costs as between the various services is striking. The pharmaceutical and general medical services have increased while the dental and ophthalmic services have decreased. The biggest rise occurred in the pharmaceutical service, where the cost increased by about £11 million between 1949/50 and 1951/2—from 22½ to 33% of the cost of the executive council services. But between 1951/2 (the year before charges were introduced) and 1953/4, it fell by about £4½ million. The increase in the general medical services between 1949/50 and 1953/4 was just over £6 million; most of this increase was due to the application of the Danckwerts award. The services which have fallen in cost (the dental and ophthalmic services) show a combined reduction since 1949/50 of £37 million. The effect of this is to reduce their share of the total executive council costs from 45 to 24 %. The ophthalmic service shows the biggest proportionate decline. In absolute terms, however, the fall in the cost of the dental service made the largest contribution to the total decrease in the cost of the executive council services. It should be noted that the decline in the cost of the dental and ophthalmic services started before charges were introduced in 1951/2.

It is clear that different factors have been at work in the different services. In general, all these trends have been affected by changes in prices and the introduction of charges. Underlying them, other and more subtle factors have been operating, the importance of which it is difficult to estimate on the information available to us. So far as is possible, however, we will consider the more obvious factors with respect to each service.

(a) *Central administration*

After making an approximate allowance for the increase in prices, the resources used by central administration (executive councils and joint pricing committees) were slightly less in 1953/4 than 1949/50.[1]

(b) *General medical services*

Table 14 gives an analysis of the general medical services designed to show the effect of eliminating changes in prices.

Table 14. *The current cost of the general medical services in actual and in 1948/9 prices (England and Wales, 1948/9–1953/4)*

(£ m.)

	1948/9*	1949/50	1950/1	1951/2	1952/3‡	1953/4‡
Cost in actual prices†	44·2	45·7	49·9	50·5	52·0	51·9
Cost in 1948/9 prices	44·2	46·6	46·7	46·8	47·3	47·1
Price index (1948/9=100)	100	98	107	108	110	110

* Annual rate—interpolated from the 270 days for which the National Health Service operated.

† The cost of the general medical service primarily covers the cost of general practitioners' services (including mileage payments) for which the doctors are paid from a central pool. The largest other item included is the cost of the maternity medical service which amounted to nearly £2·3 million in 1952/3.

‡ An upward adjustment to these figures may still be made retrospectively on account of the final settlement of payments to general practitioners.

[1] See Table 51, p. 99.

In terms of constant prices there was little difference in the cost of the services between 1949/50 and 1953/4.

To correct for changes in price raises, however, a theoretical difficulty. A choice has to be made about the unit of service to be expressed in constant prices. We have taken the unit to be 'meeting the needs of one patient throughout the year'.[1] The application, currently and retrospectively, of the Danckwerts award meant a higher capitation fee.[2] The rise of £4 million in the current cost for 1950/1 was a result of the higher 'betterment factor' applied in this year. But apart from changes in the capitation fee and changes in the population at risk it might be thought that, accepting the population at risk as the unit of service, there would be no variation from year to year in the cost of the services in constant prices. This, however, would not be the case because the capitation method of payment, though adopted in principle, has not been applied in practice. The Danckwerts award was based on the principle of maintaining the average income of doctors in the Service. As the number of doctors providing general medical services has been rising faster than the population for whom the doctors are paid, this has meant that the cost of each patient to the Service has risen.[3]

(*c*) *The pharmaceutical service*

Table 15 shows the cost of this service, including and excluding charges.

The cost of the pharmaceutical service rose steadily up to 1951/2. The following year, in which charges were introduced, shows a decrease in the cost to public funds (net cost), while the gross cost continued to rise but by a smaller amount.

As we explain in Appendix E, we have little confidence in the accuracy

[1] As we are attempting to measure the input of resources, the ideal unit would be 'doctors in whole-time equivalents'. The number of principals taking part in the Service rose from 17,566 at the end of 1949 to 18,096 on 1 July 1952. It would be very hazardous, however, to use these figures for the purpose we have in mind for two reasons. General practitioners combine with their work for this part of the Service many other activities, including the care of private patients, work in the local authority services and for other government departments, and services to industry. The scope for such work and the amount of work actually undertaken has certainly varied in the period under review. Secondly, insufficient information is available concerning assistants to principals who are excluded from the figures quoted above. We have had to use, therefore, the unit described in the text which we believe to represent the input more accurately than the figures for principals alone. Theoretically, general practice under the Service is a casual employment. In view of the number of doctors being trained at present, it would seem likely that proportionately more doctors will be employed to meet the needs of patients in the future. For any study similar to this it will, therefore, become more necessary to re-examine the unit of input of resources.

[2] See Ministry of Health, *Memorandum on the Supplementary Estimates for the Additional Sums to be Provided for the Remuneration of General Medical Practitioners in the National Health Service*, Cmd. 8599 (H.M.S.O. 1952).

[3] The fall in the price index between 1948/9 and 1949/50 arises because doctors' incomes from non-central pool sources were believed by Mr Justice Danckwerts to be lower in 1948/9 than 1949/50. His award therefore made retrospective payments at a higher annual rate for 1948/9 than for 1949/50.

or validity of the index which we have used to represent the cost of the pharmaceutical service in constant prices. It is for this reason that we do not show in the text the figures of the service in constant prices from Table 51 in Appendix B. However, we believe there is sufficient evidence to state that from 1951/2 at least the prices of pharmaceuticals have fallen fairly substantially. The fall in the net cost from 1951/2 shown in Table 15 is attributable to this factor, and it may be that the net cost continued to rise after 1950/1 *in real terms*.

Table 15. *The current cost of the pharmaceutical service including and excluding charges (England and Wales, 1948/9–1953/4)*

(£ m. in actual prices)

	1948/9*	1949/50	1950/1	1951/2	1952/3	1953/4
Gross cost of the pharmaceutical service	27·7	33·2	38·5	44·1	46·8	45·5
Less charges	—	—	—	—	−4·3	−6·0
Net cost of the pharmaceutical service	27·7	33·2	38·5	44·1	42·5	39·5

* Annual rate—interpolated from the 270 days for which the National Health Service operated.

It is extremely difficult to estimate how much greater the gross cost would have been if charges had not been imposed. The charge is based on prescription forms. But while the number of forms may decline it does not follow that the cost of the service will correspondingly decline. The same quantity and cost of pharmaceuticals may result from fewer forms. The average number of prescriptions on a form which had been running steadily at 1·6 in the first three months of 1952 rose to 1·74 in the last three months when the charge was operating. There are also indications of a rise in the quantity covered by each prescription irrespective of the number of prescriptions per form. Table 16 shows that there was some decline in the number of prescriptions dispensed after 1950/1. Without further study it is obviously impossible to interpret this trend.

Table 16. *Prescriptions dispensed in England and Wales*

(Millions in annual rates)

1948/9	191·3
1949/50	206·4
1950/1	225·1
1951/2	220·6
1952/3	219·4
1953/4	212·9

This trend is illustrated in Fig. 2, which shows prescriptions dispensed each month and a twelve-month moving average. The part played by the weather and the seasonal incidence of epidemics is very much in evidence; and these factors, when added to those already mentioned, make it even more difficult to estimate the effects of the prescription charge.

Apart from the question of charges, it is evident that the gross cost of the pharmaceutical service rose continuously up to 1952/3 (Table 15). One factor at work has been the changing composition of prescriptions dis-

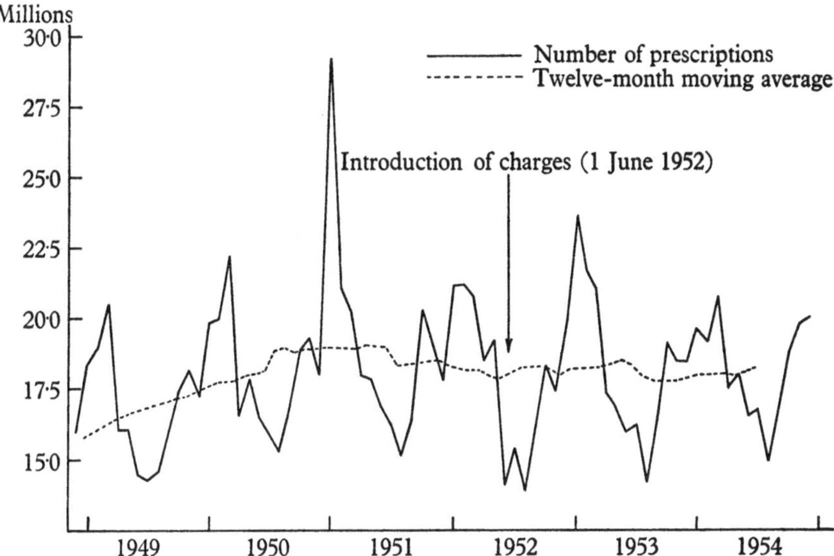

Fig. 2. The number of prescriptions dispensed in England and Wales each month and a twelve-month moving average.

pensed. The nature of the statistical material available prevents us, however, from making a simple price-quantity analysis. A more detailed study of the causes of the changes in cost between 1949/50 and 1953/4 is attempted in Appendix E, and the results are summarized in Table 17.

Table 17. *Factors accounting for the rise in the cost of the pharmaceutical service between 1949/50 and 1953/4 (England and Wales)*

Cause	Percentage of increase in cost attributable to each cause
Changes in rates of payment to pharmacists	−11
Increased quantity of ingredients	36
Changed composition of proprietaries and non-proprietaries	35
Other factors	40
Total	100

Amongst 'other factors', there is some evidence to suggest that changes in the cost of pharmaceutical ingredients have been small. Increased quantity, caused more by a larger average quantity in each prescription than a larger quantity of prescriptions issued, has been one of the two principal causes for the increased cost of the service. The other principal factor has been the increased use of proprietaries. The part which new preparations have played within this factor and among the residual factors cannot, unfortunately, be distinguished in the annual figures. Such information as is available indicates that the part they have played is an important one.

In short, we can give no complete or satisfying explanation for these trends. Having regard to the important role of the pharmaceutical service in the National Health Service it would seem desirable to call for better statistics and some study of what is taking place.

(*d*) *The dental service*

Table 18 shows the trend in the cost of the dental service including and excluding charges.

Table 18. *The current cost of the dental service including and excluding charges (England and Wales, 1948/9–1953/4)*

(£ m. in actual prices)

	1948/9*	1949/50	1950/1	1951/2	1952/3	1953/4
Gross cost of the dental service	39·0	46·4	37·7	31·6	26·5	28·6
Less charges	—	—	—	−1·7	−5·4	−6·3
Net cost of the dental service	39·0	46·4	37·7	29·9	21·1	22·3

* Annual rate—interpolated from the 270 days for which the National Health Service operated.

The cost of the dental service at current prices was obviously falling before charges were introduced, and from 1949/50 the fall in gross and net cost was £18 million and £24 million respectively.

One reason for this declining cost has been changes in the prices paid for dental work as shown in Table 19.

By 1951/2 prices had fallen 22½% below the level of 1948/9. This fall in prices was not due to free-market changes, but was caused by reduc-

Table 19. *The current gross cost of the dental service (i.e. before deduction of charges) in actual and in 1948/9 prices (England and Wales, 1948/9–1953/4)*

(£ m.)

	1948/9*	1949/50	1950/1	1951/2	1952/3	1953/4
Gross cost of the dental service in actual prices	39·0	46·4	37·7	31·6	26·5	28·6
in 1948/9 prices	39·0	49·8	46·4	40·8	34·2	36·8
Implied price index	100	93·2	81·3	77·4	77·5	77·7

* Annual rate—interpolated from the 270 days for which the National Health Service operated.

tions in the rates of payment by the Ministry of Health when it was realized that the rates originally fixed were providing dentists with greater annual remuneration than had been intended. Even after correcting for changes in prices, however, the cost of the dental service declined substantially from 1949/50 onwards.

A clearer understanding of what has been occurring in the dental service can be obtained from Table 20, which shows the public cost at constant prices allocated between 'work on prior approval' and 'other work'.

Table 20. *Break-down of the current net cost to public funds of the dental service in 1948/9 prices into prior approval and other work (England and Wales, 1948/9–1953/4)*

(£ m. in 1948/9 prices)

	1948/9*	1949/50	1950/1	1951/2	1952/3	1953/4
Prior approval	31	37	32	21	11	11
Other work	8	13	14	17	16	18
Total	39	50	46	38	27	29

* Annual rate—interpolated from the 270 days for which the National Health Service operated.

The significance of this break-down is that it serves to show as closely as the data permit the trend of the cost of providing dentures which represents the bulk of the work done on prior approval.[1] The remaining work on prior approval, for example, orthodontic treatment, is believed to have been fairly constant at £3–4 million over the six years. Allowing for this it would seem that the cost of dentures has declined from a peak of about £34 million in 1949/50 to about £8 million in 1953/4. The second category of 'other work' has been increasing steadily throughout the period.

Interpreting these data in terms of the gross cost of dental work (as shown in Table 19), it would appear that non-denture work has been expanding but that this has been offset by a greater decline in denture work. From 1949/50 onwards there has been a decline in resources used on producing dentures.

In assessing the effects of charges, it is important to note that the decline in resources used by the service started before they were introduced. There are some reasons for believing that the downward trend would have continued even if charges had not been introduced. It is estimated that by 1953 16 % of the population (nearly 7 million persons)

[1] Some of the treatment included in 'prior approval' estimates is not itself subject to prior approval (for example, fillings), and it is not known how much of this is included in estimates for partial dentures nor how much for extractions is included in denture estimates. Included in the category 'prior approval' is a mixture of treatment (for example, extractions necessitating dentures, crowns and inlays) and other treatment which happens to be added to prior approval estimates.

were wearing full dentures.[1] By 31 March 1953, nearly 6 million pairs of full dentures had been supplied under the Service.[2] Taking into account what is known about the average life of dentures, the number of sets obtained privately, mortality among those fitted with dentures after the start of the service and other factors it would seem that, by March 1953, a high proportion of persons requiring dentures had been fitted with them. Roughly, 80 % had obtained them from the National Health Service during the preceding five years.

After piecing together these and other items of information it becomes possible to make a tentative assessment of the trend in the cost of dentures. At the beginning of the Service, it looks as though the high costs were attributable to an accumulation of demand from persons with unsatisfactory dentures and persons requiring dentures. After this backlog of demand had been largely dealt with, a decline set in as a rising proportion of needs were met. The subsequent introduction of charges probably contributed to some extent, however, to a further fall in the gross cost by inducing persons either to defer obtaining dentures or to continue with unsatisfactory sets longer than they would have done had replacement been free. From Table 19 we can see that the total decline in the gross cost at constant prices between 1950/1 (the last complete financial year before charges were introduced) and 1953/4 was £10 million. At a guess, it may be that charges were responsible for about one-half of this reduction.[3]

(*e*) *The supplementary ophthalmic service*

Table 21 shows the cost of the ophthalmic service including and excluding charges.

Table 21. *The current cost of the supplementary ophthalmic service including and excluding charges (England and Wales, 1948/9–1953/4)*

(£ m. in actual prices)

	1948/9*	1949/50	1950/1	1951/2	1952/3	1953/4
Gross cost of the ophthalmic service	20·4	20·1	18·4	10·2	10·1	11·4
Less charges	—	—	—	−2·3	−3·8	−4·3
Net cost of the ophthalmic service	20·4	20·1	18·4	7·9	6·3	7·1

* Annual rate—interpolated from the 270 days for which the National Health Service operated.

[1] *Report of the Ministry of Health for the year ended 31st December, 1953, Part I,* Cmd. 9321 (H.M.S.O. 1954), p. 79.

[2] This figure does not represent 6 million different persons as more than one pair were, in a proportion of cases, supplied to the same person; the extent to which this occurred is not known for the earlier years.

[3] Further analysis of the effects of the introduction of charges and in particular of the shift in the use of resources between age groups is available in the *Report of the Ministry of Health for the year ended 31st December, 1953, Part I,* Cmd. 9321 (H.M.S.O. 1954), pp. 80–2.

As with the dental service, the cost of this service was falling before charges were introduced in 1951/2. Between 1950/1 and 1953/4 there was a fall in gross cost of £7 million and in net cost of £11 million. One reason for the decline is attributable to price changes as shown in Table 22.

Table 22. *The current gross cost of the supplementary ophthalmic service (i.e. before deduction of charges) in actual and in 1948/9 prices (England and Wales, 1948/9–1953/4)*

(£ m.)

	1948/9*	1949/50	1950/1	1951/2	1952/3	1953/4
Gross cost of the ophthalmic service in actual prices	20·4	20·1	18·4	10·2	10·1	11·4
in 1948/9 prices	20·4	22·1	21·3	12·0	11·7	13·3
Implied price index	100	91·0	86·4	85·0	86·3	85·7

* Annual rate—interpolated from the 270 days for which the National Health Service operated.

Prices fell by 14% from the start of the service until 1950/1, after which they remained steady for the next three years. Both a reduction in the scale of fees for sight testing and a cheapening in the cost of spectacles contributed to this fall in prices. After eliminating the effect of price changes it appears that the gross cost fell by £10½ million between the peak year 1949/50 and 1952/3 and then rose by £1½ million in 1953/4.

Table 23 shows the cost to public funds (net cost) in constant prices for (*a*) sight testing and (*b*) supply of spectacles.

Table 23. *Break-down of the current net cost to public funds of the ophthalmic service in 1948/9 prices into sight testing and supply of spectacles (England and Wales, 1948/9–1953/4)*

(£ m. in 1948/9 prices)

	1948/9*	1949/50	1950/1	1951/2	1952/3	1953/4
Sight testing	6·2	5·2	4·4	3·3	3·5	3·8
Supply of spectacles	14·2	16·8	16·9	6·1	3·9	4·5
Total	20·4	22·1	21·3	9·4	7·3	8·3

* Annual rate—interpolated for the 270 days for which the National Health Service operated.

The table shows that the decline in cost has come primarily from the supply of spectacles. Sight testing, which has not been subject to a charge, was at its peak in the first nine months and was almost halved in cost by 1951/2. The decline in sight testing, the essential forerunner of the supply of spectacles, is significant.

One minor explanation for the decline in the supply of spectacles has been the decline in the percentage of sight tests which result in a prescription for glasses. This fell from 95 % at the start of the service to 92 % in 1950/1 and 86 % in 1952/3. This accounts for a fall of £1 million in the cost of the supply of spectacles between 1950/1 and 1952/3. In 1953/4, however, there was a slight rise in the percentage to 87 %.

The remaining fall of £12 million from 1950/1 consists of £4½ million (in 1948/9 prices) transferred to private payments and £7½ million attributable, first, to the effects of charges on the gross cost and, secondly, to a decline which there is reason to believe would have taken place even if charges had not been introduced.

The trend of sight tests, though irregular month by month, shows a decline from a quarterly average of 1·35 million in 1949/50 to 1·15 million in the second quarter of 1951 and to a quarterly average of 0·9 million in 1952/3. By 31 March 1953 26·1 million pairs of spectacles had been supplied to a spectacle-wearing population of 19·2 million in England and Wales.[1] From a sample taken in 1948/9 it is known that in 34 % of cases one person was supplied with two pairs. Applying this rate[2] to the 26·1 million pairs, it follows that 19·5 million persons were supplied with spectacles. This figure of 19½ million persons is a minimum figure, because after 1948/9 there was a decline in the percentage of cases in which two pairs were supplied. It is, however, not possible to put a figure to this; also, the extent to which persons have had more than one issue from the service is not known. However, it may be reasonable to assume that, by 1953, a high proportion of the spectacle-wearing population had been supplied with at least one pair under the service.[3] The downward trend of demand could, therefore, be interpreted as an adjustment to normal annual needs after a back-log of demand had been met in the early years of the service. As with dentures, the average time during which spectacles remain satisfactory is not known. This, in part, depends on the standards applied by those operating the sight tests. Nevertheless, it seems likely that charges caused some postponement in demands on the service. We would hazard the estimate that the gross cost may have fallen by £5 million as a result of the introduction of charges.

All the evidence we have examined suggests the following interpretation of the trend in demands on the ophthalmic service. At the start of the service there were substantial demands from persons who had not previously had their sight tested and from persons who were overdue for a re-test. By 1951 these demands had been substantially met and the

[1] Calculated from information given in P. G. Gray, 'Who wears spectacles?', *The Lancet*, 22 September 1951, p. 537.

[2] Rate: 134 pairs per 100 persons.

[3] A sample of persons coming forward for sight tests in September 1953 showed that less than 5 % had not already received one pair of spectacles since the start of the service (see *Report of the Ministry of Health for the year ended 31st December, 1953, Part I*, Cmd. 9321 (H.M.S.O. 1954), pp. 251–3).

service was dealing more and more with normal new needs, re-testing and replacement. The introduction of charges in 1951 and their extension in 1952 caused some postponement of sight tests and some diversion of the demand for spectacles to the private sector. In 1953/4 the service expanded slightly, partly in response to the demands which had been postponed when charges were introduced and partly because the abnormally large issues at the start of the service were beginning to need replacement.

6. THE LOCAL AUTHORITY SERVICES

To complete this analysis we now briefly examine the trends in cost of these services.

Table 24 shows the cost, including and excluding charges.

Table 24. *The current cost of the local authority services including and excluding charges (England and Wales, 1948/9–1953/4)*

(£ m. in actual prices)

	1948/9*	1949/50	1950/1	1951/2	1952/3	1953/4
Gross cost of the local authority services	28·1	31·8	35·8	38·0	42·5	43·7
Less charges	−2·5	−2·4	−2·6	−2·9	−3·3	−3·3
Net cost of the local authority services	25·6	29·4	33·2	35·1	39·2	40·4

* Annual rate—interpolated from the 270 days for which the National Health Service operated.

The part which charges play in this group of services is small (less than 10 %), and the revenue from them has been virtually a constant percentage of the gross cost. In view of this and the fact that information is not available showing the particular services for which the revenue was obtained, we continue the analysis in terms of the net cost.

Table 25 shows the effect of changing prices on the net cost.

Table 25. *The current net cost to public funds of the local authority services in actual and in 1948/9 prices (England and Wales, 1948/9–1953/4)*

(£ m.)

	1948/9*	1949/50	1950/1	1951/2	1952/3	1953/4
Net cost of local authority services in actual prices	25·6	29·4	33·2	35·1	39·2	40·4
in 1948/9 prices	25·6	28·0	30·8	30·4	31·7	32·1
Implied price index	100	104·9	108·0	115·5	123·6	125·9

* Annual rate—interpolated from the 270 days for which the National Health Service operated.

The prices of the local authority services rose 26 % in the period under review compared with a rise of 29 % in the retail price index. The rise in expenditure between 1949/50 and 1953/4 is seen to be £11 million; of this, £4 million was due to a rise in the quantity of goods and services purchased, and £7 million to rising prices.

In Table 26 we show a break-down of the cost into four groups of local authority services.[1]

Table 26. *Break-down of the current net cost to public funds of the local authority services in 1948/9 prices (England and Wales, 1948/9–1953/4)*

(£ m. in 1948/9 prices)

Services	1948/9*	1949/50	1950/1	1951/2	1952/3	1953/4
Child health and maternity	12·9	13·0	13·7	12·6	13·4	12·5
Ambulance service	5·6	6·9	7·5	7·8	7·9	8·1
Domestic help service	1·5	2·4	2·8	3·1	3·4	3·8
Other	5·7	5·7	6·7	6·9	7·0	7·7
Total	25·6	28·0	30·7	30·4	31·7	32·1

* Annual rate—interpolated from the 270 days for which the National Health Service operated.

While the cost of the services as a whole has risen by 15 %, those concerned with child health and maternity (representing nearly half the total cost) have fallen by 4 %. The amount which they cost in 1953/4 (£12·5 million) was composed of £3·7 million for midwifery, £6·4 million for the care of mothers and children, and £2·4 million for health visiting.[2] Between 1949/50 and 1953/4 the cost of the care of mothers and children fell slightly, while a fall of 8 % in the cost of midwifery was balanced by a rise of 27 % in the cost of health visiting.

The fall of 8 % in the cost of midwifery can be compared with a fall of 10 % in the number of live births in England and Wales or, more usefully, with a decline of 18 % in confinements attended by domestic midwives over the same period. The number of hospital confinements steadily increased between 1949 and 1952, and fell slightly in 1953.[3] There was accordingly some under-employment of domiciliary midwives at the end of the period under review.

[1] For the main headings included in these four groups see Chapter II, p. 15.

[2] These are only very rough estimates owing to the different allocations and accounting procedures adopted by different local authorities at different periods.

[3] *Cases undertaken by midwives in hospitals in England and Wales*

Year	As midwives	As maternity nurses	Total
1949	304,543	69,523	374,066
1950	312,401	72,358	384,759
1951	318,583	78,330	396,913
1952	323,903	80,806	404,709
1953	Not available		401,116

Based on information kindly supplied by the Central Midwives Board. The number of births occurring in National Health Service hospitals without the attendance of a midwife is negligible.

The ambulance and domestic help services have each increased by over £1 million since 1949/50 and other services by £2 million. This represents an increase of 58 % for the domestic help service, 35 % for the other (mainly district nursing) services, and 17 % for the ambulance service. The rate of increase in the ambulance service has been slowing down while the domestic help service has continued to expand at much the same annual rate since 1949/50.

As with the hospital service, it is important to indicate the type of resources absorbed by the local authority services. About 85 % of the cost of the services is attributable to wages and salaries; nearly half the wages and salaries being paid to 'medical' personnel (nurses, midwives, health visitors, etc.). Since 1949/50 the consumption of goods has increased very little, but additional services have been absorbed in the form of £1 million more 'medical' workers and over £2 million more 'other' workers (mainly in the domestic help service).

The general conclusions derived from these separate analyses of the trends in cost of the different parts of the National Health Service are brought together in Chapter VI. The more important facts which have emerged are also listed in the Summary.

CHAPTER V

CAPITAL EXPENDITURE ON THE NATIONAL HEALTH SERVICE

The first part of this chapter analyses the trends in capital expenditure during the first six years of the National Health Service in England and Wales. In the second part, an attempt is made to assess the significance of this rate of expenditure in contrast to similar expenditure before the Second World War, and estimates are given of the ratio of capital to current expenditure at different times. Some comparative figures of capital expenditure on hospitals in the United States are inserted for purposes of illustration.

While current expenditure on the hospital service cannot fall below a certain minimum each year if the service is to be maintained, capital expenditure can, on the other hand, and within broad limits, be postponed without greatly affecting the running of the service for *some* period of time. In the long run, however, capital and current expenditure will have to arrive at a given relationship if the service is to continue. We shall proceed to ask, therefore, whether the level of expenditure during the first six years of the National Health Service was adequate to maintain the existing stock of capital intact.[1]

The third part of this chapter deals with the trends of capital expenditure estimated to be needed in the future to maintain the present Service.[2]

1. THE TREND IN COST, 1948–1954

The capital cost of the National Health Service (real asset expenditure)[3] is shown in Table 27 broken down into new fixed assets and changes in the value of stocks.[4]

Expenditure on new fixed assets has been fairly constant at actual prices since 1949/50. To correct for changing prices is not easy owing to the difficulty of finding an appropriate index. It seems likely, however, that between 1949/50 and 1953/4 building prices rose by at least

[1] Allowing for both depreciation and 'wear and tear'.

[2] It should be understood that in employing the term 'to maintain the present Service' we are using it as a basis for estimating trends. We neither accept nor advocate the maintenance of the Service in its present form.

[3] For definition of capital see Chapter II, p. 13.

[4] The Ministry of Health buys 'medical' goods not only for the National Health Service but for the Department of Health for Scotland and other government departments. We have accordingly made estimates of the stocks held to meet only the needs of the hospital branch of the National Health Service.

25%.[1] It follows, therefore, that in constant prices expenditure on fixed assets in 1953/4 was about three-quarters of that in 1949/50.

The rise in total capital cost between 1949/50 and 1951/2 was accounted for by additions to stocks, and between 1951/2 and 1952/3 the swing of £6 million in total capital cost was again due to changes in the rate of stock building. Stocks are, on the whole, valued at historical cost in the National Health Service; these changes represent primarily a change in the size of stock holdings, rather than changes in the value of existing stocks. There are two reasons for the sharp fall in the value of stocks in 1952/3. In part it was a response by hospital authorities to the

Table 27. *The capital cost of the National Health Service broken down into new fixed assets and changes in stocks (England and Wales, 1948/9–1953/4)*

(£ m. in actual prices)

	5 July 1948/9	Annual* rate 1948/9	1949/50	1950/1	1951/2	1952/3	1953/4
New fixed assets	7·7	10·4	11·8	11·6	12·5	11·9	11·1
Change in value of stocks	1·0	1·4	2·0	3·7	4·0	−2·2	−2·4
Total	8·8	11·8	13·7	15·3	16·5	9·8	8·8

* Interpolated from the 270 days for which the National Health Service operated.

Table 28. *The cost of new fixed assets in the National Health Service as a proportion of gross fixed capital formation (England and Wales, 1948/9–1953/4)*

(£ m. in actual prices)

	1948/9*	1949/50	1950/1	1951/2	1952/3	1953/4
(1) Gross fixed capital formation†	1295	1419	1532	1689	1874	2084
(2) Expenditure on new fixed capital assets in the National Health Service	10·4	11·8	11·6	12·5	11·9	11·1
(3) (2) as percentage of (1)	0·80	0·83	0·76	0·74	0·64	0·53

* Annual rate—interpolated from the 270 days for which the National Health Service operated.

† Gross fixed capital formation has been taken as 89% of that for Great Britain interpolated into financial years (Central Statistical Office, *National Income and Expenditure, 1955*, H.M.S.O. 1955).

[1] Two indices of building costs can be derived from Central Statistical Office, *National Income and Expenditure, 1946–1953* (H.M.S.O. 1954), p. 65. The first covers 'new housing' and rose 26% between 1948 and 1953. The second is for 'other new building and works' which rose 34% between 1948 and 1953. This last index covers a high proportion of educational building. Both in new housing and in school building, factors have been operating affecting building productivity which are probably not applicable or at least not applicable to the same extent to hospital building. As a result neither of these indices suits our purposes. It is likely, however, that the rise in the price of hospital building work has been at least as great as the rise in the price of new housing work. After considering all the evidence we were able to collect we decided to adopt a figure of 25%.

stricter financial limitations imposed upon the Service, and in part it can be attributed to letters sent by the Ministry of Health to hospital authorities in January 1953 requesting a reduction in stock values in the next financial year.

In Table 28 the new fixed assets are shown as a percentage of gross fixed capital formation in the national economy.

The table shows that the proportion of national investment devoted to the National Health Service has been negligible throughout the whole period (less than 1 %). It has steadily declined since 1949/50, and by 1953/4 was nearly 40 % lower than during the first full year of the Service.

In Table 29 expenditure on new fixed assets is analysed by services.

Table 29. *The cost of new fixed assets in the National Health Service broken down by services (England and Wales, 1948/9–1953/4)*

(£000 in actual prices)

Service	5 July 1948/9	Annual* rate 1948/9	1949/50	1950/1	1951/2	1952/3	1953/4
Hospital	5,775	7,807	9,779	9,802	10,603	9,915	9,395
Local authority	1,922	2,598	1,960	1,751	1,805	1,885	1,696
Executive council	31	42	36	25	84	139	42
Total	7,728	10,447	11,775	11,578	12,492	11,939	11,133

* Interpolated from the 270 days for which the National Health Service operated.

The bulk of new asset expenditure goes on the hospital service. The new assets in the executive council services relate only to office premises. In the local authority services about half the new assets is represented by vehicles (ambulances) and the other half by buildings.

Between July 1948 and March 1954 total expenditure on hospital fixed assets was £55 million; 91 % of this was made by the hospital authorities themselves. The remaining 9 % consisted of conversions of hospital buildings carried out by the Ministry of Works, the purchase of X-ray machines and other similar capital equipment for replacement, and capital expenditure on the bacteriological service.

Table 30 breaks down the expenditure by hospital authorities for the whole period.

Only 10 % of the expenditure over the six years has been on new hospitals and major extensions and only 21 % has been on ward accommodation. Staff quarters and amenities have absorbed 16 % of the total expenditure. In terms of housing accommodation a good part of this provision for hospital staff has the effect of relieving the housing shortage by releasing (or not using) lodgings which are thereby available for others. The relatively high rate of expenditure under this heading is partly explained by inadequacy of provision before 1948; higher standards of amenity introduced for hospital staffs after 1948, and a preference by some sections of the staff for living in.[1] Generally, some part of this expenditure might therefore be more properly allocated to 'housing' than to 'health'.

Approximately 18% of the capital expenditure was devoted to laundries, kitchens and engineering services. Some part of this expenditure had the effect of reducing current costs. There is ample scope for such 'cost-saving' expenditure. We examine this important subject in some detail in Appendix F.

Table 30. *Break-down of hospital capital expenditure**
(*England and Wales, 5 July 1948–31 March 1954*)

	Percentage of total
New hospitals and major extensions	10·2
Ward accommodation	20·7
Special medical departments (including operating theatres and diagnostic departments)	19·1
Out-patient and casualty departments	6·7
Accommodation for staff including nurse training	16·2
Laundries	2·1
Main kitchens	2·6
Engineering services	13·4
Fees for future general development	0·5
Administration (hospitals)	1·5
Miscellaneous	7·0
Total	100·0

* Including X-ray equipment, centrally supplied, and all unfixed equipment on capital account.

2. THE SIGNIFICANCE OF THE PRESENT RATE OF HOSPITAL BUILDING

In Appendix G a comparison is attempted between capital expenditure in the hospital service under the National Health Service and similar expenditure before the Second World War. There are many difficulties involved in this particular exercise, and some of them cannot be resolved because the appropriate data do not exist. In Table 31 the expenditure on a comparable basis for 1938/9 and 1952/3 is shown in 1952/3 prices.

Capital expenditure in 1938/9 was about three times the level of 1952/3. This result would not be materially altered by choosing different years either towards the end of the 1930's or during the operation of the National Health Service.

It is interesting also to compare the ratio of capital to current expenditure on hospitals before the war and under the National Health Service. This is attempted in Table 32.

[1] One reason for this preference is that board and lodging are provided substantially below cost (see Appendix C).

Table 31. *A comparison between hospital capital expenditure in 1938/9 and 1952/3* (England and Wales)*

(£ m. in 1952/3 prices)

	1938/9	1952/3	1952/3 as percentage of 1938/9
Hospital capital expenditure	32·0	10·2	32

* This table is based on a definition of expenditure approximating to that devised by the King Edward VII Fund (see Appendix G).

Table 32. *The ratio of capital to current expenditure on hospitals in 1938/9 and 1952/3 (England and Wales)*

(£ m. in actual prices)

	1938/9*	1952/3
Hospital current expenditure	46·9	249·7
Hospital capital expenditure	9·2	10·2
Capital as percentage of current	19·6	4·1

* The figures for 1938/9 are taken from Ministry of Health, *Local Government Financial Statistics, England and Wales, Summary, 1937/8* (printed for official use, 1941); *1938/9* (1942) (excluding loan charges) plus the expenditure of those voluntary hospitals reporting to the British Hospital Association for the calendar year 1938. The absolute totals are therefore incomplete, but this is unlikely to affect substantially the proportional relationship of capital and current.

On these estimates it appears that the ratio of capital to current expenditure was only 4·1 % in 1952/3 as compared with 19·6 % in 1938/9. In appraising this result it has, of course, to be remembered that current expenditure, defined in terms of what the hospitals—particularly the voluntary hospitals—themselves spent in 1938/9, is not comparable for various reasons with current expenditure after 1948. For example, nursing and medical salaries were by any standards low or non-existent in some voluntary hospitals before the war; student nurses did a great deal of domestic work; less expenditure was required to maintain equipment because less equipment was used; patients and their relatives brought food into the hospital and so reduced expenditure on provisions, and so forth. Nevertheless, the order of difference in these ratio figures, together with those given in Table 31, points to the low level of capital expenditure since 1948.

Similar data for the United States are given in Table 33. These figures can be compared only very roughly with those in Table 32, principally because the definitions employed differ in a good many respects.

It appears that in the United States capital expenditure was nearly a quarter of current expenditure in 1951. The difference between this ratio and Britain's post-1948 ratio is striking.

We now turn to compare the rate of hospital building under the National Health Service with the level required in the long run to maintain the present stock of buildings intact. On 31 December 1952, the National Health Service had a bed complement of 507,368. The cost at 1952 prices of rebuilding the present complement without any change in function, though with an inevitable improvement in design, would be about £3500 a bed.[1]

Table 33. *The ratio of capital to current expenditure on hospitals in the United States in 1951*

	$ m. in actual prices
Operating expenses of all hospitals*	3913
Value of hospital construction†	917
Construction as percentage of current expenditure	23·4

* United States President's Commission on the Health Needs of the Nation (Magnuson Commission), *Building America's Health, vol. 4, Financing a Health Program for America* (Washington, Superintendent of Documents, 1953), Table 7.4, p. 264.

† *Ibid.* Table 7.10 ,p. 274.

The total cost of rebuilding the present bed complement would therefore work out at about £1750 million. At the rate of building work in 1952/3 (about £8 million)[2] it would take about 220 years to rebuild without any extension of facilities to allow for present unsatisfied demands, technical advances, changes in the geographical distribution of population, changes in population structure and other factors.

There can be no conclusive answer to the question of how long a hospital building should be used before it is replaced. To a considerable extent this is a question of standards of treatment and accommodation and of the way in which medical care is organized. These standards[3] will inevitably vary with changes in the methods of treatment and changes in what public opinion regards as desirable. However, expert opinion would suggest that after sixty years the stage will have been reached when substantial refitting will be desirable; we must expect that the design will be ill adapted to the needs of that time if technical changes in the past provide any indication of those we may expect in the future. After ninety years, the vast majority of hospital buildings will be quite obsolescent. On this basis it follows, therefore, that the rate of capital expenditure under the National Health Service has been below half the level needed to maintain a stock of approximately 500,000 hospital beds.

[1] This is a rough average figure and covers, at one extreme of the wide range of hospital functions, the rebuilding of the fully equipped teaching hospital to, at the other, the simplest of hospital annexes. It also includes for all types the whole range of ancillary hospital buildings from nurses' hostels to doctors' dining-rooms.

[2] Furniture and equipment, including centrally supplied equipment, have been omitted from this figure.

[3] For a discussion of this subject see Nuffield Provincial Hospitals Trust, *Studies in the Functions and Design of Hospitals* (London, 1955).

3. FUTURE TRENDS IN COSTS

As stated earlier, capital expenditure can, by its nature, be postponed. There is no reason why expenditure should be up to replacement level in any particular year. But in the long run capital needs must be met if the service is to be maintained. An important factor in assessing the need for building up to or beyond replacement level now and in the future is the age of the existing stock of hospitals. If most of the hospitals in the country had been built during the last thirty years, there would obviously be no necessity to build up to replacement level at the present time. But this is far from being the case. Such information as has been collected for us by the Ministry of Health on the age of hospital buildings is neither complete nor in the form most suited for the assessment of rebuilding needs.[1] Nevertheless, it appears from these data that about 45 % of the hospitals were originally erected before 1891 and 21 % before 1861. Mental and mental deficiency hospitals are, on the average, older than other hospitals as shown in Table 34.

Table 34. *The age of hospital buildings (England and Wales)*

Percentage of hospital buildings originally erected before	Mental and mental deficiency (%)	Other (%)	Total (%)
1891	65	43	45
1861	40	18	21

This information is by no means conclusive because we do not know either the dates or the extent of the new building which took place after the original erection. Nor have we any up-to-date information about the structural condition of these hospitals. We may, however, supplement this information on age by quoting from the reports of the last national hospital survey. This took place during the Second World War. All the surveyors drew attention to the inadequate state of hospital buildings.

The surveyors of the North Western area wrote: 'Generally speaking, it must be recognized that the existing hospitals, considered as buildings, fall far short of a satisfactory standard. Indeed, considering the high place which England takes in the medical world, perhaps the most striking thing about them is how bad they are.'[2] The authors of the South Wales survey were even more explicit: 'A number of hospitals visited are so old or badly designed that they cannot be regarded as

[1] The information covers 1922 of 2750 hospitals in England and Wales in 1953. The omitted hospitals are, in the main, the smaller ones, and in total they account for only 10 % of the beds. The figures refer to the original erection dates; about half the hospitals covered had additions made to them after they were erected.

[2] Ministry of Health, *Hospital Survey, The Hospital Services of the North-Western Area* (H.M.S.O. 1945), p. 9.

worth retaining, whilst others can be improved or adapted or extended so as to satisfy modern standards without unduly heavy expenditure. In our opinion roughly one-half of the hospital accommodation, expressed in terms of hospital beds, is structurally ill-adapted for the purpose for which it is used, but, with expert advice, extension and adaptations could be undertaken which would render a fair proportion of it reasonably satisfactory. In a few instances complete demolition of the hospitals must be regarded as advisable since no tinkering with the existing structures can ever result in anything worth using for hospital purposes.' Criticism was not restricted to the old hospitals. 'We have observed that many hospitals erected in comparatively recent years are poorly designed, and do not conform to modern principles of hospital construction.'[1] The Yorkshire survey tells much the same story. 'A large number of hospitals in the region...are structurally unsuited for the adequate practice of medicine and surgery on modern lines.'[2] The West Midlands survey stated: 'New hospitals will be required in some districts, and in the coming years the older hospitals in part or whole will certainly need replacement.'[3]

In the Sheffield and East Midlands area, hospital buildings for the 'chronic' sick and for special needs were particularly criticized. 'Some of these special hospitals are however very bad indeed. We have seen isolation hospitals unworthy of use for any human occupation, and over-crowded, ill-adapted and structurally unsuitable maternity homes which should have perished long since. As a group the chronic hospitals are probably the worst.'[4] In the North Eastern area it was said: 'Many of the beds...are in accommodation which should be closed or rebuilt.'[5] The London surveyors summed up by saying: 'The general conclusion to be drawn from all this evidence can only be that either in quantity or quality deficiencies in all types of accommodation were widespread in 1938.'[6]

It may be concluded from all this evidence that hospital building cannot continue much longer at a figure well below replacement level if it is desired to maintain the service at a reasonable standard. About £30 million a year would represent a replacement level of building with

[1] Ministry of Health, Welsh Board of Health, *Hospital Survey, The Hospital Services of South Wales and Monmouthshire* (H.M.S.O. 1945), p. 11.

[2] Ministry of Health, *Hospital Survey, The Hospital Services of the Yorkshire Area* (H.M.S.O. 1945), p. 22.

[3] Ministry of Health, *Hospital Survey, The Hospital Services of the West Midlands Area* (H.M.S.O. 1945), p. 2.

[4] Ministry of Health, *Hospital Survey, The Hospital Services of the Sheffield and East Midlands Area* (H.M.S.O. 1945), p. 14.

[5] Ministry of Health, *Hospital Survey, The Hospital Services of the North-Eastern Area* (H.M.S.O. 1946), p. 8.

[6] Ministry of Health, *Hospital Survey, The Hospital Services of London and the Surrounding Area* (H.M.S.O. 1945), p. 11.

a sixty-year depreciation period, and at least £20 million a year with a ninety-year depreciation period. But considering the age and condition of the existing stock of hospitals and the low level of investment during and after the war, figures £10 million or £20 million higher might be thought necessary according to the rate at which it is desired to raise hospital capital to an adequate standard.

Another factor which requires examination is the effect of population changes on the need for hospital beds. Estimates of the future population have been derived from the population projection published by the General Register Office at the end of 1953. These are shown in Table 35.[1]

Table 35. *Projected civilian population* (England and Wales, 1956/7, 1961/2, 1971/2)*

Year	Numbers (millions)	Percentage of 1951/2
1951/2	43·31	100·0
1956/7	43·98	101·5
1961/2	44·46	102·7
1971/2	45·26	104·5

* These questions of population size and structure in relation to the National Health Service are further discussed in Chapter VI and Appendices H and I.

The population is expected to increase by 2 million (4½%) over twenty years. Applying this rate of increase to the 462,000 available beds in 1951 gives a round figure of 21,000 more beds by 1972.

Another relevant factor is the changing age structure of the population. The number and proportion of older people is expected to increase and, because it is generally understood that the old make proportionately larger demands on hospital accommodation, some allowance should accordingly be made for this factor in estimating future needs.

The subject of population change is examined in some detail in Appendix I in relation to the future cost of the National Health Service. The assumptions adopted and the methods employed in making such estimates are stated in this appendix. Here we limit ourselves to showing the results of a calculation of the effects of changes in the size and structure of the population on the existing complement of hospital beds.

Table 36 shows that, after age and sex adjustments have been made to the estimated population changes on the basis of *who was in hospital at the time of the 1951 Census*, about 51,000 additional occupied hospital beds will be needed by 1971/2—an increase of 11% or about ½% per year. It is an estimate which makes the fundamental assumption that all other factors are unchanged; standards and methods of medical care, the incidence of diseases and injuries, the geographical distribution of

[1] Published in General Register Office, *The Registrar General's Quarterly Return for England and Wales*, 4th qtr. 1953, no. 420, p. 29.

Table 36. *The effects of changes in population size, age and sex structure on the demand for hospital beds** (*England and Wales, 1956/7, 1961/2, 1971/2*)

Year	Occupied hospital beds	Increase over 1951/2	Percentage of 1951/2
1951/2	462,000	—	100
1956/7	476,000	14,000	103
1961/2	485,000	23,000	105
1971/2	513,000	51,000	111

* Based on Table 92, which gives the 1951 hospital population by age and sex. As the Registrar General's population projection assumes constant natality we have assumed that the number of maternity beds will remain unchanged at the 1951 figure.

the population, and many other imponderable elements, discussed in Appendix I.

For what it is worth, however, this exercise suggests that population changes over this period are, in themselves, a relatively unimportant factor in relation to the future rate of capital expenditure. The number of hospital beds at the end of 1952 closed 'due to lack of staff' (23,000) and 'temporarily closed for other reasons' (16,000) represents a high proportion of the figure of 51,000. Moreover, 'improved bed turnover' between 1949 and 1953 was, according to the Ministry of Health, equivalent to providing 40,000 extra beds. On the other hand, present waiting lists are large and some hospitals are overcrowded. While bearing all these considerations in mind it would, nevertheless, seem that the age of the hospitals themselves now and over the next twenty years is likely to constitute a more important factor in determining capital expenditure than any foreseeable change in the age composition of the population needing hospital care.

CHAPTER VI

CONCLUSIONS

PART I. THE MAIN FACTS

In this final chapter, we bring together the main facts which have emerged from the analysis of the different parts of the National Health Service, explain the changes in cost which are revealed, and assess their relationship to the national economy.

In a concluding section, we briefly consider the results of two special studies (Appendices H and I) of the relationships between population change, social structure and present and future demands on the National Health Service. Finally, we draw attention to the need to expand and intensify the study of contemporary problems of medical care, its organization and administration.

We begin this chapter by following the same arrangement of material as was used in earlier chapters. First, we discuss the role of charges; secondly, we show the proportion of the national income devoted to the Service; thirdly, we discuss the effect of changing prices, and fourthly, we consider changes in the type of resources used.

1. THE CURRENT COST OF THE NATIONAL HEALTH SERVICE AND THE REVENUE FROM CHARGES

Table 37 shows the current cost of the Service, including and excluding charges.

Table 37. *The current cost of the National Health Service including and excluding charges (England and Wales, 1948/9–1953/4)*

(£ m. in actual prices)

	5 July 1948/9	1948/9*	1949/50	1950/1	1951/2	1952/3	1953/4
Gross current cost of the National Health Service	246·4	333·2	376·6	395·7	411·7	436·7	453·4
Less charges	−4·0	−5·4	−5·0	−5·2	−9·6	−19·8	−23·1
Net current cost of the National Health Service	242·5	327·8	371·6	390·5	402·1	416·9	430·3

* Annual rate—interpolated from the 270 days for which the National Health Service operated.

Between 1948 and 1951, the charges yielded about £5 million a year. They covered only payments for accommodation in hospital (including payments under the Road Traffic Acts) and payments under the local authority services for domestic help, etc. Charges for dentures and spectacles were introduced on 21 May 1951 and increased the revenue by £4 million between 1950/1 and 1951/2. More extended charges were introduced in the middle of 1952, bringing the total revenue up to £23 million in 1953/4 (the first full year for which these charges had operated). It should be noted that even in that year charges represented

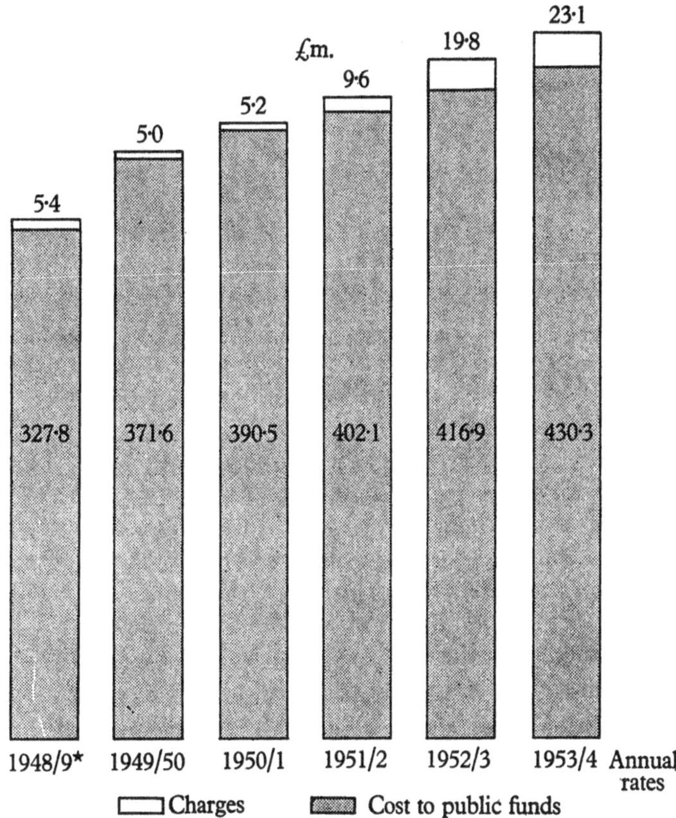

Fig. 3. The current cost of the National Health Service including and excluding charges.

only about 5 % of the gross cost of the Service. Between 1950/1 and 1953/4, gross expenditure rose by £58 million, but as a result of the new charges net expenditure rose by only £40 million. It has been shown in Chapter IV that the introduction of the charges had some effect in reducing demand. A slowing down in the rate at which gross expenditure was rising was, however, already well in evidence before the charges were imposed. The main features of Table 37 are brought out in Fig. 3.

2. THE COST OF THE NATIONAL HEALTH SERVICE IN RELATION TO THE NATIONAL INCOME

In Table 38 the current cost to public funds (net cost) is shown as a proportion of the gross national product—the generally accepted measure of total national resources.

Table 38. *The current net cost to public funds of the National Health Service as a proportion of the gross national product (England and Wales, 1948/9–1953/4)*

(£ m. in actual prices)

	1948/9*	1949/50	1950/1	1951/2	1952/3	1953/4
Gross national product†	9,349	9,907	10,539	11,560	12,487	13,273
Net cost of the National Health Service	327·8	371·6	390·5	402·1	416·9	430·3
Net cost as percentage of gross national product	3·51	3·75	3·71	3·48	3·34	3·24

* Annual rate—interpolated from the 270 days for which the National Health Service operated.

† These figures represent 89% of the gross national product for Great Britain (Treasury, *Preliminary Estimates of National Income and Expenditure 1948 to 1954*, Cmd. 9423 (H.M.S.O. 1955)) interpolated into financial years. The deduction of 11% applies to Scotland and Northern Ireland.

The year in which the highest proportion (3·75%) of national resources was taken by the National Health Service was the first full year, 1949/50. Since then the proportion has fallen each year. Again it can be seen that the fall began before the new charges were introduced. The total fall between 1949/50 and 1953/4 in the proportion amounts to 14%. Had the proportion of resources devoted to the Service in 1953/4 been the same as in 1949/50 the net cost would have been £67 million higher.

In Table 39 the gross cost of the Service is similarly shown as a proportion of the gross national product.

Table 39. *The current gross cost of the National Health Service (i.e. before deduction of charges) as a proportion of the gross national product (England and Wales, 1948/9–1953/4)*

(£ m. in actual prices)

	1948/9*	1949/50	1950/1	1951/2	1952/3	1953/4
Gross national product	9,349	9,907	10,539	11,560	12,487	13,273
Gross cost of the National Health Service	333·2	376·6	395·7	411·7	436·7	453·4
Gross cost as percentage of the gross national product	3·57	3·80	3·75	3·56	3·50	3·42

* Annual rate—interpolated from the 270 days for which the National Health Service operated.

The gross cost was also at its peak in 1949/50, and by 1953/4 had fallen, in the proportion used, by 10%. Had the gross cost been proportionately the same in 1953/4 as in 1949/50 the total would have been higher by £51 million. In Chapter IV we made certain tentative estimates of the extent to which the new charges may have lowered the gross cost by 1953/4. We suggested £5 million for the dental service,[1] and also £5 million for the ophthalmic service.[2] If forced to make a guess for the pharmaceutical service, we would put it at £4 million. We considered these estimates to represent the maximum possible

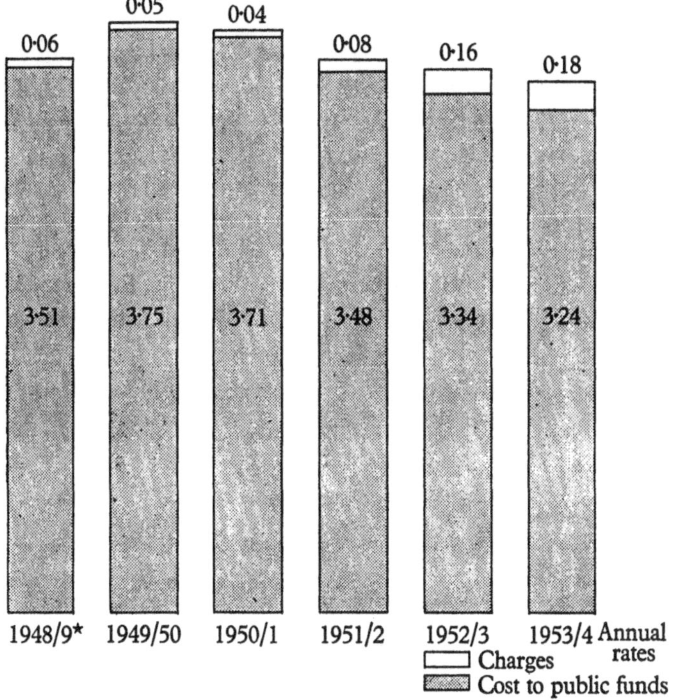

Fig. 4. The current cost of the National Health Service including and excluding charges as a proportion of the gross national product.

indirect effects of the new charges. The total of £14 million may be compared with the foregoing figure of £51 million. The indirect effects of these charges, therefore, in cutting down demand can account for less than a third of the decline in the proportion of the national income devoted to the National Health Service. This conclusion would not be substantially altered by correcting for price changes.

The figures in both Tables 38 and 39 are shown graphically in Fig. 4.

[1] See p. 42. [2] See p. 44.

3. THE EFFECTS OF CHANGING PRICES

The trends of prices in the three branches of the Service are brought together and shown in Table 40.

Notwithstanding the tentative nature of these indices the estimated price rises between 1948/9 and 1953/4 may be compared with a rise of 29 % in the retail price index. The rise in prices in the local authority services comes closest to that for the retail index. The rise in the hospital services index is slightly less. Some of the reasons for this are discussed in Chapter IV. Prices in the executive council services, however, fell by 9 % between 1948/9 and 1950/1, rose by 4 % by 1952/3 and then fell by 3 % in 1953/4. These fluctuations represent the combined results of different trends within the executive council services. While prices in the general medical service rose slightly, prices in the pharmaceutical, dental and ophthalmic services fell markedly owing to downward adjustments in scales of payment. The effect of changing prices on the cost of the executive council services as a whole is illustrated in Fig. 5 and on the three branches of the National Health Service in Fig. 6.

Table 40. *Implied price indices by services (based on net costs)**
(England and Wales, 1948/9–1953/4)

Service	1948/9	1949/50	1950/1	1951/2	1952/3	1953/4
Hospital	100·0	104·8	107·0	114·8	121·2	123·5
Executive council	100·0	94·6	91·3	95·1	95·7	92·6
Local authority	100·0	104·9	108·0	115·5	123·6	125·9

* For details see Table 50, p. 96. The indices have been derived by dividing the figures under items 43, 56 and 67 in Table 48 by the corresponding totals in Table 51 and multiplying by a hundred.

In Table 41 the cost of the Service to public funds (net cost) is shown in actual and constant prices.

In terms of 1948/9 prices, the net cost of the National Health Service to public funds reached its peak in 1950/1. It fell during the next two years to a level approximately the same as in the first full year of the Service. In 1953/4 there was a small rise. This table is shown graphically in Fig. 7.

In Table 42 the gross cost of the Service is shown in actual and constant prices.

This table shows that the gross cost in constant prices rose by 5 % in 1950/1, was at a lower level during the next two years, and rose again in 1953/4. In other words, the figure has fluctuated between 2 and 9 % above the 1949/50 level.

Table 41. *The current net cost to public funds of the National Health Service in actual and in 1948/9 prices (England and Wales, 1948/9–1953/4)*

(£ m.)

	1948/9*	1949/50	1950/1	1951/2	1952/3	1953/4
Current net cost of the National Health Service in actual prices	327·8	371·6	390·5	402·1	416·9	430·3
In 1948/9 prices	327·8	369·8	388·3	374·1	370·6	380·8

* Annual rate—interpolated from the 270 days for which the National Health Service operated.

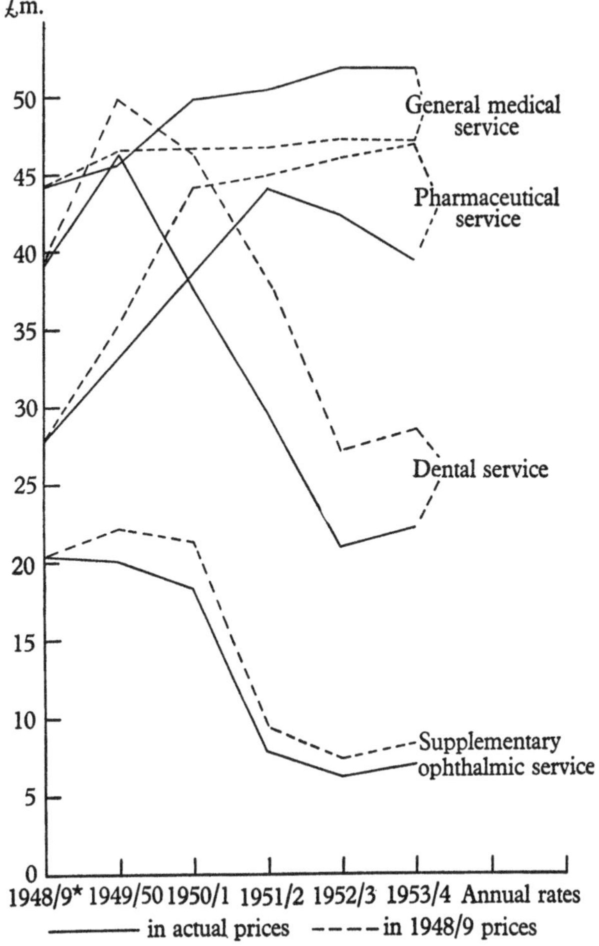

Fig. 5. The current net cost to public funds of the executive council services in actual and in 1948/9 prices.

Table 42. *The current gross cost of the National Health Service (i.e. before deduction of charges) in actual and in 1948/9 prices (England and Wales, 1948/9–1953/4)*

(£ m.)

	1948/9*	1949/50	1950/1	1951/2	1952/3	1953/4
Current gross cost of the National Health Service in actual prices	333·2	376·6	395·7	411·7	436·7	453·4
In 1948/9 prices	333·2	374·3	393·1	383·6	391·9	406·4

* Annual rate—interpolated from the 270 days for which the National Health Service operated.

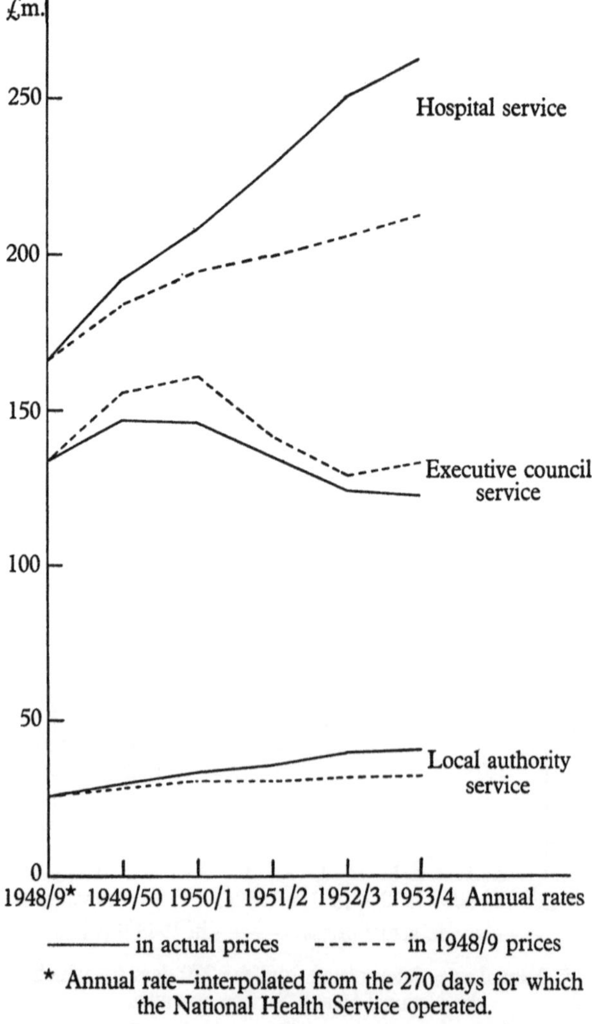

Fig. 6. The current net cost to public funds of the National Health Service by services in actual and in 1948/9 prices.

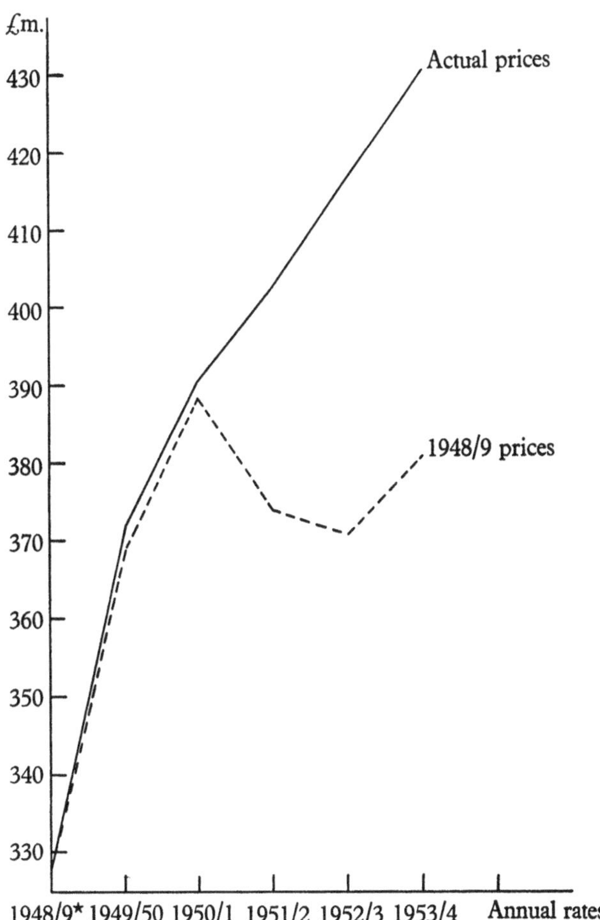

Fig. 7. The current net cost to public funds of the National Health Service in actual and in 1948/9 prices.

4. THE CHANGE IN RESOURCES USED

From Table 42 we saw that the gross cost of the National Health Service in 1948/9 prices rose by £32 million between 1949/50 and 1953/4. This represents the total of additional resources consumed. How was this total made up of different types of resources? Using the classification into types described in Chapter II[1] we present, in Table 43, the broad results of a break-down into these categories. In effect, this table brings together the main features of the separate analyses for the different

[1] Chapter II, pp. 16–17.

Table 43. *Changes in resources used in the current gross cost of the National Health Service (i.e. before deduction of charges) between 1949/50 and 1953/4 in 1948/9 prices** *(England and Wales)*

(£ m. in 1948/9 prices)

	Medical	Other	Total
Wages and salaries	14 (A)	11 (B)	25
Goods and contracts:			
Pharmaceutical service	19	—	19
Spectacles†	− 7	—	− 7
Other	5 (C)	4	9
Contracted services:			
Dental	−13	—	−13
General medical services and sight testing	− 1 (D)	—	− 1
Totals	17	15	32

* This table cannot be reconciled with Table 51, p. 98, for two reasons. First, it is concerned with the gross cost of the National Health Service, while Appendix B deals with the cost to public funds. Secondly, the elimination of trading activities other than charges to the public shown in Appendix C has been applied. In consequence, the items are stated only in round figures.

† The figure of £7 million differs from the decline of £12 million shown in Table 51 because the present table is concerned with the gross cost of the National Health Service, whereas Table 51 is concerned with the net cost or cost to public funds. In other words, £5 million of spectacles were paid for by charges in 1953/4.

These items are, in round figures, chiefly made up as follows:

(A) Nurses and midwives (£7 million), doctors (£4 million), medical auxiliaries (£2 million—all in the hospital services) and health visitors, nurses, etc., in the local authority services (£1 million).

(B) Other workers (mainly domestic staff) in the hospital services (£8½ million) and other workers—mainly domestic helps—in the local authority services (over £2 million).

(C) Drugs, dressings, equipment, etc., in the hospital services (£3 million), appliances and other goods provided by the Ministry of Pensions (£1½ million) and goods and contracts in the local authority services (£½ million).

(D) An increase of £½ million in the general medical services and a decrease of £1½ million in sight testing.

branches of the Service relating to changes in the consumption of resources.[1] These were given in Chapter IV.

It will be seen that the dominating changes have been: an increase of £25 million on wages and salaries; an increase of £24 million on drugs and medical goods; and a decrease of £20 million on dentures and spectacles. Allowing for the fact that some part of the total increase was accounted for by the use of additional labour who were unlikely to have found employment elsewhere (married women, part-time workers, Irish and other overseas workers specially recruited) it would seem that the net diversion of resources to the National Health Service between 1949/50 and 1953/4 was relatively negligible. It is also relevant that this small diversion of resources took place during a period when the population of England and Wales increased by about 800,000.

[1] Detailed estimates for the hospital service are shown in Table 66, p. 116.

5. THE EFFECTS OF CHANGING POPULATION

We now turn to consider this further factor of population change which has to be taken into account in studying trends in costs and the use of productive resources.

The proportion of the population making use of some or all of the different parts of the National Health Service is not known. It probably varies between the different parts and has no doubt undergone some change since 1948/9. In respect to medical care (the field of dental care is even more complicated) a proportion of the population—and perhaps an increasing proportion—makes use of both a National Health Service practitioner and a private practitioner. As the extent of private practice in general is not known we have, in Table 44, related the costs to the population liable to call on the Service. This population rose by nearly 2 % between 1948/9 and 1953/4.[1] Table 44 gives estimates of the gross and net costs per head in constant prices.

Table 44. *Estimated current costs per head of the National Health Service including and excluding charges in 1948/9 prices (England and Wales, 1948/9–1953/4)*

	1948/9	1949/50	1950/1	1951/2	1952/3	1953/4
Current gross cost of the National Health Service per head	£7. 16*s*.	£8. 14*s*.	£9. 2*s*.	£8. 17*s*.	£9	£9. 7*s*.
Current net cost of the National Health Service per head	£7. 13*s*.	£8. 12*s*.	£8. 19*s*.	£8. 13*s*.	£8. 11*s*.	£8. 15*s*.

This adjustment for population change shows that expenditure per head in constant prices was highest in 1950/1 for net cost and 1953/4 for gross cost. There is no consistent trend in either set of figures. The gross cost figures show a general tendency to rise; the net cost figures were, on the other hand, lower in 1952/3 than in the first full year of the Service and only 3*s*. per head higher in 1953/4. The main impression that this table leaves is the relative smallness of the movements in cost per head since 1949/50. This general conclusion is in accord with the results of our analysis of the important question of changes in the consumption of resources used. Contrary to public opinion, the net diversion of resources to the National Health Service since 1949/50 has been of relatively insignificant proportions.

[1] Estimates of the total civilian population of England and Wales. The figures were kindly supplied by the General Register Office.

PART II. SOCIAL FACTORS AND FUTURE TRENDS

In the Summary we list some of the principal conclusions that have emerged from this study of the trend of expenditure on the National Health Service. It has been, as we emphasized in Chapter 1, a limited study. For good reasons of time, resources and competence, we set ourselves against any discussion or study of the wider social and medical aspects of the national health. In particular, we had to omit any detailed consideration of the problem of 'demand' or 'need' for the various services provided by or through the operation of the National Health Service. To what extent and at what standards the Service has or has not been successful in meeting 'need' since 1948 are questions outside our self-imposed terms of reference. Our concern has been to trace the changing pattern of expenditure and, from time to time, to ask questions and seek explanations for specific changes that have been identified. In doing so, we have, however, been led—sometimes reluctantly because of the paucity of data—to examine certain aspects of 'demand'. Thus, we essayed, for example, to estimate the effect of charges on the cost of (and demand for) some branches of the National Health Service. But these estimates were of a tentative nature, and we attempted no more than an examination of such material as was available to us. To have aimed at firmer estimates would have called for a large programme of field studies and statistical research. We shall refer again to this matter of research in relation to the operation of the various services.

The one factor in demand we have considered at some length and in different parts of this study is the factor of population. This it was essential to do for the limited purposes of our expenditure analysis. Changes in the population at risk are clearly relevant to changes in levels of expenditure. They cannot be left out of account, for instance, in any attempt to measure secular changes in expenditure when it is desired to express such changes in constant terms. But to analyse the effects of population change simply on the basis of total numbers is to use an extremely crude instrument. Everything that is known about the complex pattern of health and disease demonstrates the importance of age and sex as factors in the determination of demand for medical care. As we explain in Appendix H, we found ourselves constantly asking questions about the age and sex structure of the patient population in studying the widely varying costs of services provided by different types of hospitals. We did so again when we considered the question of capital expenditure on hospital buildings. We wanted also to know the structure of the non-patient hospital population when we came to consider the subsidy involved in providing accommodation for staff.

To a limited extent, therefore, and with the assistance of the General Register Office, we have sought in various parts of this study to take account of the factors of age and sex in relation to the current use of different branches of the Service. We have also done so in undertaking the task for the Guillebaud Committee of estimating the order of magnitude of additional future costs to the Service solely as a result of projected population change. It is doubtful whether this particular exercise would have been suggested at all but for the influence of what is sometimes called 'the problem of ageing'. So much alarm has been provoked in recent years about the possible effects of 'an ageing population' that it seemed worth while to hazard even some preliminary estimates for others to criticize. These are set out in terms of cost in Appendix I, and we hope we have made explicit there the various assumptions and reservations in material and method on which the estimates insecurely rest. By studying in this way the effects on current costs of expected changes in population over the next twenty years as an independent, isolated factor we reach the conclusion that, on the basis of what is known at present about age and sex differences in demand (which, incidentally, is lamentably little), there is no justification for the alarm that has been expressed about the impact of 'an ageing population' on the cost of the National Health Service. Changes in age structure by themselves are calculated to increase the present cost of the Service to public funds by 3½ % by 1971/2. A further increase of 4½ % is attributable to the projected rise in the total population of England and Wales (using the official projection figures).

One reason why the additional costs of more old people (a projected increase of some 1½ million persons aged 65 and over) are insignificant is because only about one-fifth of expenditure is currently devoted to this age group. No doubt the figure would have been higher had it been possible to allow for the generally accepted fact that this age group makes heavier demands on the general practitioner than younger people. But this we were not able to do in the absence of any representative studies of the work of general practitioners.

A second explanation of the relatively low costs of medical care for the elderly has to be sought in the field of quality and standard of service. These are matters of fundamental importance which quite obviously we could not pursue in this documentary study. But in so far as, by-and-large, the older age group are currently receiving a lower standard of service than the main body of consumers and that there are also substantial areas of unmet need among the elderly, then it would follow that the estimates we present are even less indicative of future trends in cost. The material we analyse in Appendix H on the hospital population does suggest that, in terms of age groups, the scope for raising standards of service is greater among the elderly than among other groups in the population. It was shown, for example, that about two-thirds of all the hospital accommodation in the country for those aged 65 and over is taken by the single, the widowed and divorced, and that most of these people in 'dependent' situations are to be found in the population of 'chronic' and mental hospitals.[1] It is known that standards of active treatment and rehabilitation are low in many of these hospitals.

Elsewhere we have expressed the view that, in studies of this kind, to consider the factor of age in isolation from other related factors is not a fruitful approach to the analysis of social institutions. Age—or old age in this context—is only one of many important social and demographic factors determining the level of demand for health and other social services. We are fortified in this view by the results of our analysis in Appendix H, which suggests that, other things being equal, the demand for hospital care is more influenced by the social situation of a person than by the age of a person. Irrespective of the changing incidence of disease, concepts of ill-health, standards of diagnosis and treatment and attitudes to medical care, all these 'social' factors of age, sex, family relationships, class and income play a variety of roles in determining the pattern of demand. They do not all work in the same direction; more old people may mean more demands on some services but not on others; more children and a higher birth-rate affect the different branches of the Service in different ways; less hospitalized sickness may mean more expenditure on welfare services; a larger proportion of the population with middle-class standards and aspirations may mean more *expressed* demand for some forms of medical care; a lower marriage rate and smaller families may mean increased demands for hospital care; changes in the proportions of men and women who are single, widowed, divorced and childless may represent in the future more important factors in influencing demand for medical care than any foreseeable changes in the age structure of the population as a whole. These are some of the suggestions which are thrown up by our studies of the 1951 hospital population.

It was not, unfortunately, possible to develop our estimates of the future costs of the Service by taking account of these 'social' factors. Little is known about variations in the demand for and the cost of different forms of medical, dental, ophthalmic and other services from different groups in the population by age, sex, marital state, dependency, social class and other characteristics. Appendices H and I throw a glimmering of light on some of these questions. We summarize briefly some of the points that emerged from the former:

(1) Compared with the demands made by single men and women (and, to a lesser extent, the widowed) the proportion of married men and women in hospital even at age 65 and over is extremely small.

[1] Appendix H, p. 146.

(2) Among married men and women, the rise in the proportion in hospital with advancing age is not at all dramatic and, contrary to the assumptions often made, does not reach very high levels even after age 75. It is also noteworthy—again, contrary to expectation—that, age by age, there is little difference between married men and women.

(3) After age 45 the proportions in hospital of single people (particularly men) and, to a lesser extent, of the widowed and divorced, diverge more and more sharply with advancing age from those of married people.

(4) For all types of hospital and in relation to their numbers in the total adult population, the single, widowed and divorced make about double the demand on hospital accommodation compared with married people.

(5) About two-thirds of all the hospital beds in the country occupied by those aged over 65 are taken by the single, widowed and divorced.

(6) The bulk of the population of mental and 'chronic' hospitals are single people. Of the single and widowed aged over 65 needing hospital care most of them are to be found in these two types of hospital. Marriage and its survival into old age appears to be a powerful safeguard against admission to hospitals in general and to mental and 'chronic' hospitals in particular.

(7) In respect to certain characteristics, the population of teaching hospitals (and to a somewhat lesser extent general hospitals) is different from that of all hospitals. They have a younger population; a much less noticeable progression with age, and apparently admit only a small fraction of elderly people.

(8) Among other factors of demand for hospital care which are outside the power of the National Health Service to control, accidents and injuries represent one of the most important elements in the total demand.

(9) Men aged 25–64 in social classes I, II and III appear to be making full use of National Health Service hospitals, whereas semi-skilled and unskilled men of these ages in classes IV and V are making fewer demands than might have been expected from their relatively higher morbidity and mortality rates.

(10) For all types of hospital, the proportion of resident staff to inmates was at least 22% in 1951. It varied from over 50% for all teaching hospitals to 6 and 7% for mental deficiency and mental hospitals respectively. It may be that a reduction in the proportion of staff which is resident to 30% in those hospitals which now exceed this figure might be as important in terms of hospital space as any likely changes in the national population or its age composition during the next decade.[1]

[1] See Appendix C.

(11) An analysis of the Government Actuary's estimates of the population of Great Britain in 1979 shows that among those who make by far the heaviest claims on hospital accommodation, the number of single women of pensionable ages will actually decline, while the number of single men of such ages will increase by only a negligible figure.

(12) If detailed adjustments were made to our figures of gross and net current costs per head for 1949/50–1953/4 (Table 44) to take account of changes in population structure they would not materially alter the general picture. Between these years the population aged 15–44 declined by about 700,000; there was a corresponding increase in the age group 45–64; the number of children rose by 500,000, and the number of people aged over 65 rose by about 300,000. The combined effect of these changes would involve a downward adjustment in the gross and net cost figures per head for 1953/4 of about 2*s*. primarily because of the increase in the child population which, in terms of hospital care, is the most expensive age group.[1] We estimated in Table 44 that the net cost per head of the National Health Service was £8. 12*s*. in 1949/50 and £8. 15*s*. in 1953/4. Changes in the population, therefore, are sufficient to account for the increase in the cost of the National Health Service to public funds between 1949/50 and 1953/4, which, as we have shown, has been of relatively insignificant proportions.

In interpreting these results it is necessary to bear in mind that as they relate only to people in hospital on census night 1951 they do not indicate the proportion of people in any given category who had some stay in hospital during the year. This is one of several qualifications (not least being the factor of selection of patients for hospital care) to which attention is drawn in Appendices H and I.

Finally, we conclude with some brief reference to the need for research. It is natural that we should do so, for with a monotony that at times has seemed exaggerated we have repeatedly drawn attention to defects and inconsistencies in the material on which this study is based. Continuously we have had to make adjustments to the original data and to supplement them with estimates. Many of the comments we have made should not, however, be taken to imply criticism of the Ministry of Health and other authorities. It would have been, to say the least, presumptuous of us to have expected that material collected for purposes of administration and financial control should be arranged and classified in such a form as to be suitable for the purposes of this study.

Every year in which the National Health Service has operated there has been a steady improvement in the quantity and quality of information available to the administrator and, to a somewhat lesser extent, to the public. This, of course, as we have recognized, has added to our

[1] This calculation is based upon the figures quoted in Appendix I (Table 105) and is subject to all the qualifications stated in that appendix.

difficulties in studying trends in expenditure—a price which any research worker should be willing to pay. There is no doubt that as a result of these improvements we now know far more than we did as recently as 1939 about the social and economic problem of medical care. Then, virtually nothing was known about the costs of medical care; about the various hospital systems, and about the organization and economy of general practice. Now we can at least see the dimensions of these and allied problems.

The new knowledge that has accumulated since 1948 has, paradoxically, been partly responsible for the public alarm about the cost of the National Health Service. Much of it has been crude and undiscerning in quality; a defect inevitable in the early stages of this new Service. Much of it again has been circumscribed to fit conventional and often ill-fitting frames of reference. In a number of important sectors the results have, at the very least, given rise to much misunderstanding; in others they have at best been difficult to interpret. We gave some examples in Chapter II of the errors that can arise from any attempt to interpret trends in cost of the Service in terms of payment statistics. We also showed in Appendix A that adjustments in the region of £70–80 million a year need to be made to account for the divergence between the net cost of the Service as stated in the Appropriation Accounts and our estimates of the cost to public funds. It is hardly surprising that misunderstanding should arise when changes of this magnitude have to be made in order to reach a less ambiguous and more consistent concept of cost.

It seems to us that now the National Health Service is seven years old, with a more skilled and technically experienced corps of administrators behind it, the stage has been reached for a further step forward in the collection, classification and analysis of facts. What is now needed is refinement, analysis and operational study rather than more routine statistics.

We do not suggest that statistical and accounting intelligence in combination with *ad hoc* research modifies in any way the need for skilled administration. But we do believe that administration at most levels—regionally, locally and at the centre—is capable of some improvement if aided with the results of a discriminating statistical service. The diversity of the National Health Service makes it particularly dangerous to assume that any unit or any piece of activity is typical of the whole. We often found in pursuing this study that commonly held opinions were disproved when the appropriate facts were collected and analysed in a meaningful way. It was also instructive to see how our inquiries stimulated an interest in the exploration of various fields of Health Service activity which had hitherto not been examined in any detail. We hope that the publication of this study will make some contribution to fostering and expanding this interest both nationally and locally.

APPENDIX A

A CLASSIFIED RECONCILIATION BETWEEN THE COST OF THE NATIONAL HEALTH SERVICE TO PUBLIC FUNDS IN PRODUCTIVE RESOURCES AND THE APPROPRIATION ACCOUNTS

The purpose of this appendix is to account for the divergence between the cost of the National Health Service as stated in the Appropriation Accounts and our estimate of the 'cost of the Service to public funds'. The reason for our choice of the concept of cost as meaning the use of current productive resources is explained in Chapter II.

The text of this appendix is intended to serve as a guide to Table 45, which gives details of the adjustments made and groups together adjusted items of a similar nature. Broadly the classifications adopted originate from the factors responsible for causing the divergence. As this is essentially an accounting table, the totals have not been rounded, even though the margin of error in certain of the estimates demands rounding of the grand totals to the nearest £1 million.

1. THE CHOICE OF CONCEPT FROM THE APPROPRIATION ACCOUNTS

Three concepts of cost can be derived from the Appropriation Accounts, and it was necessary to select one of these as a basis for reconciliation:

The gross total of the vote. For the first two years of the Service this recorded all the cash provided on the National Health Service votes without taking account of any receipts. During the next three years, certain trading receipts were subtracted. For this and other reasons the gross total of the vote figures are not comparable from year to year.

The net total of the vote. This is the gross total of the vote minus the appropriations-in-aid applied. Appropriations-in-aid applied are credits to the National Health Service vote which can be used to help finance the Service. These are estimated credits; and when a credit is greater than the original estimate it cannot be used in aid of the Service. As a result the net total of the vote does not show the net cost of the vote to the Exchequer; nor are the figures comparable from year to year.

The true net cost of the vote. This is the gross total of the vote less all the credits actually received (both appropriations-in-aid and extra-Exchequer receipts).

We have chosen to work from the true net cost of the vote, as the figures are more comparable from year to year than those yielded by the other two concepts. Notwithstanding this, it does not, as it stands, provide the concept of cost we have in mind. We are attempting to measure the total expenditure of the government (central and local) on the National Health Service as a whole. Corrections are therefore necessary so as to include all public expenditure on resources used in providing the Service, and as a consequence of applying a consistent definition of the National Health Service throughout the period under review.

2. THE RECONCILIATION EXPLAINED

The adjustments which have to be made to the true net cost of the vote to transform it into our concept of cost are substantial. A detailed account of these adjustments and the reasons for them are given below. The figures in brackets refer to the items listed in Table 45.

(a) *Adjustments made in arriving at an appropriate and consistent definition of the National Health Service*

As we are adjusting from the net total of the vote, the first step was to add back the contributions from other public funds used to finance the Service. The National Insurance Fund (2) has provided about £36 million a year. The War Damage Commission (3) has contributed small sums never amounting to more than £½ million. The Hospital Endowments Fund (4) paid £6½ million in 1949/50, and sums in the neighbourhood of £1 million in succeeding years. Since charges were introduced in 1951, a small part of the cost of the Service has been transferred to the National Assistance Board (5). In 1952/3, charges amounting to approximately £700,000 were paid by the Board for those persons in need of assistance.

Under the conventions of government accounting the central administrative costs of running the Service are not charged to the vote. Estimates of the cost of Ministry of Health salaries (7), of the upkeep of its buildings (9), the expenses of the Board of Control (8), and all allied services (9), have, therefore, to be included. Similarly, both the capital (16) and current costs (15) of local authority services have to be added. The current costs shown in Table 45 cover total expenditure on local authority services and not (as in the Appropriation Accounts) just the grants made by the central government.

The problem of defining the field of responsibility of the National Health Service was discussed in Chapter II. Here we repeat the main points. Expenditure from non-Exchequer funds (6) on hospital purposes and amenities has been included as part of the cost of the Service. Certain costs not attributable to the peace-time role of the Service have been subtracted, namely, civil defence and strategic stock piling (12). To achieve consistency, we decided to define the Service by its scope and content in the year 1951/2. When votes were charged with different responsibilities in other years, the items of cost in question have been added to or subtracted from the accounts for these other years. Thus, the cost of Broadmoor Institution (13) has been included throughout, although it was transferred to the Health Service from the Home Office only in April 1949. For the first two years certain training expenses (14) were carried by the main Ministry of Health vote but were later transferred to the Health Service vote. Additions have therefore been made for these two years. Similarly, in 1948/9 the Ministry of Works (10) carried on its own vote the cost of certain hospital building work charged in later years to the Health Service. An addition has been made for 1948/9.

Certain stores are purchased centrally by the Ministry of Health. Some of these are passed to the Department of Health for Scotland and other government departments. The cost of stores (11) has been adjusted to ensure that only those purchased for use by the Health Service in England and Wales are included.

In the figures for the first year of the Service, expenditure attributable to the period between 1 April and 4 July 1948 has been omitted as far as possible.

The combined effect of all adjustments under this heading (18) is to increase the true net cost of the vote by £39 million for the first nine months and about £60 million annually in later years.

(*b*) *The adjustments made to ensure a correct valuation of resources*

The superannuation contributions of both employer and employees are subtracted in the 'true net cost of the vote'. We have added these back (19) so as to value the resources used more correctly. We treat these contributions as part of *current* costs, as they are a form of remuneration for the employee. The prospects of superannuation are among the factors which are taken into account when employment is accepted. In effect, we regard these contributions as income of the employee compulsorily saved and deposited with the employer. In total they amounted to £22½ million in 1952/3.

A somewhat different kind of adjustment is involved in treating various retrospective payments. These have been allocated back to the years in which the relevant services were rendered. The rates of payment to general practitioners were revised in 1952/3 by the Danckwerts award (20) which applied to all payments from the start of the Service. Approximately £24 million has been transferred from 1952/3 to earlier years. Similarly, distinction awards to specialists (21) were made in 1950/1 covering the whole period from the start of the service, and these have been redistributed. There was also a retrospective award to nurses and midwives made in 1950/1 for the two previous years. An estimated adjustment (22) has therefore been made to allocate the award to the appropriate years.

The effect of all adjustments under this heading (23) is to increase the cost of the first four years by approximately £14, £23, £24 and £27 million respectively, and to decrease the cost for 1952/3 by about £1 million.

(*c*) *The adjustments due to delays in payment*

In the executive council services there is a delay between the use of resources and payment for them. In the case of expenditure on the pharmaceutical service (24), the work of joint pricing committees became seriously in arrears. Chemists were accordingly paid on the basis of estimated amounts due to them, and adjustments were later made by the joint pricing committees. Closer estimates of the value of goods and services used each month have therefore been made by us; they are derived from the figures which have subsequently emerged as the prescriptions for each month have been priced.

In both the dental (26) and ophthalmic (25) services delays in payment also arise. In the case of the dental service a course of treatment can be lengthy; only on its completion is it reported for payment. In the supply of both dentures and surgical appliances (27) considerable resources are used for 'work in progress' which are not paid for until some time later. Detailed adjustments have been made in all these instances of delayed payments.

The introduction of the National Health Service in 1948 presented great problems for the accounting administration of the Ministry of Health, such as the need to standardize and summarize the accounts of many hospitals which had previously operated on diverse systems and under managements of varying efficiency. As a result, in the earlier years of the Service corrected figures were very late in reaching the Ministry. The Appropriation Accounts had, therefore, to be closed on incomplete information. The adjustments needed for these accounting delays concern principally expenditure incurred by hospitals (29) and receipts for services rendered (30).

The effect of all adjustments under this heading (33) is to increase the true net cost of the vote by £21½ million and £2½ million for the first nine months and 1949/50 respectively, and to reduce the vote by roughly £¾, £4 and £2 million for the remaining three years.

(*d*) *Adjustments for expenditures and receipts not involving the use of current productive resources*

On the appointed day in 1948 the Minister undertook certain heavy financial liabilities which, during the early years of the Service, were gradually liquidated. He undertook to compensate general practitioners (34, 35) for loss of the right to sell their practices, and he compensated other persons for loss of office (36). The total of these compensation payments have varied from £3 to £6½ million (including interest) since 1949/50. The Minister agreed to pay local authorities for certain stores (37) taken over on the appointed day. This cost nearly £6 million during the first five years and payments were still being made in 1952/3. The Minister also undertook to meet the debts of the voluntary hospitals (38) as well as taking over their credits. Paying off these debts cost £34½ million in the first five years. Even as late as 1952/3 over £4 million was paid off. On the other hand, credits and certain other debt transactions (44) brought in a net gain of £20 million by the end of March 1953, most of it, however, during the first nine months. All these expenditures have, of course, had certain economic effects which would repay investigation, but they do not involve the use of current productive resources by the National Health Service, and, therefore, must be excluded from our concept of the cost to public funds. We must also exclude transactions in assets (48) which existed before the current period. These transactions with the private sector also have economic effects, but they are of a different kind from those with which we are at present concerned.

In taking over the superannuation commitments for the staff transferred on the appointed day, the Minister received approximately £31 million up to March 1953 in respect to pre-1948 contributions. He has also been paying out pensions and allowances to retired staff. As we are treating current contributions as part of current costs, all other superannuation transactions (56) must be excluded from the true net cost of the vote. In the first nine months of the Service the Minister made a net gain of £17 million from these complicated superannuation transactions; in subsequent years the amounts involved were much smaller (56).

In the first year of the Service it was found necessary for hospitals to increase their cash balances by £9 million. Variations in cash holdings are not relevant to the measure of resources currently consumed and adjustments have been made accordingly (57).

There are also a number of other accounting adjustments, e.g. bringing more stores into account, which have called for corrections in Table 45.

3. THE PRELIMINARY CLASSIFICATION OF THE COST OF THE NATIONAL HEALTH SERVICE TO PUBLIC FUNDS IN PRODUCTIVE RESOURCES

In Tables 46 and 47 the necessary adjustments shown in Table 45 and described in § 2 above are carried out. The cost is classified into current (Table 46) and capital (Table 47). The basis of the distinction is described in Chapter II. Within each table a break-down is given for the three administrative branches of the Service. These two tables are also accounting tables with the purpose of showing the basis of classification rather than of indicating those items which happened to be significant in the period under review. It is for this reason that the figures have not been rounded.

TABLES 45–47

Table 45. *Reconciliation between the gross total of the vote less appropriations-in-aid less extra-Exchequer receipts realized and the total (capital and current) cost to public funds of the National Health Service in productive resources*

(£)

Number	Item	5 July 1948/9	1949/50	1950/1	1951/2	1952/3	1953/4
1	True net total of the vote	176,876,613	305,033,006	330,022,476	346,302,875	383,860,401	366,731,753
	(*a*) The definition of the National Health Service						
2	National Insurance Fund	24,696,000	35,534,730	36,355,670	36,930,000	35,938,000	36,218,000
3	War Damage Commission	—	3,472	451,829	127,956	5,019	5,720
4	Hospital Endowments Fund	—	6,500,000	1,375,000	774,704	725,000	168,500
5	National Assistance Board	—	—	—	170,820	697,674	975,707
6	Non-Exchequer funds	679,000	1,323,000	1,562,000	2,222,000	2,436,000	2,942,000
7	Ministry of Health salaries	900,000	1,200,000	1,400,000	1,400,000	1,400,000	1,600,000
8	Board of Control	24,211	34,464	36,489	39,503	41,702	36,006
9	Allied services	600,000	800,000	900,000	1,100,000	800,000	700,000
10	Ministry of Works hospitals	292,656	—	—	—	—	—
11	Stores adjustment	−627,203	−368,355	87,561	−256,069	313,446	281,168
12	Less defence expenditure included in the vote	—	−271	−121,341	−978,672	−7,121,877	−4,426,731
13	Broadmoor and Ministry of Pensions	51,833	—	—	—	—	−1,965,465
14	Training	30,000	50,000	—	—	—	—
15	Consolidating local authorities	9,650,591	15,096,777	17,597,270	18,242,967	20,618,914	20,238,124
16	Local authority (capital)	2,540,000	2,795,000	2,434,000	2,329,000	2,142,000	1,908,000
17	Administration in executive council services	2,519	−3,002	−3,053	−31,843	—	−1,072
18	Total (*a*)	38,839,607	62,965,815	62,075,425	62,070,366	57,995,878	58,679,957
	(*b*) The valuation of resources						
19	Superannuation contribution	9,897,854	17,396,597	18,307,571	18,783,651	22,460,981	21,773,005
20	General medical services Danckwerts award	3,584,476	4,033,404	7,856,115	8,372,531	−23,846,526	—
21	Distinction award	874,000	1,219,000	−2,093,000	—	—	—
22	Nurses award	—	500,000	−500,000	—	—	—
23	Total (*b*)	14,356,330	23,149,001	23,570,686	27,156,182	−1,385,545	21,773,005
	(*c*) Lag in payments						
24	Pharmaceutical	4,574,881	1,709,897	3,678,267	−1,220,206	−706,214	−679,268
25	Ophthalmic	3,938,493	−1,633,620	−1,172,405	−683,145	2,454	9,408
26	Dental	11,065,830	3,384,408	−3,027,672	−2,098,125	−1,610,383	−45,942
27	Ministry of Pensions	150,000	−90,000	−40,000	−20,000	—	—
28	Sale of land and buildings	−23,984	−103,740	−101,904	45,970	—	—
29	Hospital expenditure	−180,690	87,413	−1,956,265	54,309	24,327	37,813
30	Service receipts	2,174,492	−1,009,390	507,424	−106,401	42,718	437,074
31	Other	569	165,260	−165,829	—	65,830	28,712
32	Appropriation from earlier years	—	—	1,566,754	—	2,365	2,875
33	Total (*c*)	21,699,591	2,510,228	−711,630	−4,027,598	−2,178,903	−209,328

	(d) Expenditures not involving the use of productive resources						
	(i) Liabilities:						
34	General Practitioners' practices: capital	−3,687,471	−4,565,816	−1,691,890	−3,893,522	−2,423,553 }	−2,783,642
35	interest	—	−2,157,684	−1,360,058	−1,287,252	−1,576,948 }	
36	Loss of office	−493	−29,847	−35,625	−37,148	−41,834	−40,658
37	Local authorities for stores	−2,197,000	−3,181,441	−276,500	−62,093	−2,238	−4,652
38	Hospital liabilities	−19,623,260	−3,854,839	−3,671,528	−3,444,095	−4,036,982	−2,436,521
39	Adjustments to above	−31,343	−103,421	134,764	—	—	—
40	Total (i)	−25,539,567	−13,893,048	−6,900,837	−8,724,110	−8,081,555	−5,265,473
	(ii) Creditor debtor position:						
41	Loan repayments	—	—	1,528	550	550	11,144
42	Other	18,087,572	2,642,752	−1,485,187	131,233	466,941	453,647
43	Insurance	—	—	—	102,797	—	—
44	Total (ii)	18,087,572	2,642,752	−1,483,659	234,580	467,491	464,791
	(iii) Transactions in existing assets:						
45	Purchases of land, hospitals and equipment	−211,754	−1,128,885	−945,478	−1,797,812	−685,851	−1,337,974
46	Sales of above	24,000	121,000	237,000	200,000	215,291	197,848
47	Purchases in local authority services	−618,000	−835,000	−683,000	−524,000	−257,000	−212,000
48	Total (iii)	−805,754	−1,842,885	−1,391,478	−2,121,812	−727,560	−1,352,126
	(iv) Superannuation account:						
49	Transfer receipts	16,934,194	3,630,736	4,103,760	2,799,134	2,442,831	1,824,096
50	Transfer payments	−141	−217,237	−504,214	−691,564	−625,996	−3,413,097
51	Refund receipts	—	12,586	15,391	3,066	1,566	2,152
52	Refund payments	−138,454	−705,858	−914,882	−1,267,054	−1,446,565	—
53	Funds received	1,074,219	131,334	63,479	31,344	7,998	12,090
54	Pensions and allowances	−449,508	−1,017,801	−1,376,716	−1,834,750	−2,334,908	−3,049,670
55	F.S.S.N., etc.	−461,854	−866,414	−920,799	−842,349	−803,703	—
56	Total (iv)	16,958,456	967,346	466,019	−1,802,173	−2,758,777	−4,624,429
57	(v) Change in cash position	−8,863,559	1,174,467	254,495	−486,240	−472,631	2,885,290
58	(vi) Sale of securities	—	8,834	9,528	61,642	40	30
	(vii) Accounting adjustments:						
59	Incorrectly charged	−386,169	2,242,934	−158,522	−11,359	−1,689	5,724
60	Stores, cash, creditors, etc.	—	368,226	46,860	−30,109	9,506	−25,683
61	Total (d)	−549,021	−8,331,374	−9,157,594	−12,879,581	−11,565,175	−7,911,876
62	Grand total adjustment	74,346,507	80,293,670	75,776,887	72,319,369	42,866,255	72,331,758
63	Vote plus adjustment	251,223,120	385,326,676	405,799,363	418,622,244	426,726,656	439,063,511
64	Rounding errors	11	−2	0	−4	−3	2
65	Total cost (capital and current)	251,223,131	385,326,674	405,799,363	418,622,240	426,726,653	439,063,513

Table 46. *The current net cost to public funds of the National Health Service in productive resources*

(£)

Number	Item	5 July 1948/9	1949/50	1950/1	1951/2	1952/3	1953/4
	I. Central and miscellaneous						
1	Ministry salaries	900,000	1,200,000	1,400,000	1,400,000	1,400,000	1,600,000
2	Allied services	600,000	800,000	900,000	1,100,000	800,000	745,661
3	Central Health Services Council	454	2,249	2,007	2,721	2,173	1,840
4	Training services (adjustment)	1,040	6,054	63,413	72,431	84,493	83,571
5	Training addition	30,000	50,000	—	—	—	—
6	Training adjustment	—	1,215	−1,215	—	—	—
7	Rampton, Moss Side, Broadmoor	284,709	404,161	516,807	526,671	971,363	1,113,973
8	Receipts for (7)	−16,931	−24,844	−46,286	−48,475	−51,308	−55,756
9	Board of Control	24,211	34,464	36,489	39,503	41,702	36,006
10	Miscellaneous payments	12,368	61,860	31,131	29,282	30,618	28,014
11	Adjustment to (10)	2,593	−1,850	−743	—	—	—
12	Miscellaneous receipts	−9,021	−2,917	−4,391	−3,974	−2,727	−2,307
13	Total I	1,829,423	2,530,392	2,897,212	3,118,159	3,276,314	3,551,002
	II. Hospital Service						
14	Hospital maintenance expenditure	115,398,598	184,677,695	204,164,603	219,528,549	239,784,260	251,742,262
15	Specialist services	7,898,261	12,062,732	13,837,485	16,243,843	17,073,407	17,950,059
16	Distinction award adjustment	874,000	1,219,000	−2,093,000	—	—	—
17	Nurses adjustment	4,100,000	500,000	−500,000	—	1,367,014	1,144,845
18	Current stores adjustment	504,926	611,896	504,764	671,939	1,016,384	1,098,208
19	Miscellaneous	15,000	20,000	41,808	31,876	81,889	87,083
20	Non-Exchequer funds	679,000	1,323,000	1,562,000	2,222,000	2,436,000	2,942,000
21	Payments of patients	−2,034,882	−2,483,947	−2,422,087	−2,441,721	−2,806,020	−2,983,935
22	Road Traffic Acts	−52,327	−113,274	−136,544	−176,162	−195,359	−227,025
23	Other trading receipts	−11,272,506	−17,007,482	−20,179,951	−21,950,318	−24,068,931	−24,649,443
24	Other appropriations	—	−1,779	−8,108	−14,659	−28,973	−22,952
25	Administration	2,935,664	5,014,742	5,572,231	6,471,178	6,838,715	7,056,989
26	Hospitals not vested	831,558	1,445,263	1,647,660	1,847,628	2,059,005	2,114,763
27	Blood transfusion	365,484	632,726	710,130	808,398	914,155	973,651
28	Mass radiography, miscellaneous	1,383,070	1,421,910	1,228,091	1,445,284	1,711,641	1,833,922
29	Ministry of Pensions	644,649	2,307,387	3,107,278	3,285,312	3,061,178	3,139,851
30	Adjustment to (29)	150,000	−90,000	−40,000	−20,000	—	−36,854
31	Ministry of Works	—	181,505	70,947	—	—	—
32	Research	25,136	31,360	34,334	25,360	29,787	29,855
33	Bacteriological	577,374	674,771	850,911	946,400	921,116	950,746
34	Public Health Laboratory receipts	−14,745	−9,298	−6,422	−9,039	−8,811	−7,219
35	Tuberculosis abroad	—	—	—	28,401	96,387	88,495
36	Total II	123,008,260	192,418,207	207,946,130	228,944,269	250,282,844	263,225,301

	III. Executive Council Services						
	(a) Central:						
37	Administration	1,560,842	1,861,434	1,947,180	2,527,618	2,342,424	2,312,691
38	Tribunal	—	1,055	1,450	900	1,151	946
39	Rents	—	−1,750	−3,536	−1,098	−2,708	−1,562
40	Waste paper	—	—	−1,012	−2,663	−1,720	−912
41	Total (a)	1,560,842	1,860,739	1,944,082	2,524,757	2,339,147	2,311,163
	(b) General medical services:						
42	Payments	29,126,249	41,643,427	42,071,535	42,122,554	75,631,435	51,719,179
43	Danckwerts award	3,584,476	4,033,404	7,856,115	8,372,531	−23,846,526	—
44	Central Register	—	—	—	—	197,081	145,114
45	Medical Practices Committee	4,427	6,485	6,507	7,143	8,204	8,103
46	Health centre receipts	—	—	—	−6,429	−5,225	−7,302
47	Total (b)	32,715,152	45,683,316	49,934,157	50,495,799	51,984,969	51,865,094
	(c) Pharmaceutical:						
48	To pharmacists	19,465,113	31,674,326	36,904,678	42,404,159	44,735,846	43,532,123
49	Other	1,002,969	1,550,348	1,583,786	1,705,571	2,069,967	2,044,455
50	Charges	—	—	—	—	−4,625,047	−6,429,634
51	Charges paid by National Assistance Board	—	—	—	—	296,640	397,563
52	Total (c)	20,468,082	33,224,674	38,488,464	44,109,730	42,477,406	39,544,507
	(d) Dental:						
53	Resources	28,600,000	46,000,000	37,300,000	31,046,049	25,943,819	27,979,922
54	Other	10,614	12,807	9,759	35,946	78,710	35,042
55	Charges	—	—	—	−1,746,049	−5,543,819	−6,479,922
56	Charges paid by National Assistance Board	—	—	—	67,500	160,830	217,872
57	Estimates Board	209,806	354,095	398,852	478,492	501,325	500,680
58	Total (d)	28,820,420	46,366,902	37,708,611	29,881,938	21,140,865	22,253,594
	(e) Ophthalmic:						
59	Resources	15,100,000	20,100,000	18,400,000	10,232,666	10,100,000	11,438,757
60	Charges	—	—	—	−2,432,666	−4,062,843	−4,638,757
61	Charges paid by National Assistance Board	—	—	—	103,320	227,790	335,797
62	Total (e)	15,100,000	20,100,000	18,400,000	7,903,320	6,264,947	7,135,797
63	Total III	98,664,496	147,235,631	146,475,314	134,915,544	124,207,334	123,110,155
	IV. Local Authority Services						
64	Health centres	22,191	1,046	21,934	−14,000	9,000	41,554
65	Care of mothers and children	4,971,934	7,455,408	7,648,204	7,654,000	9,188,000	8,090,742
66	Midwifery	3,118,828	4,322,526	4,768,256	4,497,000	4,680,000	4,757,861
67	Health visiting	1,431,744	2,022,439	2,525,455	2,562,000	2,781,000	3,002,822
68	Home nursing	2,353,450	3,401,231	4,172,670	4,424,000	4,757,000	5,250,752
69	Vaccination and immunization	212,587	324,725	469,249	456,000	473,000	582,787
70	Ambulance service	4,114,040	7,003,450	7,877,210	8,811,000	9,592,000	10,000,546
71	Prevention of illness	624,753	1,080,727	1,322,563	1,584,000	1,721,000	1,890,742
72	Domestic help	1,129,003	2,435,983	2,959,742	3,484,000	4,061,000	4,720,721
73	Mental help	915,537	1,291,617	1,312,497	1,556,000	1,731,000	1,940,302
74	Other	60,594	69,165	140,406	115,000	179,000	137,733
75	Total IV	18,954,661	29,408,317	33,218,186	35,129,000	39,172,000	40,416,562
76	Grand total current	242,456,840	371,592,547	390,536,842	402,106,972	416,938,492	430,303,020

Table 47. *The capital cost of the National Health Service in productive resources*

(£)

Number	Item	5 July 1948/9	1949/50	1950/1	1951/2	1952/3	1953/4
	I. Hospital Services						
1	Hospital authorities	5,347,436	8,682,775	8,846,560	9,655,547	9,140,332	8,771,271
2	Ministry of Works	292,656	539,463	438,057	448,199	306,212	176,444
3	Mass radiography and blood transfusion	38,828	203,242	145,979	36,010	27,681	187,056
4	Bacteriological	39,631	41,717	88,198	198,456	155,619	117,000
5	X-ray	56,828	311,664	283,241	265,179	247,759	94,495
6	Change in value of stocks (centrally purchased)	−172	−44,438	54,915	−52,302	231,613	6,000
7	Change in value of stocks (hospital)	1,037,874	2,003,254	3,629,321	4,074,912	−2,384,178	−2,379,260
8	Blood-drying units	—	—	—	—	37,661	49,140
9	II. Local Authority Services	1,922,000	1,960,000	1,751,000	1,805,000	1,885,000	1,696,000
	III. Executive Council Services						
10	Premises (executive councils and joint pricing committees)	31,210	28,892	19,957	47,467	30,473	27,767
11	Dental Estimates Board	—	7,558	5,293	36,800	109,989	14,580
12	Total	8,766,291	13,734,127	15,262,521	16,515,268	9,788,161	8,760,493
13	Total (capital and current)	251,223,131	385,326,674	405,799,363	418,622,240	426,726,653	439,063,513

APPENDIX B

THE CURRENT COST OF THE NATIONAL HEALTH SERVICE TO PUBLIC FUNDS IN PRODUCTIVE RESOURCES EXPRESSED IN CONSTANT PRICES

1. DIFFICULTIES OF ANALYSIS

The purpose of this appendix is to analyse the change in expenditure between (1) changes in quantities of goods and services bought and (2) changes in their prices, and to draw attention to some of the particular problems in the National Health Service of eliminating the effects of changing prices.

It was first necessary to rearrange the data in Appendix A, Table 46, in a form suitable for the application of price indices. This is done in Table 48 and a note is attached to this appendix showing the reconciliation with Table 46, Appendix A.

The bases for the classification adopted in arranging Table 48 and throughout this appendix were discussed in Chapter II: the principal objective is to distinguish between (*a*) goods and contracts and (*b*) services. It is not, however, possible to do so as accurately as we should like owing to the following reasons:

The varying nature of accounting subdivisions. The accounts do not always show a clear division between goods and services. For example, the remuneration of laundry staff at *individual* hospitals is shown under wages and salaries, while the remuneration of similar staff employed by a *group* of hospitals is included with the cost of contracted laundry under the 'objective' heading of 'laundry'. We have therefore had to allocate such items to 'goods and contracts'. Similar problems arise with expenditure on works and maintenance and farms and gardens. The way in which expenditure in various of these fields is allocated in the accounts between subheads is sometimes quite arbitrary and is subject to change from year to year. Special researches have therefore had to be made so as to fit these items as far as possible into the framework of our classification.

The heterogeneous nature of accounting subdivisions. Certain subdivisions of expenditure are too large and heterogeneous to allow, without further analysis, the application of price indices. This defect is particularly apparent in the accounts for the first year or so of the National Health Service. For example, the hospital service subhead for 'other staff' groups together remuneration ranging from the middle-range salaries to the lowest wages paid. Other difficulties in applying price indices are specified later under salaries and wages.

The varying nature of the terms on which goods are purchased. Purchases are made by different hospital managements on different terms—retail, wholesale and by contract. Moreover, practice varies from year to year. These differences have been taken into account in the construction and application of price indices.

Changes in the composition of accounting subdivisions. In certain cases, substantial changes have occurred since 1948/9 in the composition of subdivisions. Thus, major changes in medical treatment have led to marked switches in expenditure from year to year under such subheads as 'drugs and dressings' and 'medical and surgical appliances' in the hospital services and payments to chemists in the executive council services. Similar difficulties arise also in the dental and ophthalmic services as a result of changes in the type and quality of the goods supplied. Difficulties of this kind make these particular items unsuitable for composite index treatment; they require, instead, the re-pricing of each component.

Inadequate data on hospital trading activities. Because of the inadequate data on which we had to work we were faced with considerable difficulties here in attempting to express the use of productive resources in constant prices. Some of the particular difficulties are specified in Appendix C.

2. THE CONSTRUCTION AND APPLICATION OF PRICE INDICES

In addition to the difficulties described above in classifying the data for price treatment there are further difficulties to be faced in finding appropriate bases on which to construct particular price indices. For items (7)–(20) in Table 50, we have used for the changes in prices between 1952/3 and 1953/4 the unpublished index of hospital costs prepared by the Scottish Statistical Office. As this index is based on a sample of the expenditure of hospitals in Scotland we believe that it provides a more reliable indication of changes in the price of purchases made by hospitals in England and Wales than the indices which we have developed for the earlier years. In the following notes we explain briefly how we have dealt with the more important categories of goods and contracts for the period between 1948/9 and 1952/3 and with items not covered by the Scottish index. As emphasized in Chapter III, the special price indices we have devised are not the result of extensive field work and we have no doubt that with more study they could be improved. So far as possible and in as many cases as possible, however, care has been taken to ascertain from various spending authorities[1] the composition and market of purchase of particular categories of goods. In other cases we have used existing indices published by the Central Statistical Office, the Board of Trade and the Ministry of Labour.

In the following account of the price index treatment of the quantitatively more important categories[2] the serial numbers refer to the items in the tables attached to this appendix.

(*a*) *Goods and contracts*

Provisions (7). A detailed comparison was made between the food weights used in the Ministry of Labour retail price index and the weights which

[1] Hospital authorities, local authorities, the Ministry of Health and other government departments.

[2] The majority of categories under which expenditure has at any time exceeded £2 million per year.

emerged from an analysis of the foods actually consumed during the same year (1953) in two general hospitals in the Paddington (London) Hospital Group. The two sets of weights broadly agreed except for milk. In these hospitals expenditure on milk was nearly 20 % (which agrees generally with other hospital expenditure) as compared with a weight of 10 % in the Ministry of Labour index. For hospital provisions, therefore, we used this index modified to take account of the additional weight for milk.

Drugs and dressings (10). This item caused difficulty and for two reasons. First, the rapidly changing pattern of consumption renders the item unsuitable for treatment by an index with constant weights. For example, in one hospital studied the percentage of expenditure devoted to antibiotics rose from about 10 % at the start of the Service to about 40 % in 1952/3. Moreover, the prices of individual antibiotic preparations fell sharply during this period. Secondly, no index is available to represent adequately all expenditure on drugs and dressings. Rather than make no allowance for changing prices at all, we have applied the index of basic drug prices which is used in the Ministry of Health in connexion with the pharmaceutical service.[1] We are conscious of its unsuitability for this particular purpose. The error introduced as a result may therefore be large in proportion to the expenditure involved.

Fuel, light and power (12). The bulk of this expenditure is coal and coke. The National Coal Board states that prices of both domestic and boiler fuel have been moving roughly in the same proportion. For hospital consumption we have therefore used domestic coal and coke prices. Prices of coal, gas and other fuels have moved closely together but electricity has lagged considerably behind. In the fuel and light component of the interim price index (operating until 1952) electricity had a weight of about 10 % of the total. The 1952 index raised it to over 20 %. The Central Statistical Office[2] found it to be over 25 % of consumer expenditure on fuel and light in 1952. It seems reasonable to assume that electricity constituted about 25 % of hospital fuel expenditure throughout the period under review. The Central Statistical Office index of market prices of fuel and light has, therefore, been applied to hospitals and not the fuel and light component of the Ministry of Labour index.

Laundry (13). This item in the hospital accounts covers only 'laundry contracted outside'. The Institute of British Launderers has supplied us with the trend figures of maximum prices for the country as a whole. This series is very close to another series based on costing for army contracts. Though hospitals get their contracts considerably below maximum prices, it seems safe to assume that the prices they paid have moved throughout the period in proportion to maximum prices.

Domestic repairs (15). This item consists primarily of furniture and such items as crockery and cleaning materials. The Central Statistical Office and retail price indices for durable household goods have moved closely together since 1948. Such indices are probably overweighted with textiles and carpets

[1] See Appendix E.

[2] All references to Central Statistical Office indices relate to those published in the Blue Book on *National Income and Expenditure*, annual.

while hospital purchases were primarily beds, bedding and ward furnishings. The following Central Statistical Office indices have therefore been used:

75 % Central Statistical Office: Durable household goods
25 % Central Statistical Office: Other household goods (to represent matches, soap and cleaning materials)

Rent, rates and water (16). The Ministry of Labour index for rent and rates has been used for this item, although it is not satisfactory. Some proportion of the rents paid by hospitals is for housing used as nurses' homes.

Printing and stationery (17). Over half the cost of this item appears to consist of medical records. The British Federation of Master Printers has kindly supplied an index for the cost of such work. For the main ordinary stationery needs, indices supplied by H.M.S.O. have been used.

The index has been built up as follows:

50 %	B.F.M.P.	Quality work
20 %	H.M.S.O.	Paper printing
10 %	H.M.S.O.	Envelopes
10 %	H.M.S.O.	Carbons
10 %	H.M.S.O.	Pencils

Canteens and shops (19). An index has been developed from the following Central Statistical Office indices weighted as follows:

40 % beverages
10 % books, newspapers, magazines
10 % food
20 % sugar, preserves, confectionery
20 % tobacco

Miscellaneous (22). We have not been able to ascertain in any detail the items covered by this heading. The composition varies widely between one hospital and another. Though largely guesswork, we have applied the Ministry of Labour retail price index.

Non-Exchequer funds (32). There is no information available indicating the type of purchases made under this heading. So far as we know, a great deal of expenditure on hospital maintenance is supplemented by expenditure from these funds. From various inquiries we have made but without any detailed facts we have given equal weight to three indices—provisions (7), domestic repairs (15), user agreements (21),[1] and to the Central Statistical Office index of durable household goods.

Hospitals not vested (35). This index is based upon the implied index of hospital maintenance expenditure (excluding the cost of medical staff).

Appliances and invalid tricycles (38). An index has been calculated using 1948/9 weights of the cost of surgical boots and appliances supplied through the Ministry of Pensions. We are grateful to the Ministry of Pensions for the detailed information supplied from which this calculation was made.

General medical services (47). The rate of payments under the maternity

[1] Expenditure on user agreements represents the cost to hospital authorities of institutions used partly as hospitals and partly as Part III institutions under the National Assistance Act.

medical services has not changed during the period under review. For the remaining payments an index has been constructed from information given in the White Paper on the Danckwerts award.[1] The total for the central pool for Great Britain plus the amount given by the Danckwerts award has for each year been divided by the civilian population.

Pharmaceutical (*48*). The index for basic drug prices used by the Ministry of Health has been applied with certain adaptations to allow for changes in oncost and in the container allowance.

Dental (*49*). The prices paid for dental work are negotiated by the Ministry of Health. The index we have used is based on information supplied by the Ministry.

Sight testing (*53*). As with the dental service, prices paid for sight testing are negotiated by the Ministry of Health. Different fees are payable to the four categories of persons who undertake this work. The Ministry of Health has kindly developed an index for us based on the weights of the work performed during the first twelve months of the Service.

Supply of spectacles (*54*). The Ministry of Health has also calculated the cost of one type of lens and frame commonly dispensed by the Service; the cost of this type has been traced throughout the period under review. The total cost of one pair, two pairs, and bifocals has been assessed in relation to the proportions of these different kinds of work carried out in the first twelve months of the Service.

(*b*) *Salaries and wages*

Medical (*4*). There was no change in the rate of remuneration during the period under review.

Nurses and midwives (*5*). This index, made in co-operation with the Ministry of Health, is based on the trend of remuneration of five different grades of nurses weighted by the proportions of each grade employed in the Services.

Others (*6*). This index has been developed by weighting together three sub-indices which have been devised for this purpose. The first sub-index is intended to represent medical auxiliaries and is based upon the trend of remuneration of three large classes—radiographers, physiotherapists and medical laboratory technicians. The second (to represent domestic workers) is based on weighted rates for male and female workers (group III) in London, urban areas and rural areas. The third (to represent administrative and clerical staff) is based upon the trend of per capita earnings from 1950/1 onwards, and between 1948/9 and 1950/1 on the trend of earnings of employees in national and local government.[2] These three sub-indices have been weighted in accordance with the estimated expenditure on these different categories of staff in 1952/3.

Administrative wages (*33*). The index applied to this item is the administrative and clerical component of the 'others' index described above.

[1] Ministry of Health, *Memorandum on the Supplementary Estimates for the Additional Sums to be Provided for the Remuneration of General Medical Practitioners in the National Health Service*, Cmd. 8599 (H.M.S.O. 1952).

[2] See *Ministry of Labour Gazette*, March 1949, p. 84; March 1950, p. 78; March 1951, p. 90.

(*c*) *The local authority services* (*57–66*)

We have attempted a rough break-down of the cost of the different services into wages and salaries, administration, and goods and contracts, by adjusting the data contained in the returns published by the Institute of Municipal Treasurers and Accountants.[1] Separate indices have been applied to these items which are similar, in appropriate instances, to those described above. For wages and salaries we have developed indices for the remuneration of district nurses, health visitors, midwives and ambulance drivers, and a separate index for workers in the domestic help service.

The statistical material, arranged for re-pricing, is shown in Table 48, to which are attached detailed notes explaining the reconciliation with Table 46 of Appendix A.

Table 49 shows the trends of current cost in actual prices and the change between 1949/50 and 1953/4.

Table 50 shows the indices which we have applied.

Table 51 shows current cost in the prices ruling between 5 July 1948 and 31 March 1949.

Table 52 shows the trends of current cost in 1948/9 prices and the change between 1949/50 and 1953/4.

[1] In doing so we have had to make certain corrections for those authorities rendering incomplete returns (Institute of Municipal Treasurers and Accountants, *Local Health Services Statistics*, annual).

TABLES 48–52

Table 48. *The current net cost to public funds of the National Health Service in actual prices (England and Wales, 1948/9–1953/4)*

(£000 in actual prices)

Number	Item	5 July 1948/9	Annual rate 1948/9	1949/50	1950/1	1951/2	1952/3	1953/4
	I. Central and Miscellaneous							
1	(a) Wages	1,100	1,487	1,600	1,890	1,890	1,960	2,200
2	(b) Other	729	985	930	1,007	1,228	1,316	1,351
3	Total I	1,829	2,472	2,530	2,897	3,118	3,276	3,551
	II. Hospital Services							
	A. Maintenance							
	(a) Salaries and wages:							
4	Medical (including specialists)	13,866	18,745	23,246	23,554	24,972	26,047	27,217
5	Nurses and midwives	27,799	37,580	45,682	48,611	51,132	56,242	59,152
6	Others	33,078	44,717	52,082	58,105	65,746	72,225	75,752
	(b) Goods and contracts:							
7	Provisions	13,958	18,869	21,882	23,559	27,128	30,940	32,863
8	Staff uniforms and clothing	759	1,026	1,193	1,499	1,762	1,718	1,705
9	Patients' clothing	924	1,249	1,300	1,399	1,615	1,669	1,606
10	Drugs and dressings	5,329	7,204	7,645	8,785	10,431	10,112	9,647
11	Medical and surgical appliances	4,275	5,779	6,355	6,713	6,804	7,888	8,435
12	Fuel, light and power	7,425	10,037	10,103	11,267	12,601	13,867	14,728
13	Laundry	1,224	1,655	1,807	2,228	2,612	2,943	3,252
14	Maintenance of buildings	5,049	6,825	6,618	8,152	7,834	8,961	10,682
15	Domestic repairs	5,652	7,641	7,105	7,488	7,916	8,622	8,516
16	Rent, rates and water	2,388	3,228	3,626	3,758	3,985	4,211	4,637
17	Printing and stationery	1,915	2,589	2,768	1,670	2,070	2,066	1,919
18	Ambulance and transport	609	823	1,076	1,067	987	1,106	1,131
19	Canteens and shops	812	1,098	1,489	1,631	1,993	2,129	2,225
20	Farms and gardens	873	1,180	1,174	1,262	1,434	1,548	1,595
21	User agreements	906	1,225	1,321	1,334	1,290	1,342	1,346
22	Miscellaneous	1,639	2,216	2,271	3,447	3,695	3,827	3,981
23	General Nursing Council	—	—	—	—	—	1,367	1,145
24	Total A	128,480	173,686	198,743	215,529	236,007	258,830	271,534
	(c) Receipts:							
25	Payments of staff	−5,381	−7,274	−8,208	−10,812	−11,724	−13,313	−13,567
26	Payments of patients and Road Traffic Acts	−2,087	−2,821	−2,597	−2,559	−2,618	−3,014	−3,186
27	Local authorities	−1,773	−2,397	−2,479	−2,477	−2,553	−2,564	−2,540
28	Canteens and shops	−981	−1,326	−1,814	−2,050	−2,340	−2,522	−2,630
29	Farms and gardens	−1,596	−2,158	−2,478	−2,624	−2,848	−3,146	−3,320
30	Other	−1,244	−1,682	−1,697	−1,834	−2,047	−2,102	−2,216
	Total receipts	−13,062	−17,658	−19,273	−22,356	−24,130	−26,661	−27,459
31	Net total A	115,418	156,028	179,470	193,173	211,877	232,169	244,075

	B. Other							
32	Non-Exchequer funds	679	918	1,323	1,562	2,222	2,436	2,942
33	Administration: (*a*) Wages	1,716	2,320	3,921	4,472	5,251	5,629	5,850
34	(*b*) Goods	1,220	1,649	1,094	1,100	1,220	1,210	1,207
35	Hospitals not vested	832	1,125	1,445	1,648	1,848	2,059	2,115
36	Blood transfusion:							
	(*a*) Wages	231	312	407	442	506	549	615
37	(*b*) Goods	134	181	226	268	302	365	359
38	Appliances and invalid tricycles	795	1,075	2,399	3,138	3,265	3,061	3,103
39	Bacteriological	563	761	665	844	937	912	944
40	Miscellaneous:							
	(*a*) Wages	100	135	170	212	256	263	331
41	(*b*) Goods	1,323	1,788	1,301	1,084	1,259	1,628	1,685
42	Total B	7,593	10,264	12,951	14,770	17,066	18,112	19,151
43	Total II	123,011	166,292	192,421	207,943	228,943	250,281	263,226
	III. Executive Council Services							
	Central:							
44	Wages	1,142	1,544	1,455	1,546	2,053	1,922	1,902
45	Other	419	566	406	398	472	417	409
46	Total	1,561	2,110	1,861	1,944	2,525	2,339	2,311
47	General medical services	32,715	44,226	45,683	49,934	50,496	51,985	51,865
48	Pharmaceutical	20,468	27,670	33,225	38,488	44,110	42,477	39,545
	Dental:							
49	Dental resources	28,611	38,678	46,013	37,310	29,403	20,640	21,753
50	Dental Estimates Board: Wages	178	241	285	325	408	434	439
51	Other	32	43	69	74	70	67	62
52	Total	28,821	38,962	46,367	37,709	29,881	21,141	22,254
	Ophthalmic:							
53	Sight testing	4,600	6,218	4,600	3,900	2,800	2,900	3,199
54	Supply of spectacles	10,500	14,194	15,500	14,500	5,103	3,365	3,937
55	Total	15,100	20,412	20,100	18,400	7,903	6,265	7,136
56	Total III	98,664	133,379	147,236	146,475	134,916	124,207	123,110
	IV. Local Authority Services							
57	Care of mothers and children	4,972	6,721	7,455	7,648	7,654	9,188	8,091
58	Midwifery	3,119	4,216	4,323	4,768	4,497	4,680	4,758
59	Health visiting	1,432	1,936	2,022	2,525	2,562	2,781	3,003
60	Home nursing	2,353	3,182	3,401	4,173	4,424	4,757	5,251
61	Vaccination and immunization	213	287	325	469	456	473	583
62	Ambulance services	4,114	5,562	7,003	7,877	8,811	9,592	10,001
63	Prevention of illness	625	845	1,081	1,323	1,584	1,721	1,891
64	Domestic help	1,129	1,526	2,436	2,960	3,484	4,061	4,721
65	Mental health	916	1,238	1,292	1,312	1,556	1,731	1,940
66	Other	83	112	70	162	101	188	179
67	Total IV	18,955	25,624	29,408	33,218	35,129	39,172	40,417
68	Total current real resources	242,459	327,767	371,595	390,533	402,106	416,936	430,304

Table 49. *The trend of the current net cost to public funds of the National Health Service in actual prices (England and Wales, 1948/9–1953/4. 1949/50=100)*

Number	Item	Annual rate 1948/9	1949/50	1950/1	1951/2	1952/3	1953/4
	I. Central and Miscellaneous						
1	(*a*) Wages	93	100	118	118	123	138
2	(*b*) Other	106	100	108	132	142	145
3	Total I	98	100	115	123	129	140
	II. Hospital Services						
	A. Maintenance						
	(*a*) Salaries and wages:						
4	Medical (including specialists)	81	100	101	107	112	117
5	Nurses and midwives	82	100	106	112	123	129
6	Others	86	100	112	126	139	145
	(*b*) Goods and contracts:						
7	Provisions	86	100	108	124	141	150
8	Staff uniforms and clothing	86	100	126	148	144	143
9	Patients' clothing	96	100	108	124	128	124
10	Drugs and dressings	94	100	115	136	132	126
11	Medical and surgical appliances	91	100	106	107	124	133
12	Fuel, light and power	99	100	112	125	137	146
13	Laundry	92	100	123	145	163	180
14	Maintenance of buildings	103	100	123	118	135	161
15	Domestic repairs	108	100	105	111	121	120
16	Rent, rates and water	89	100	104	110	116	128
17	Printing and stationery	94	100	60	75	75	69
18	Ambulance and transport	76	100	99	92	103	105
19	Canteens and shops	74	100	110	134	143	149
20	Farms and gardens	101	100	107	122	132	136
21	User agreements	93	100	101	98	102	102
22	Miscellaneous	98	100	152	163	169	175
23	General Nursing Council	—	—	—	—	—	—
24	Total A	87	100	108	119	130	137
	(*c*) Receipts:						
25	Payments of staff	89	100	132	143	162	165
26	Payments of patients and Road Traffic Acts	109	100	99	101	116	123
27	Local authorities	97	100	100	103	103	102
28	Canteens and shops	73	100	113	129	139	145
29	Farms and gardens	87	100	106	115	127	134
30	Other	99	100	108	121	124	131
31	Net total A	87	100	108	118	129	136

No.	Item						
	B. Other						
32	Non-Exchequer funds	69	100	118	168	184	222
33	Administration: (*a*) Wages	59	100	114	134	144	149
34	(*b*) Goods	151	100	101	112	111	110
35	Hospitals not vested	78	100	114	128	142	146
36	Blood transfusion: (*a*) Wages	77	100	109	124	135	151
37	(*b*) Goods	80	100	119	134	162	159
38	Appliances and invalid tricycles	45	100	131	136	128	129
39	Bacteriological	114	100	127	141	137	142
40	Miscellaneous: (*a*) Wages	79	100	125	151	155	195
41	(*b*) Goods	137	100	83	97	125	130
42	Total B	79	100	114	132	140	148
43	Total II	86	100	108	119	130	137
	III. Executive Council Services						
	(*a*) Central:						
44	Wages	106	100	106	141	132	131
45	Other	139	100	98	116	103	101
46	Total (*a*)	113	100	104	136	126	124
47	(*b*) General medical services	97	100	109	111	114	114
48	(*c*) Pharmaceutical	83	100	116	133	128	119
	(*d*) Dental:						
49	Resources	84	100	81	64	45	47
50	Dental Estimates Board: Wages	85	100	114	143	152	154
51	Other	62	100	107	101	97	90
52	Total (*d*)	84	100	81	64	46	48
	(*e*) Ophthalmic						
53	Sight testing	135	100	85	61	63	70
54	Supply of spectacles	92	100	94	33	22	25
55	Total (*e*)	102	100	92	39	31	36
56	Total III	91	100	99	92	84	84
	IV. Local Authority Services						
57	Care of mothers and children	90	100	103	103	123	109
58	Midwifery	98	100	110	104	108	110
59	Health visiting	96	100	125	127	138	149
60	Home nursing	94	100	123	130	140	154
61	Vaccination and immunization	88	100	144	140	146	179
62	Ambulance services	79	100	112	126	137	143
63	Prevention of illness	78	100	122	147	159	175
64	Domestic help	63	100	122	143	167	194
65	Mental health	96	100	102	120	134	150
66	Other	160	100	231	144	269	256
67	Total IV	87	100	113	119	133	137
68	Total current real resources	88	100	105	108	112	116

Table 50. *Price indices (1948/9 = 100)*

Number	Item	1948/9	1949/50	1950/1	1951/2	1952/3	1953/4
	I. Central and Miscellaneous						
1	(*a*) Wages	100	105	107	119	127	133
2	(*b*) Other	100	101	108	128	130	131
	II. Hospital Services						
	A. Maintenance						
	(*a*) Salaries and wages:						
4	Medical (including specialists)	100	100	100	100	100	100
5	Nurses and midwives	100	116	116	116	128	131
6	Others	100	102	104	114	121	125
	(*b*) Goods and contracts:						
7	Provisions	100	108	114	131	151	156
8	Staff uniforms and clothing	100	104	107	123	112	112
9	Patients' clothing	100	104	107	124	116	119
10	Drugs and dressings	100	96	96	109	102	92
11	Medical and surgical appliances	100	103	116	134	126	124
12	Fuel, light and power	100	103	106	113	122	133
13	Laundry	100	100	102	108	113	117
14	Maintenance of buildings	100	101	107	128	133	131
15	Domestic repairs	100	102	108	120	124	120
16	Rent, rates, and water	100	101	102	104	109	114
17	Printing and stationery	100	98	111	156	146	149
18	Ambulance and transport	100	102	110	120	129	128
19	Canteens and shops	100	101	104	112	120	126
20	Farms and gardens	100	104	108	119	123	123
21	User agreements	100	105	107	116	123	125
22	Miscellaneous	100	102	106	117	126	129
23	General Nursing Council	100	110	110	113	121	126
	(*c*) Receipts:						
25	Payments of staff	100	104	109	122	134	138
26	Payments of patients and Road Traffic Acts	100	105	107	116	123	125
27	Local authorities	100	105	107	116	123	125
28	Canteens and shops	100	102	104	113	121	127
29	Farms and gardens	100	103	105	116	123	123
30	Other	100	102	105	113	128	130

	B. Other						
32	Non-Exchequer funds	100	104	110	123	131	130
33	Administration: (*a*) Wages	100	102	104	121	128	135
34	(*b*) Goods	100	101	108	128	130	131
35	Hospitals not vested	100	105	107	116	123	125
36	Blood transfusion: (*a*) Wages	100	102	103	114	120	124
37	(*b*) Goods	100	103	109	120	131	133
38	Appliances and invalid tricycles	100	88	83	83	75	78
39	Bacteriological	100	102	106	117	126	124
40	Miscellaneous: (*a*) Wages	100	102	103	114	120	124
41	(*b*) Goods	100	103	106	117	126	129
	III. Executive Council Services						
	Central:						
44	Wages	100	102	104	121	128	135
45	Other	100	101	108	128	130	131
47	General medical services	100	98	107	108	110	110
48	Pharmaceutical	100	94	87	98	92	84
	Dental:						
49	Resources	100	93	81	77	77	77
50	Dental Estimates Board: Wages	100	102	104	121	128	135
51	Other	100	101	108	128	130	131
	Ophthalmic:						
53	Sight testing	100	88	88	84	84	84
54	Supply of spectacles	100	92	86	84	87	87
	IV. Local Authority Services						
57	Care of mothers and children	100	105	107	117	124	126
58	Midwifery	100	107	111	117	126	128
59	Health visiting	100	108	110	114	123	126
60	Home nursing	100	108	112	118	127	129
61	Vaccination and immunization	100	108	112	118	127	129
62	Ambulance services	100	101	105	113	121	123
63	Prevention of illness	100	108	112	118	127	129
64	Domestic help	100	102	104	114	121	125
65	Mental health	100	108	110	114	123	126
66	Other	100	108	110	122	125	128

Table 51. *The current net cost to public funds of the National Health Service revalued in 1948/9 prices (England and Wales, 1948/9–1953/4)*

(£000 in 1948/9 prices)

Number	Item	5 July 1948/9	Annual rate 1948/9	1949/50	1950/1	1951/2	1952/3	1953/4
	I. Central and Miscellaneous							
1	(*a*) Wages	1,100	1,487	1,524	1,766	1,588	1,543	1,654
2	(*b*) Other	729	985	921	932	959	1,012	1,031
3	Total I	1,829	2,472	2,445	2,698	2,547	2,555	2,685
	II. Hospital Services							
	A. Maintenance							
	(*a*) Salaries and wages:							
4	Medical (including specialists)	13,866	18,745	23,246	23,554	24,972	26,047	27,217
5	Nurses and midwives	27,799	37,580	39,381	41,906	44,079	43,939	45,154
6	Others	33,078	44,717	51,061	55,870	57,672	59,690	60,602
	(*b*) Goods and contracts:							
7	Provisions	13,958	18,869	20,261	20,666	20,708	20,490	21,066
8	Staff uniforms and clothing	759	1,026	1,147	1,401	1,433	1,534	1,522
9	Patients' clothing	924	1,249	1,250	1,307	1,222	1,439	1,350
10	Drugs and dressings	5,329	7,204	7,964	9,151	9,570	9,914	10,486
11	Medical and surgical appliances	4,275	5,779	6,170	5,787	5,078	6,260	6,802
12	Fuel, light and power	7,425	10,037	9,809	10,629	11,151	11,366	11,074
13	Laundry	1,224	1,655	1,807	2,184	2,419	2,604	2,779
14	Maintenance of buildings	5,049	6,825	6,552	7,619	6,120	6,738	8,154
15	Domestic repairs	5,652	7,641	6,966	6,933	6,597	6,953	7,097
16	Rent, rates and water	2,388	3,228	3,590	3,684	3,832	3,863	4,068
17	Printing and stationery	1,915	2,589	2,824	1,505	1,327	1,415	1,288
18	Ambulance and transport	609	823	1,055	970	823	857	884
19	Canteens and shops	812	1,098	1,474	1,568	1,779	1,774	1,766
20	Farms and gardens	873	1,180	1,129	1,169	1,205	1,259	1,297
21	User agreements	906	1,225	1,258	1,247	1,112	1,091	1,077
22	Miscellaneous	1,639	2,216	2,227	3,250	3,158	3,037	3,086
23	General Nursing Council	—	—	—	—	—	1,130	909
24	Total A	128,480	173,686	189,171	200,400	204,257	211,400	217,678
	(*c*) Receipts:							
25	Payments of staff	−5,381	−7,274	−7,892	−9,919	−9,610	−9,935	−9,831
26	Payments of patients and Road Traffic Acts	−2,087	−2,821	−2,473	−2,392	−2,257	−2,450	−2,549
27	Local authorities	−1,773	−2,397	−2,361	−2,315	−2,201	−2,085	−2,032
28	Canteens and shops	−981	−1,326	−1,778	−1,971	−2,071	−2,084	−2,071
29	Farms and gardens	−1,596	−2,158	−2,406	−2,499	−2,455	−2,558	−2,699
30	Other	−1,244	−1,682	−1,667	−1,753	−1,807	−1,640	−1,705
31	Net total A	115,418	156,028	170,594	179,551	183,856	190,648	196,791

	B. Other							
32	Non-Exchequer funds	679	918	1,272	1,420	1,807	1,860	2,263
33	Administration: (*a*) Wages	1,716	2,320	3,844	4,300	4,340	4,398	4,333
34	(*b*) Goods	1,220	1,649	1,083	1,019	953	931	921
35	Hospitals not vested	832	1,125	1,376	1,540	1,593	1,674	1,692
36	Blood transfusion: (*a*) Wages	231	312	399	429	444	458	496
37	(*b*) Goods	134	181	219	246	252	279	270
38	Appliances and invalid tricycles	795	1,075	2,726	3,781	3,934	4,081	3,978
39	Bacteriological	563	761	652	796	801	724	761
40	Miscellaneous: (*a*) Wages	100	135	167	206	225	219	267
41	(*b*) Goods	1,323	1,788	1,263	1,023	1,076	1,292	1,306
42	Total B	7,593	10,264	13,001	14,760	15,425	15,916	16,287
43	Total II	123,011	166,292	183,595	194,311	199,281	206,564	213,078
	III. Executive Council Services							
	(*a*) Central:							
44	Wages	1,142	1,544	1,426	1,487	1,697	1,502	1,409
45	Other	419	566	402	369	369	321	312
46	Total (*a*)	1,561	2,110	1,828	1,856	2,066	1,823	1,721
47	(*b*) General medical services	32,715	44,226	46,615	46,667	46,756	47,259	47,150
48	(*c*) Pharmaceutical	20,468	27,670	35,346	44,239	45,010	46,171	47,077
	(*d*) Dental:							
49	Resources	28,611	38,678	49,476	46,062	38,186	26,805	28,251
50	Dental Estimates Board: Wages	178	241	279	313	337	339	325
51	Other	32	43	68	69	55	52	47
52	Total (*d*)	28,821	38,962	49,823	46,444	38,578	27,196	28,623
	(*e*) Ophthalmic:							
53	Sight testing	4,600	6,218	5,227	4,432	3,333	3,452	3,808
54	Supply of spectacles	10,500	14,194	16,848	16,860	6,075	3,868	4,525
55	Total (*e*)	15,100	20,412	22,075	21,292	9,408	7,320	8,333
56	Total III	98,664	133,379	155,687	160,498	141,818	129,769	132,904
	IV. Local Authority Services							
57	Care of mothers and children	4,972	6,721	7,100	7,148	6,542	7,410	6,421
58	Midwifery	3,119	4,216	4,040	4,295	3,844	3,714	3,717
59	Health visiting	1,432	1,936	1,872	2,295	2,247	2,261	2,383
60	Home nursing	2,353	3,182	3,149	3,726	3,749	3,746	4,071
61	Vaccination and immunization	213	287	301	419	386	372	452
62	Ambulance services	4,114	5,562	6,934	7,502	7,797	7,927	8,131
63	Prevention of illness	625	845	1,001	1,181	1,342	1,355	1,466
64	Domestic help	1,129	1,526	2,388	2,846	3,056	3,356	3,777
65	Mental health	916	1,238	1,196	1,193	1,365	1,407	1,540
66	Other	83	112	65	147	83	150	140
67	Total IV	18,955	25,624	28,046	30,752	30,411	31,698	32,098
68	Total current real resources	242,459	327,767	369,773	388,259	374,057	370,586	380,765

Table 52. *The trend of the current net cost to public funds of the National Health Service revalued in 1948/9 prices (England and Wales, 1948/9–1953/4. 1949/50 = 100)*

Number	Item	Annual rate 1948/9	1949/50	1950/1	1951/2	1952/3	1953/4
	I. Central and Miscellaneous						
1	(*a*) Wages	98	100	116	104	101	109
2	(*b*) Other	107	100	101	104	110	112
3	Total I	101	100	110	104	104	110
	II. Hospital Services						
	A. Maintenance						
	(*a*) Salaries and wages:						
4	Medical (including specialists)	81	100	101	107	112	117
5	Nurses and midwives	95	100	106	112	112	115
6	Others	88	100	109	113	117	119
	(*b*) Goods and contracts:						
7	Provisions	93	100	102	102	101	104
8	Staff uniforms and clothing	89	100	122	125	134	133
9	Patients' clothing	100	100	105	98	115	108
10	Drugs and dressings	90	100	115	120	124	132
11	Medical and surgical appliances	94	100	94	82	101	110
12	Fuel, light and power	102	100	108	114	116	113
13	Laundry	92	100	121	134	144	154
14	Maintenance of buildings	104	100	116	93	103	124
15	Domestic repairs.	110	100	100	95	100	102
16	Rent, rates and water	90	100	103	107	108	113
17	Printing and stationery	92	100	53	47	50	46
18	Ambulance and transport	78	100	92	78	81	84
19	Canteens and shops	74	100	106	121	120	120
20	Farms and gardens	105	100	104	107	112	115
21	User agreements	97	100	99	88	87	86
22	Miscellaneous	100	100	146	142	136	139
23	General Nursing Council	—	—	—	—	—	—
24	Total A	92	100	106	108	112	115
	(*c*) Receipts:						
25	Payments of staff	92	100	126	122	126	125
26	Payments of patients and Road Traffic Acts	114	100	97	91	99	103
27	Local authorities	102	100	98	93	88	86
28	Canteens and shops	75	100	111	116	117	116
29	Farms and gardens	90	100	104	102	106	112
30	Other	101	100	105	108	98	102
31	Net total A	91	100	105	108	112	115

	B. Other						
32	Non-Exchequer funds	72	100	112	142	146	178
33	Administration: (*a*) Wages	60	100	112	113	114	113
34	(*b*) Goods	152	100	94	88	86	85
35	Hospitals not vested	82	100	112	116	122	123
36	Blood transfusion: (*a*) Wages	78	100	108	111	115	124
37	(*b*) Goods	83	100	112	115	127	123
38	Appliances and invalid tricycles	39	100	139	144	150	146
39	Bacteriological	117	100	122	123	111	117
40	Miscellaneous: (*a*) Wages	81	100	123	135	131	160
41	(*b*) Goods	142	100	81	85	102	103
42	Total B	79	100	114	119	122	125
43	Total II	91	100	106	109	113	116
	III. Executive Council Services						
	(*a*) Central:						
44	Wages	108	100	104	119	105	99
45	Other	141	100	92	92	80	78
46	Total (*a*)	115	100	102	113	100	94
47	(*b*) General medical services	95	100	100	100	101	101
48	(*c*) Pharmaceutical	78	100	125	127	131	133
	(*d*) Dental:						
49	Resources	78	100	93	77	54	57
50	Dental Estimates Board: Wages	86	100	112	121	122	116
51	Other	63	100	101	81	76	69
52	Total (*d*)	78	100	93	77	55	57
	(*e*) Ophthalmic						
53	Sight testing	119	100	85	64	66	73
54	Supply of spectacles	84	100	100	36	23	27
55	Total (*e*)	92	100	96	43	33	38
56	Total III	86	100	103	91	83	85
	IV. Local Authority Services						
57	Care of mothers and children	95	100	101	92	104	90
58	Midwifery	104	100	106	95	92	92
59	Health visiting	103	100	123	120	121	127
60	Home nursing	101	100	118	119	119	129
61	Vaccination and immunization	95	100	139	128	124	150
62	Ambulance services	80	100	108	112	114	117
63	Prevention of illness	84	100	118	134	135	146
64	Domestic help	64	100	119	128	141	158
65	Mental health	104	100	100	114	118	129
66	Other	172	100	226	128	231	215
67	Total IV	91	100	110	08	113	114
68	Total current real resources	89	100	105		100	103

RECONCILIATION WITH APPENDIX A, TABLE 46

Number in Appendix B	Number in Appendix A, Table 46
1	1, 3, 4, 5, 6, part 7, 9
2	2, part 7, 8, 10, 11, 12
4	part 14, 15, 16
5	part 14, 17 for 1948–51
6, 7, 8, 9	part 14
10, 11, 17	part 14, 18
12–16, 18–22	part 14
23	17 for 1952–3
25, 27–30	23
26	21, 22
32	20
33, 34	25
35	26
36, 37	27
38	29–31
39	33, 34
40, 41	14, 24, 28, 32, 35
44	part 37, 38
45	part 37, 39, 40
47	47
48	52
49	53–56
50, 51	57
53, 54	62
57–66	64–75

APPENDIX C

TRADING ACTIVITIES IN THE HOSPITAL SERVICE[1]

In analysing the activities of the hospital service it is necessary to know not only the size of changes in real resources used, but also in which categories of resources the changes have primarily taken place. To discover this, a detailed examination is needed of trading activities in the service. The essential facts are not, however, collected centrally. This obviously limits the possibilities of interpreting the accounts on a national scale, or of measuring accurately the impact of the Health Service on the national economy. Moreover, the absence of trading accounts renders the subhead a loose system of national or regional control over expenditures for different purposes. It follows too that it is less possible to assess the efficiency of those activities undertaken by hospital authorities which lend themselves to some measurement of value.[2] And it becomes more difficult to estimate the effects of policy or price changes on the Service.

1. STAFF PAYMENTS

The purpose of this appendix is to examine these accounting questions in respect to some of the more important trading activities with a view to eliminating such expenditure from hospital maintenance costs. We begin with staff payments. The major difficulty here is that we know in the aggregate what hospital staffs paid for board and lodging but we do not know the cost of providing food, fuel, laundry, domestic assistance and other services. This is an important and hitherto neglected matter. With a limited amount of hospital 'space' for all accommodation needs, the higher the proportion of resident staff the lower will be the amount of space available for patients and medical services in general. The large rise since 1948 in the ratio of total hospital staff (particularly nurses) to in-patients means—on the assumption of a constant proportion of resident staff—that a larger proportion of certain resources consumed by the hospitals has been used to provide board and lodging for staff. In other words, it means that this particular trading activity has been playing a more important role in the economy of the hospital, and it is, therefore, more necessary to know whether the receipts are meeting the full costs of the services provided. Unfortunately, however, no information is available centrally which shows the number and proportion of resident hospital staffs. This was one of the reasons why we sought the help of the General Register Office who tabulated for us a special analysis of the 1951 Census material relating to the population of hospitals and other institutions.[3] Some of the results of this analysis are summarized in Table 53.

[1] This appendix relates to all trading activities other than the provision of hospital services at private cost (see tables in Appendix B).

[2] For a study of this aspect of hospital accounting see Nuffield Provincial Hospitals Trust, *Report of an Experiment in Hospital Costing* (London, 1952).

[3] See Appendix H for an analysis of the patient population.

Table 53. *Resident staff by sex related to the 'inmate' population in different types of hospital on the census night 1951*

Type of hospital	Inmate population	Resident staff: Male	Female	Total	Resident staff as percentage of inmate population
Teaching	22,308	801	11,041	11,842	53
Wholly general	64,433	1,620	25,982	27,602	43
Mainly general	51,393	1,201	12,548	13,749	27
Mainly chronic	14,678	224	1,193	1,417	10
Chronic	17,784	274	1,547	1,821	10
Convalescent	2,445	64	750	814	33
Isolation	1,970	61	1,159	1,220	62
Maternity	8,863	85	2,625	2,710	31
Orthopaedic	3,794	129	1,608	1,737	46
Tuberculosis	17,901	1,055	4,323	5,378	30
Tuberculosis and isolation	5,746	223	2,293	2,516	44
Ear, nose and throat	195	8	94	102	52
Children	4,036	60	1,961	2,021	50
Eye	507	10	182	192	38
Other special hospitals	9,632	292	2,860	3,152	33
Other establishments	205	2	61	63	31
Contracted institutions	3,986	325	1,284	1,609	40
Mental	141,062	2,821	6,979	9,800	7
Mental deficiency	50,158	942	2,239	3,181	6
Total	421,096	10,197	80,729	90,926	22

These, it should be emphasized, are minimum figures. It is possible that substantial numbers of staff provided with accommodation in separate hostels, nurses' homes, annexes and private houses detached from the main hospital buildings were not enumerated as resident staff at the time of the Census. We cannot, however, estimate the numbers involved without an intensive study of the census schedules and other sources of information.

For all types of hospitals combined, the proportion of resident staff to inmates was at least 22 % in 1951. We do not know what it was before or after.

Table 53 also shows that the proportion varies very greatly as between different types of hospital. Excluding the small group of isolation hospitals, it will be noted that the proportion is highest in teaching hospitals with one resident staff to two patients. At the other extreme are the two big groups of mental and mental deficiency hospitals with only 7 and 6 % respectively of resident staff. The proportion is much lower in hospitals catering mainly for elderly patients—the so-called 'chronic' hospitals (10 %)—than in specialist hospitals for children (50 %). Any attempt to estimate future needs for hospital space cannot ignore these factors. In considering, for example, the effects of population changes, account would have to be taken of the widely different demands for resident staff from different types of hospitals. Attention may also be drawn to the fact that a reduction in the proportion of staff which is resident to, say, 30 % in those hospitals which now exceed this figure might well be as important in terms of hospital space as any likely changes in the national population and its age composition during the next ten years or so.[1] It is not known, however, to what extent staff space in hospital premises could be adapted for other uses.

To return to the question of receipts and expenditure for staff in residence, we note that in 1951 there were at least 91,000 staff accommodated in all types of hospitals.

We do not know the composition of this figure by category of staff, remuneration and payments made for board and lodging. In 1952/3 these payments brought in £13·3 million.[2] This sum covered both payments by resident staff for board and lodging and payments by non-resident staff for meals and other services. In an attempt to assess the subsidy element in the remuneration of staff the first step is to break down the total of £13·3 million for resident and non-resident staff and by grade of staff.

(*a*) *Resident staff*

The largest category of staff concerned is 'nurses and midwives'. The whole-time staff on 31 December 1953 is shown by grade and sex in Table 54.

Table 54. *Whole-time nurses and midwives by grade and sex on 31 December 1953**

	Nurses			
Grade	Male	Female	Midwives	Total
Staff nurses and other senior staff	12,038	37,578	5,274	54,890
Student nurses	3,818	44,474	3,733	52,025
Enrolled assistant nurses	2,706	8,069	—	10,775
Pupil assistant nurses	219	3,318	—	3,537
Nursing assistants	2,295	4,081	—	6,376
Other nursing staff	3,355	13,594	—	16,949
Total	24,431	111,114	9,007	144,552
Number resident	3,110	70,738	6,641	80,489

* Staff returns for the end of a year may not be typical of a year as a whole. We do not know, however, to what extent such figures differ from annual averages.

There are no statistics available showing the number of resident staff in each grade. In Table 55, however, we make certain estimates from data provided by the Ministry of Health and also of the mean payment for board and lodging appropriate to each grade in 1952/3.

The total payments by resident nurses and midwives are estimated at about £9½ million for 1952/3.

From the census figures in Table 53 it seems that there were at least 91,000 resident staff (81,000 women and 10,000 men). Comparing these figures with those in Table 54 and assuming that the number of resident staff remained constant between 1951 and 1953 we are therefore left with an unaccounted number of 7000 men and over 3000 women. Some of the men were junior medical staff[3] for whom payments are not negotiated centrally

[1] These matters are further discussed in Appendix H.

[2] Appendix B, Table 48, item 25.

[3] For house officers a fixed charge for board and lodging is specified centrally. In February 1955 it was £125 a year.

and vary widely. Table 56 shows such information as is available on this question. From these figures it would appear that the mean is about £150. We use this figure as a rough approximation in the absence of detailed information. The majority of the remaining unaccounted 11,000 were resident workers (mainly domestic) paying about £75 a year. We have accordingly estimated for all these 11,000 staff an average payment of £90 a year bringing in a total of £1 million.

Total payments from resident staff in 1952/3 are, therefore, raised to £10½ million.

Table 55. *Estimates of staff payments by resident nurses and midwives in different grades*

Grade	Number in grade 31 December 1953	Estimate of number resident	Mean payment in 1952/3 per annum	Total payment 1952/3 (£ m.)
Staff nurses and other senior staff	54,890	25,000	£145	3·63
Student nurses	52,025 }	45,000*	£106†	4·77
Pupil assistant nurses	3,537 }			
Enrolled assistant nurses	10,775	4,000	£130	0·52
Nursing assistants	6,376	2,000	£120	0·24
Other nursing staff	16,949	4,000	£80‡	0·32
Total	144,552	80,000	£119	9·48

* Student nurses are normally resident in their first and second years. Residence may be optional in the third year.

† The payment by students was increased from £100 to £108 on 1 January 1952.

‡ There is no negotiated payment for unqualified staff but it is believed that the payment approximates to that made by domestic workers. This is negotiated by the Ancillary Staffs Council.

(*b*) *Non-resident staff*

The major difficulty in analysing payments by non-resident staff is to estimate the number of meals taken. On the basis of data supplied by the South West Metropolitan Regional Hospital Board it would appear that, in terms of 'day-meals', the number taken by non-resident staff represented about one-tenth of the meals taken by patients and about one-half of all meals taken by the staff.[1] In the absence of more information, we assume that this region is typical of the country as a whole.[2] This implies that the day-meals consumed by non-resident staff of all grades amounted to 50,000 daily.

Non-resident nurses and midwives (of whom there were about 60,000)[3] paid on the average about £28[4] a year for meals taken while on duty and for laundry. Part-time nurses, in general, make no payment for meals occurring during their hours of duty.[5] After making allowance for a proportion of nurses who did not take their meals on duty and paid only a laundry charge

[1] See Chapter III, Table 8.

[2] As this region has proportionately more mental hospitals than other regions, it may have a lower proportion of resident staff.

[3] The total of whole-time nurses and midwives was 140,964 on 31 December 1952.

[4] Before 1 June 1952, £20 a year and, subsequently, £30 a year.

[5] This factor is taken into account in determining their rates of pay.

of £5 a year and certain other factors, we concluded that total payments by non-resident nurses and midwives came to about £1½ million in 1952/3. While it is extremely difficult to represent the meals taken by these nurses and midwives in terms of day-meals we would hazard the guess that, in 1952/3, they accounted for roughly 20,000 day-meals. This leaves 30,000 day-meals for other staff.

Only in the case of ancillary workers is there a negotiated price for meals. From inquiries we have made among hospitals in the south of England it

Table 56. *Emolument values for resident medical staff**

	£100	£115	£120	£130	£135	£140	£145	£150	£155
1. Newcastle	—	—	—	—	—	—	—	—	—
2. Leeds	—	—	—	†	†	†	†	†	—
3. Sheffield	—	1	—	2	1	1	4	11	2
4. East Anglian	—	—	—	—	—	—	—	—	—
5. North West Metropolitan	1	—	—	3	2	3	—	1	—
6. North East Metropolitan	—	—	—	†	—	—	—	—	—
7. South East Metropolitan	—	—	—	—	—	—	—	—	—
8. South West Metropolitan (Western Area)	—	—	—	—	—	—	—	—	—
8. South West Metropolitan (Eastern Area)	1	—	2	1	—	—	—	4	—
9. Oxford	2	—	1	2	—	1	—	6	—
10. South Western (Northern Area)	—	—	2	—	—	—	—	2	—
10. South Western (Southern Area)	—	—	—	—	—	—	—	—	—
11. Welsh	—	—	—	—	—	—	—	—	—
12. Birmingham	—	—	—	†	—	†	—	†	—
13. Manchester	—	—	—	†	—	—	—	—	—
14. Liverpool	—	—	—	8	—	—	—	3	—

	£160	£165	£170	£175	£180	£200	£210	£250
1. Newcastle	—	—	—	—	—	—	—	—
2. Leeds	—	—	—	—	—	—	—	—
3. Sheffield	—	—	1	1	—	1	—	—
4. East Anglian	—	—	—	—	—	—	—	—
5. North West Metropolitan	—	—	—	1	—	1	1	—
6. North East Metropolitan	—	—	—	—	—	†	—	—
7. South East Metropolitan	—	—	—	—	—	—	—	—
8. South West Metropolitan (Western Area)	—	—	—	—	—	—	—	—
8. South West Metropolitan (Eastern Area)	1	3	1	1	3	—	—	—
9. Oxford	1	—	—	—	—	—	—	—
10. South Western (Northern Area)	—	—	—	—	—	2	—	1
10. South Western (Southern Area)	—	—	—	—	—	—	—	—
11. Welsh	—	—	—	—	—	—	—	—
12. Birmingham	—	†	—	—	—	—	—	—
13. Manchester	—	—	—	—	—	—	—	—
14. Liverpool	—	—	—	—	1	—	—	—

* Source: National Association of Hospital Management Committee Group Secretaries.
† Number of cases unknown.

appears that in general the prices fixed for these workers tend to be applied to all other grades of staff because of the difficulty of making different charges. In the ordinary way, therefore, in many hospitals all grades from cleaners to consultants paid the same prices, e.g. 1*s*. 5*d*. for lunch[1] and 5*d*. for supper, etc. (see Table 58). In 1952/3 the negotiated price for meals for ancillary workers averaged 2*s*. 11*d*. a day.[2] For 30,000 day-meals, this works out at £1·6 million for 1952/3.

We now bring together all these hazardous calculations for staff payments (Table 57).

Table 57. *Estimated staff payments classified by rate of payment (England and Wales, 1952/3)*

(£ m. in actual prices)

	Payment
Resident staff:	
Annual payment £90 or under	1·3
Annual payment £106	4·8
Annual payment £120–£130	0·8
Annual payment £135 or over	3·6
Non-resident staff:	
Nurses and midwives for meals on duty and laundry at £28 a year	1·5
Other staff meals at 2*s*. 11*d*. a day	1·6
Total	13·6
Error	0·3
Actual staff payments in 1952/3	13·3

Table 58. *Staff payments: ancillary workers in the hospital service (1946–1954)*

	With effect from				
	1 August 1946	1 October 1951	8 December 1952	16 November 1953	13 December 1954
Breakfast	6*d*.	8*d*.	9*d*.	10*d*.	11*d*.
Dinner	1*s*.	1*s*. 3*d*.	1*s*. 5*d*.	1*s*. 7*d*.	1*s*. 8*d*.
Tea	5*d*.	6*d*.	7*d*.	7*d*.	8*d*.
Supper	3*d*.	4*d*.	5*d*.	5*d*.	6*d*.
	1 August 1946	1 October 1951	21 November 1952	21 September 1953	7 September 1954
Total board	15*s*. 2*d*.	19*s*. 3*d*.	22*s*. 2*d*.	23*s*. 11*d*.	26*s*. 3*d*.
Lodging	5*s*. 10*d*.	7*s*.	7*s*. 7*d*.	7*s*. 7*d*.	8*s*. 2*d*. (7*s*. 8*d*.)*
Laundry†	2*s*.	2*s*. 9*d*.	3*s*. 3*d*.	3*s*. 3*d*.	3*s*. 7*d*.
Total	23*s*.	29*s*.	33*s*.	34*s*. 9*d*.	38*s*. (37*s*. 6*d*.)*

* A differential rate for women was introduced on 13 December 1954.

† The laundry charge (average 2*s*. 11*d*. for 1952/3) seems low when compared with the cost of the average domestic bundle estimated by the Institute of British Launderers at 5*s*. in 1952/3.

[1] In some hospital groups, however, we found that consultants were charged 2*s*. for lunch.

[2] Up to 8 December 1952, 2*s*. 9*d*. a day and, subsequently, 3*s*. 2*d*.

Even greater difficulties are involved in estimating the cost of the services provided for which these payments were made. First we show in Table 58 the details of the negotiated payments for ancillary workers.

According to the hospital cost statements of the South West Metropolitan Regional Hospital Board it appears that in 1952/3 the cost of food alone per patient per week varied from 26*s*. in tuberculosis hospitals to 15*s*. in mental hospitals. It would thus seem that the charge for full board for ancillary workers roughly met the cost of the provisions consumed. This is broadly confirmed by a cost study of twenty-nine hospitals in nine regions carried out in 1951/2 by the Secretaries and Treasurers of Regional Hospital Boards who kindly supplied us with the following details:

	£	*s.*	*d.*
Food	1	1	0
Preparation and service of food		6	9
Uniform		2	6
Laundry		3	7
Domestic service		9	6
Domestic renewals, etc.		3	10
Fuel, light, heat and water ...		3	4
Rent and rates		2	6
	£2	13	0

This total covers the cost of providing accommodation, full board and other services for whole-time resident ancillary staff. It takes no account of repairs and redecoration to buildings, and the allowance for rent excludes the attributable rent of hospital buildings.[1] It would thus appear that these staffs were paying under half of the cost in 1951/2.

We have also obtained from the South West Metropolitan Regional Hospital Board the results of certain studies of the actual costs of maintaining nurses' homes. These relate to seven hospital groups. They provide not only cost figures but the payments actually made by the nurses benefiting from the expenditure. The Finance Officers were asked to record all expenditure which could be identified as relating to the nurses' homes. The difficulties encountered in doing so have again, it is believed, resulted in some understatement of costs. The attributable rent is again omitted, and in the case of provisions the same cost has been assumed for the average member of the staff as for the average patient. This results in some understatement because such investigations as have been made into feeding costs for patients and staff all point to the conclusion that the cost is greater for staff than for patients. In Table 59 we show the costs falling on the National Health Service as a percentage of costs paid by the staff.

The extent of the subsidy ranges from 44 to 96 % and averages 72 %. This represents an annual rate of £75 per nurse. If these groups were representative of the country as a whole, the annual subsidy on the 80,000 resident nurses and midwives would be costing £6 million.

[1] See Chapter III, p. 20. We estimate for repairs, redecorations and rent an average weekly cost of 16*s*. to 20*s*. for a bed in a nurses' home erected under the National Health Service (60-year depreciation average; 3 % interest; buildings only). This would absorb a high proportion of the payments made by nurses which range from 40*s*. to 60*s*. a week.

Similar data concerning the costs of nurses' homes have also been provided for us by the North West Metropolitan Regional Hospital Board. Once again, not all expenditure is included, but the figures are based upon the actual costs of feeding the staff as distinct from a figure derived from averaging expenditure on both patients and staff. The weekly cost per resident in a nurses' home in St Albans was £3. 0*s*. 8*d*. in February 1955 when there were forty-nine residents and £4. 2*s*. 10*d*. in September 1954 when there were thirty-one residents. For another nurses' home (in Uxbridge) the weekly cost was estimated to be about £4. 15*s*. per resident in 1953/4.

Table 59. *The percentage subsidy on the charge for board and accommodation in seven hospital groups in the South West Metropolitan Region during the six months ended 30 September 1952*

Type of hospital	Area	Number of nurses in residence	Cost per resident per week	Percentage subsidy after deducting staff payments
General	London	169	£3. 0*s*. 9*d*.	44
General	Surrey	130	£3. 11*s*. 5*d*.	88
General	Surrey	61	£3. 7*s*. 7*d*.	71
Special (children's)	Surrey	306	£3. 6*s*. 5*d*.	87
General	Western	149	£2. 17*s*. 8*d*.	56
Mental deficiency	Surrey	24	£4. 3*s*. 1*d*.	96
Special (mental)	Surrey	14	£3. 9*s*. 6*d*.	69
Total		853		72

These scattered pieces of information indicate that expenditure on resident staff varies widely, depending on the number in residence, the type of accommodation provided and many other factors. It would seem hazardous to assume that the national position could be estimated by averaging the information we have managed to collect. We have therefore adopted a different approach to the problem of estimating the amount of the subsidy. We sought information which would allow us to calculate a 'reasonable subsistence minimum' (as we call it) for full board and lodging for resident staff. Obviously, this approach ignores questions of differential standards of service and amenity provided in different hospitals and for different categories of staff.[1] It has, however, the merit of enabling us to estimate a *minimum* subsidy element.

Data relating to board and lodging charges were collected from many diverse sources. For purposes of illustration three are specified here:

(i) A study of twenty advertisement boards in central and working class areas of London in February 1954 revealed very few offers of full board (excluding the weekday dinner) below £2. 5*s*. 0*d*. a week. None at this price offered exclusive use of a room and not all offered exclusive use of a bed. After taking account of the higher costs of London, the profit element, the cost of the six dinners, and of the personal laundry provided for hospital staff, we concluded that a reasonable subsistence minimum would be at least £3 a week.

[1] For example: higher quality meals for medical staff; furnished flats for matrons with a full-time maid; free transport; secretarial services and so forth.

(ii) From June 1952 the National Assistance Board was paying 35*s*. a week for a single person. This excludes rent, and makes no allowance for laundry and staff costs in the preparation and service of meals in hospital. Again we concluded that at least £3 a week was a reasonable subsistence figure.

(iii) We obtained from the Ministry of Labour and National Service the charges and costs per resident in hostels provided for industrial workers managed by the National Service Hostels Corporation Ltd. In standard hostels, men and women were paying 40*s*.[1] and 35*s*. a week respectively for cubicled accommodation and board comprising two main meals per day and an additional main meal on Sundays. No personal laundry services were provided. At industrial hostels of all kinds the total overall costs of board and accommodation for men and women averaged about £3 per week in 1952/3.[2]

From all the evidence brought together in this appendix we believe that a 'reasonable subsistence minimum' for the range of goods and services provided for hospital staff was over £3 a week in 1952/3. Student nurses paying on the average £106 a year in this financial year would have needed to pay at least 50 % more to meet the cost of board and lodging provided.

It has been the purpose of this exercise to eliminate trading activities from the hospital accounts. We must therefore take into account the fact that hospital authorities do not pay full rent for the premises they use.[3] In view of this, and also of our inability to compare the payments made by higher grades of staff with the cost of providing the facilities they use, we have decided to assume that, for each year of the National Health Service, the cost of providing these goods and services was 40 % higher than the payments made by the staff for them. We present this as a minimum figure; it obviously understates the true position.

This average percentage of 40 for all resident staff, together with an allowance for the subsidy involved in the meals and other services provided for non-resident staff, represents, in round figures, an annual subsidy of £5 million.

2. FARMS AND GARDENS

The Public Accounts Committee, in its examination of this trading activity, has drawn attention to an apparent loss on farms and gardens as shown in the Ministry of Health's Section 55 accounts.[4] To enable us to investigate the problem more fully, the Treasurer of the South West Metropolitan Regional Hospital Board kindly provided us with detailed information on farms and gardens in this region. Table 60 gives the figures as prepared in accordance with Section 55 requirements.

A number of committees in the region, principally mental hospital groups, own or rent large areas of land which have been developed as mixed farms. The detailed farm trading accounts prepared by these committees show that

[1] 47*s*. (men), 42*s*. (women) a week from 13 April 1953. 54*s*. (men), 49*s*. (women) a week from 18 October 1954.

[2] The occupancy of these hostels is about 80 %.

[3] See Chapter III, p. 20.

[4] See *Third Report from the Committee of Public Accounts Session 1952–53*, H.C. Paper 203 (H.M.S.O. 1953).

the statutory accounts give a misleading picture of the results of these trading activities. The chief reasons are:

(1) All expenditure on farms and gardens is not included under that heading (e.g. oil fuel for tractors is allocated to fuel, light, power, and the like; rents and rates of farm buildings, cottages and land are allocated to rents and rates). In addition, because hospitals are owned by the Ministry, certain items of expenditure in a private farmer's account are not incurred (e.g. road-fund licences and insurances).

Table 60. *Expenditure on and receipts from farms and gardens as prepared for the Section 55 accounts (South West Metropolitan Regional Hospital Board 1951/2 and 1952/3)**

(£)

	1951/2	1952/3
Expenditure:		
Salaries and wages	198,023	205,751
Other	163,485	174,319
Total	361,508	380,070
Less direct credits	308,519	346,710
Apparent loss	52,989	33,360

* The figures cover all hospital management committees in the region and include those committees operating market gardens.

(2) The statutory accounts fail to distinguish accurately between capital and current items of expenditure. Many purchases are made to maintain and improve farm equipment, but the accounts show neither a dead stock valuation nor a depreciation charge. Stock values for livestock and garnered crops only are shown and all other stock purchases are immediately written off to expenditure, thus inflating the expenditure on the farms and gardens account.

(3) The value placed on produce transferred from hospital farms to hospitals for consumption is based on wholesale prices ruling at the time of transfer, and not on prices paid to private farmers. The difference mainly consists of food subsidies, the principal items involved being milk, meat and eggs. As the farms in the region produce annually about 750,000 gallons of milk, 1,000,000 eggs and 200 tons of meat it is clear that this factor is an important one.

Table 61 summarizes the farm trading accounts prepared by sixteen

Table 61. *Trading accounts for farms and gardens for sixteen hospital groups (South West Metropolitan Regional Hospital Board 1951/2 and 1952/3)*

(£)

	1951/2	1952/3
Expenditure:*		
Salaries and wages	104,432	112,183
Other	366,760	373,468
Total	471,192	485,651
Income	478,560	510,057
Profit and loss	7,368 profit	24,406 profit

* No allowance is made for central administrative expenditure; the amount involved is, however, thought to be insignificant.

hospital groups in the region based on all expenditures for seed, fertilizers, feeding stuffs, new machinery, repairs, livestock, fuel, rent, rates, property repairs, interest on capital, subsidies, and full stock valuations.

Although the figures relate only to the main hospital farming activities carried out in the region and therefore exclude most of the garden accounts, they show that the statutory accounts give a seriously misleading picture of the true value of these trading activities.

In addition to the farms controlled by hospital management committees in the region, the Board directly administers a large area of farmland totalling some 3600 acres, excluding woodlands, in Surrey. This land, mostly adjacent to a number of mental hospitals, is organized into three farm units collectively known as 'grouped farms'. They were developed in this way by the London County Council before the appointed day.

The factors we have mentioned as making the statutory accounts misleading do not all apply to the Board's farms because all expenditure incurred on these farms is allocated to 'farms'. The reason for this is that the Board's expenditure is shown in Table C of the Board's statutory accounts, whereas Management Committees are required to include farm and garden expenditure in Table B (Hospital Maintenance Expenditure). This point apart, similar comments to those already made apply to the presentation of the Board's trading activities. Table 62 shows the Board's statutory accounts for these grouped farms.

Table 62. *Expenditure on and receipts from grouped farms as prepared for the Section 55 accounts (South West Metropolitan Regional Hospital Board 1950/1–1952/3)*

(£)

	1950/1	1951/2	1952/3
Expenditure:			
Salaries and wages	56,036	59,399	64,381
Other	64,812	61,314	66,434
Total	120,848	120,713	130,815
Income	103,560	108,310	119,470
Apparent loss	17,288	12,403	11,345

This table should be compared with the trading account figures given in Table 63.

In Table 63 certain figures are given for the estimated value of patients' labour; these are thought to be too high. A number of patients could not have worked outside the hospital farm, and those who could would need to be accompanied by a trained nurse. However, the value in terms of economic resources of any alternative to the present arrangements is probably very small.

The conclusions we reach from the examination of this and other material on expenditure and receipts on farms and gardens are broadly two: first, that for the particular purposes of this study over the period 1948–53 the statutory form of accounts is seriously misleading[1] and, secondly, that in the area of the

[1] A form of trading account for farms and gardens was introduced by the Ministry of Health in 1954 (H.M. (54) 38). This it is thought will, in the future, mark an improvement in representing the facts.

South West Metropolitan Regional Hospital Board expenditure and receipts on farms and gardens have just about balanced during the period in question. Had time and resources permitted it would clearly have been desirable to have investigated the problem in all hospital regions. But this was not possible. We are therefore assuming that what obtains in this region obtains in all regions. Thus, in eliminating expenditure and receipts on trading activities from hospital maintenance expenditure we have assumed for the whole period that the operation of farms and gardens was exactly covered by receipts.

Table 63. *Trading accounts of grouped farms (South West Metropolitan Regional Hospital Board 1950/1–1952/3)*

(£)

	1950/1	1951/2	1952/3
Expenditure:			
Salaries and wages	56,036	59,399	64,381
Other	169,882	167,020	176,749
Total	225,918	226,419	241,130
Income	219,953	225,349	242,643
Profit or loss	5,965* loss	1,070 loss	1,513 profit
Estimated value of patients' labour not included in this table	3,520	3,343	3,010

* Partly due to a reduction of £3600 in stock value.

3. CANTEENS AND SHOPS

In examining this type of trading activity we find that the form of accounts does not show all the expenditure involved in running canteens and hospital shops. The particular items not allocated are salaries and wages, light, heat and rent.

The Treasurer of the South West Metropolitan Regional Hospital Board has again assisted us with information and Table 64 gives, for this region, the figures as shown in the Section 55 accounts.

Table 64. *Expenditure on and receipts from canteens and shops as prepared for the Section 55 accounts (South West Metropolitan Regional Hospital Board 1950/1–1952/3)*

(£)

	1950/1	1951/2	1952/3
Expenditure	266,048	311,096	312,333
Direct credits	319,991	352,095	361,464
Profit	53,943	40,999	49,131

A study of several canteen trading accounts compiled by management committees according to the procedure laid down in H.M.C. (48) 34 shows that 'other' charges, excluding rent which is not chargeable, amount to between 5 and 8% of the total expenditure shown in the Section 55 accounts.

After making allowance for these charges it emerges that the operation of canteens and shops in this region produced some income for the Treasury, and this reduced to a slight extent the cost of the hospital service. There are, however, a number of reasons (which we will not pursue here) for believing that this region is not typical of other regions in this respect. On balance, therefore, we decided to assume for the purposes of our calculations that expenditure on all hospital canteens and shops was exactly covered by receipts during the whole period of this study.

4. ALL OTHER RECEIPTS

We have assumed that other services falling within the definition of 'trading activities' have been exactly at cost. We have allocated throughout the relevant items of expenditure according to the proportions they bear to total expenditure. The amount involved was less than £5 million each year.

5. CONCLUSION

From the evidence presented in this appendix it is clear that to allocate expenditure on trading activities in conformity with the requirements of the statutory accounts involves a substantial error. For the purposes of this study it would, however, be pointless—and immensely time-consuming—to attempt a detailed allocation to fit all the itemized headings shown in Appendix B. Instead, we content ourselves with an allocation on the basis of the broad categories of goods and contracts described in Chapter 1. Table 65 shows expenditure on hospital maintenance in 1949/50 and 1953/4 in these broad

Table 65. *Adjustments to hospital maintenance expenditure to eliminate trading activities (England and Wales, 1949/50 and 1953/4)*

(£ m. in actual prices)

	1949/50			1953/4		
	Total expenditure (i)	Adjustment for trading activities (ii)	Expenditure not on trading activities (iii) (i) + (ii)	Total expenditure (iv)	Adjustment for trading activities (v)	Expenditure not on trading activities (vi) (iv) + (v)
Salaries and wages:						
Medical (including specialists)	23·2	—	23·2	27·2	—	27·2
Nurses and midwives	45·7	2·1	47·8	59·2	4·6*	63·8
Other	52·1	−5·7	46·4	75·8	−7·2	68·6
Goods and contracts:						
Medical goods	14·0	—	14·0	18·1	—	18·1
Other	63·8	−13·4	50·4	91·3	−21·6	69·7
Total†	198·8	−17·0	181·8	271·6	−24·2	247·4

* Part of the adjustment to this item in 1952/3 and 1953/4 is accounted for by treating item 23 in the tables of Appendix B on a basis comparable with the earlier years.

† The difference between the totals of columns (iii) and (vi) and item 31 in Table 48 of Appendix B is accounted for by item 26 which is excluded from the above table.

categories; the adjustments required to eliminate expenditure on trading activities; and expenditure after these activities have been eliminated.

For comparability with the constant price figures in Appendix B, the adjusted figures in columns (iii) and (vi) of the above tables are also shown in constant prices in Table 66. The figures have been rounded to the nearest £1 million, as the errors involved do not justify more precise estimates.

Table 66. *Hospital maintenance expenditure with trading activities eliminated in 1948/9 prices (England and Wales, 1949/50 and 1953/4)*

(£ m. in 1948/9 prices)

	1949/50	1953/4
Salaries and wages:		
Medical (including specialists)	23	27
Nurses and midwives	42	49
Other	45	55
Goods and contracts:		
Medical goods	14	17
Other	49	51
Total*	173	199

* The difference between these totals and item 31 in Table 51 of Appendix B is accounted for by item 26 which is excluded from the above table.

APPENDIX D

PART-TIME AND WHOLE-TIME MEDICAL AND DENTAL STAFF IN THE HOSPITAL SERVICE

1. ANALYSIS OF THE STATISTICS

In Chapter IV, p. 34, reference was made to the increase in medical and dental staff in the hospital service. This appendix analyses the causes and costs of the increase.

The accounts presented in this book show an increase in expenditure on hospital medical and dental staff of £4 million between 1949/50 and 1953/4. As there was little change in the rates of remuneration between the appointed day and 1 April 1954, this figure represents an increase both in actual and 1948/9 prices. It has therefore to be analysed in relation to changes in the number and category of staff employed.

Considerable difficulties are encountered in analysing and interpreting such statistics. There are two broad categories—whole-time and part-time staff. The statistics for part-timers are recorded in two different series. The first series (published in the *Annual Reports of the Ministry of Health*) shows part-time appointments. One individual may hold appointments with one or more than one hospital. Such appointments may be for one or more than one half-day. It is clear, therefore, that comparative statistics of appointments are only a very rough guide to changes in the number of man-hours used by the Service. Moreover, this series has now become less useful for comparative purposes as a result of the transfer of responsibility for making returns from hospital management committees to regional boards. The first figures affected by this change are those for 31 December 1953. In consequence, some appointments at different hospitals in one group recorded as separate appointments in the earlier returns were counted as one appointment in the figures for 1953.

The second series of part-time staff statistics, though more reliable, is not published. It shows the number of notional hours worked by part-timers during the week. To convert these hours into whole-time equivalents, we can divide them by 35.[1] Table 67 shows the total staff each year in whole-time equivalents and compares this in percentage terms with the trend in costs.

The staff figures in this table are for 31 December of each year and the cost figures are for the financial years. It is therefore not surprising that the two trends do not exactly correspond. The staff figures show an increase of 18½ %, while the cost figures have increased slightly less—by 17 %.

Table 68 shows staff in whole-time equivalents in 1949 and 1953 and the percentage change between these years broken down into whole-time and part-time categories.

The role of different grades, and the role of whole-time and part-time

[1] It is assumed that the whole-timer works eleven half-days of 3½ hours during the week—a total of 38½ hours. It is further assumed that the part-timer spends one-eleventh of his time in travel.

service within these grades, have undergone considerable changes since 1949. For example, a number of senior registrars and part-time senior hospital medical officers have been promoted to the consultant grade, a number of house officers have been promoted to the senior house officer grade, and many medical superintendents have been re-graded as consultants. We will, however, confine our discussion to the changing roles of whole-time and part-time service.

Table 67. *Medical and dental staff in whole-time equivalents compared with the trend of resources used (England and Wales, 1949–1954)*

Staff in whole-time equivalents			Cost (£ m.)		
Year	Number	Percentage of 1949	Year	Cost	Percentage of 1949/50
1949	12,694	100·0	1949/50	23·2	100
1950	13,478	106·2	1950/1	23·6	101
1951	14,324	112·8	1951/2	25·0	107
1952	14,871	117·1	1952/3	26·0	112
1953	15,040	118·5	1953/4	27·2	117

Table 68. *Medical and dental staff broken down by grade and into whole-time and part-time (England and Wales, 31 December 1949 and 31 December 1953)*

(Whole-time equivalents*)

	1949		1953		Percentage change 1949–53	
Grade	Whole-time	Part-time	Whole-time	Part-time	Whole-time	Part-time
Consultants	1310	2463	1728	3140	32	28
Senior hospital medical officers and senior hospital dental officers	686	524	1167	459	70	−12
Senior registrars	1308	158	966	62	−26	−61
Registrars	1478	71	2102	61	42	−14
Senior house officers	784	20	1675	22	114	10
Junior hospital medical officers	402	—	475	—	18	—
Medical superintendents	153	20	29	7	−81	−65
Deputy medical superintendents	85	5	16	1	−81	−80
House officers	2633	23	2553	9	− 3	−61
Others (including general practitioners)	115	456	30	538	−74	18
Total	8954	3740	10,741	4299	20	15

* For part-timers the hours recorded per week have been divided by 35.

In total, whole-time work has increased by 20 % and part-time work by 15 % since 1949. But taking together the first three grades of staff shown in the table, whole-time and part-time service have increased by about the same proportion (between 16 and 17 %). Among part-timers the increase has occurred almost entirely in the consultant grade.

Table 69 shows for the consultant grade alone the changes in the different specialities.

Table 69. *Number of consultants broken down by speciality or department and into whole-time and part-time service (England and Wales, 31 December 1949 and 31 December 1953)*

(Whole-time equivalents)

Speciality or department	1949 Whole-time (i)	1949 Part-time (ii)	1949 Total (iii)	1953 Whole-time (iv)	1953 Part-time (v)	1953 Total (vi)	(vii)† (vi) ÷ (iii)	1949 (viii)‡ (i) as percentage of (iii)
General medicine	124	259	383	110	366	476	124	32
General surgery	142	415	557	121	515	636	114	25
Gynaecology and obstetrics	59	215	274	56	259	315	115	21
Paediatrics	24	77	101	25	111	136	135	24
Psychiatry	200	71	271	353	91	444	163	74
Cardiology	—	8	8	—	11	11	137	—
Dentistry	14	52	66	17	52	69	105	21
Dermatology	3	63	66	6	79	85	129	5
Diseases of chest	132	45	177	236	31	267	151	75
Ear, nose and throat	12	189	201	13	217	230	114	6
Infectious diseases	27	4	31	37	4	41	132	87
Neurology and neurosurgery	13	45	58	5	61	66	114	22
Ophthalmology	1	150	151	3	180	183	121	1
Plastic surgery	9	17	26	2	26	28	108	35
Radiotherapy	54	23	77	56	33	89	116	70
Thoracic surgery	8	28	36	8	54	62	172	22
Traumatic and orthopaedic surgery	29	167	196	29	213	242	123	15
Venereal diseases	16	49	65	29	34	63	97	25
Geriatrics	4	1	5	18	8	26	520	80
Pathology	240	64	304	315	71	386	127	79
Anaesthetics	80	295	375	112	457	569	151	21
Physical medicine	12	25	37	21	37	58	157	32
Radiology	76	161	237	136	193	329	139	32
Others	31	38	69	18	39	57	83	45
Total*	1310	2463	3773	1726	3140	4866	129	35

* Some totals do not add up owing to rounding.

† Total whole-time equivalents in 1953 as a percentage of the total in 1949.

‡ Whole-time as a percentage of total whole-time equivalents.

Strikingly different changes have been operating in different specialities. But as may be seen by studying the last two columns, the table shows one fairly consistent trend. The specialities in which the role of whole-time service is greatest show in general the greatest expansion. The largest absolute increases in whole-time consultants have occurred in psychiatry (152) and diseases of the chest (104)—specialities where the role of whole-timers is at least twice that of part-timers. Between 1949 and 1953, psychiatry expanded by 63 % and diseases of the chest by 51 %, as compared with an expansion in all specialities of 29 %. The largest absolute increases in part-time consultants have occurred in anaesthetics (162), general medicine (107) and general surgery (100)—predominantly part-time specialities. But while the expansion in anaesthetics was above average (51 %), the expansion in general medicine was 24 % and in general surgery 14 %. In seven major specialities taken together (general medicine, general surgery, gynaecology and obstetrics, paediatrics, ear, nose and throat, ophthalmology, and traumatic and orthopaedic surgery) the total of whole-timers fell from 391 to 357—a fall of 9 %, while the total of part-timers (in whole-time equivalents) rose from 1472 to 1861—a rise of 26 %.

We have calculated the changes that would have occurred in whole-time and part-time service if each speciality had developed equally by 29 % since 1949 though still showing the relative changes in the role of part-time and whole-time service that occurred between 1949 and 1953 in each speciality.[1] This calculation indicates an increase in whole-time service of 17 % and an increase in part-time service of 34 %. The greater relative increase of whole-time consultants shown in Table 68 has been caused, therefore, by specialities which are mainly staffed by whole-timers expanding more than specialities staffed mainly by part-timers. If each speciality had expanded to the same extent part-time service by consultants would have increased twice as much as whole-time service and the increase in part-time medical and dental staff would have been greater than the increase in whole-time staff.

These figures take account, of course, of new appointments, retirements and changes in existing contracts. Where switches have occurred these, it would seem, have been overwhelmingly from whole-time to part-time service. National figures are available of transfers from whole-time to part-time service within regional boards but not of transfers from part-time to whole-time service. In answer to a question in 1954, the Parliamentary Secretary to the Ministry of Health gave the information shown in Table 70.[2]

Table 70. *Transfers of consultants from whole-time to part-time service (Regional Hospital Boards in England and Wales, 1951–1953)*

Year	Transfers
1951	42
1952	61
1953	46
Total	149

These figures do not, however, represent the total number of transfers that have occurred within the National Health Service. The consultant who resigned a whole-time appointment with one Regional Board to take on a part-time appointment with another board would not be included in these figures.

More detailed information has been provided for us by the South West Metropolitan Regional Hospital Board. Table 71 summarizes the position from the start of the Service until the end of 1953.

[1] To be more precise, we have assumed a linear relation between the number of whole-time (or part-time) consultants and the total number of consultants in each speciality except venereal diseases and 'others'—the two contracting specialities. In the case of venereal diseases we have allocated the whole increase to whole-time consultants, and in the case of 'others' we have allocated the whole increase to part-time consultants.

[2] *H.C. Deb.* 8 April 1954, col. 65.

Table 71. *The disposal of applications for transfers by specialists between whole-time and part-time service (South West Metropolitan Region, July 1948–December 1953)*

	Total number of applications received	Number approved	Number not approved	Number still under consideration
Whole-time to part-time	45	22	22	1
Part-time to whole-time	3	3	—	—

It appears from the information for this region that the trend of both applications for transfer and transfers effected has been overwhelmingly from whole-time to part-time.

At first sight this conclusion may seem to conflict with the staff data in Table 68. However, a reconciliation becomes apparent when it is remembered that there have been substantial staff changes during the five years; many retirements, promotions and new appointments have occurred. The majority of the new appointments have been whole-time. An increase of 237 in the number of whole-time consultants between 31 December 1950 and 31 December 1953 was greater than the total transfers to part-time service recorded in the same period, namely, 149 (Table 70). About half the increase in whole-time consultants was, however, in mental and mental deficiency hospitals. In all other hospitals, therefore, part-time service increased at a greater rate than whole-time service. Transfers from whole-time to part-time service contributed to this trend. What is also significant is that much of the expansion of whole-time consultant service took place between 31 December 1949 and 31 December 1950. Since then, part-time consultant service has been increasing more rapidly than whole-time service. Measured in hours of work, over two-thirds of all part-time hospital service now relates to the consultant grade. Part-time service in lower grades has decreased substantially since 1949.

In summary, it is becoming more frequent for service below the consultant grade to be on a whole-time basis. When the consultant grade is reached, however, transfer to part-time service is becoming common.

There are various reasons for this: the higher social and professional prestige believed to be attached to part-time service; the opportunities to engage in private practice in combination with access to beds in the National Health Service; payments for National Health Service domiciliary consultations; travelling time allowances; income-tax concessions and so forth.

2. THE RELATIVE COSTS OF WHOLE-TIME AND PART-TIME SERVICE

Because of these financial incentives part-time service is on average more costly to the National Health Service than whole-time service. It is difficult, however, to measure the extent of this, for the reason that the information available about the work done by specialists is scanty and often unreliable. Special inquiries have, therefore, had to be made to collect additional information. We now consider several factors which contribute to the higher costs of part-time service per notional[1] hour of work.

First, the salary scale itself provides for greater remuneration of the part-timer per half-day. Table 72 shows the percentage increase in the rate of remuneration of part-time specialists compared with whole-time specialists calculated in accordance with the formula set out in the *Terms and Conditions of Service*.[2]

Table 72. *Percentage increase in the rate of remuneration of part-time specialists over whole-time specialists*

Notional half-days	Percentage increase of part-timer (operative during the period 5 July 1948–31 March 1954)	Percentage increase of part-timer (from 1 April 1954)
1	25	25
2	25	25
3	25	25
4	25	19
5	25	15
6	21	12½
7	14	11
8	9	9
9	6	6

The percentage increase was somewhat reduced in the middle ranges from 1 April 1954, but, during the period we are considering, the part-timer with five or less half-days was paid 25 % more than the whole-timer. For part-timers doing more than five half-days, the differential fell to only 6 % for nine half-days.

A second advantage of the part-timer arises in payment for time spent in travelling.[3] In arriving at the appropriate contract to be given to a part-time specialist, travelling time is taken into account. A part-time specialist cannot be paid travelling time for a journey of more than half-an-hour each way to his main hospital. From the maximum of an hour per day it follows that the ceiling on session time spent in travelling can be assumed to be two sessions a week for any one individual.

If the time allowed for the actual work performed, and the time spent in travelling to and from work are added together and total fractionally more than a whole session, the specialist has a right to a contract for the next full number of sessions. The following example illustrates the point:

Assessment of work actually performed per week, say two sessions at 3½ hours per session	= 7 hours
Add: Travelling time per week, say	½ hour
Total to be covered	= 7½ hours

[1] By 'notional' hour we mean the hour of work for which the specialist is paid. We assume a working week of 38½ hours for the whole-time specialist.

[2] Ministry of Health, *Terms and Conditions of Service of Hospital Medical and Dental Staff* (*England and Wales*) (London, 1952), par. 5.

[3] Payment for time spent in travelling is included in superannuation rights.

As this exceeds two sessions, assessed at 7 hours, the consultant can get a contract for three sessions. Cases like this may be rare in new contracts, but such contracts were made in the early years of the National Health Service.

A third advantage of the part-timer also concerns travel. Not only is the part-time specialist paid for his time spent in travel, but the expenses of travel are met by the regional boards. The expenses of the whole-timer in travelling between his hospital appointments are also met by the boards, but in general he is expected to travel to and from his main hospital at his own expense. There are few parallels in the whole field of employment of workers having the cost of travel to and from work paid for them. These travel expenses for part-timers are subject to a limit of ten miles each way.[1] If, therefore, the specialist lives ten miles or more from his main hospital and travels by car of more than ten horse-power (which is usually the case) he can be paid a maximum of £161[2] for travel expenses during the year. In the South West Metropolitan Region in 1952/3 travel expenses were running at a rate of nearly £200 per whole-time equivalent[3] of part-time services. Travel expenses of whole-timers were £64 per head for journeys made between hospital appointments and to undertake domiciliary consultations. Part of this difference could be accounted for by the tendency for part-time appointments to be made more frequently when duties are to be performed with more than one hospital. If we guess that the part-timer is paid £100 per whole-time equivalent for expenses which would have been paid if a whole-time specialist had undertaken the same work, it would follow that part-timers are being paid about £100 per whole-time equivalent for travel to and from their main hospital.

To explain the full advantages of these travel expenses, it is necessary to take account of their tax treatment. Where the whole-timer is paying, for example, £100 per year for travel to work, he is paying it out of taxed income. A maximum part-timer does not pay tax on the £100 which he may be paid for travel to work. The whole-timer would need to be paid about £230[4] more than the part-timer to leave him in the same financial position in this respect. The relative advantage of the maximum part-timer, so far as travel allowances are concerned, is therefore about £230.

To illustrate how these various factors can operate together to the advantage of the part-timer we take, for example, an extreme case. Let us assume that there are eleven half-days of hospital work to be done. This work could be done by a whole-time consultant at a cost of £2750. Alternatively, it might be done by two part-timers undertaking three half-days each and one part-timer undertaking five half-days as their sole contribution to the hospital service. Each of the consultants giving three half-days will be paid

[1] In certain cases where the specialist has a private consultation room in his main hospital, no travel expenses are paid.

[2] Twenty miles per day, for five days per week, for forty-six weeks per year = 4600 miles. Expenses are paid at the rates of 9¼*d.* per mile for the first 2000 miles, 7¾*d.* per mile for the next 5000 and 6¼*d.* thereafter.

[3] A whole-time equivalent is taken here as eleven half-days per week.

[4] The maximum salary of a whole-time consultant was £2750 excluding any merit award, before 1 April 1954.

for four half-days to cover travelling time. Each half-day will be paid at a rate of 25 % above the equivalent rate for a whole-time appointment. The consultant giving five half-days will be paid for seven at a rate (before 1 April 1954) again 25 % higher than the equivalent rate for a whole-timer. In all, there are fifteen sessions. The cost is £4687. Considering the number of consultants involved travel expenses may be £150[1] and the tax concessions on these expenses perhaps another £100. The cost to public funds of having the work done in this way would be about 80 % higher than appointing a whole-timer. This estimate excludes the additional superannuation benefits which will accrue to the part-time consultant.

It may be that such cases are infrequent. There are, however, many contracts in existence under which seven half-days of work are given. The part-timer is paid for nine half-days at a rate 6 % above whole-time rates. If a whole-timer did the work in the course of his duties, the attributable cost would be £1750.[2] The part-timer is paid £2375 and may get a relative gain on travel expenses of £200.

A part-timer cannot be paid for more than nine notional half-days. It is known from national figures that two-thirds of part-time appointments are maximum appointments. Some of the others are cases like the example given above. Some make no payment for travelling time; in other words, the duties specified in the contract involve nine half-days of work. There are other cases in which the duties expected or the services given are more than nine half-days, even though payment is made for only nine half-days. It is becoming more common for vacancies to be advertised offering the option for the post to be taken either as a whole-time or as a maximum part-time appointment. Moreover, the medical press has, in certain cases, been exercising pressure (in advertising posts) for notices of whole-time appointments to include an option of maximum part-time.[3] Some of the transfers from whole-time to part-time service which have taken place involve the specialist in the same duties after the transfer. In other cases, the transfer may be made to allow the whole-timer to lighten his load of work for the National Health Service. Another advantage of part-time employment is that the consultant can engage in private practice. In considering these transfers it is frequently argued that the maximum part-time appointment which, in practice, involves whole-time duties is cheaper for the taxpayer. The whole-timer would be paid £2750, and the part-timer £2375. There seems at first sight to be a saving of £375. This is not always the case and for two reasons. First, there are the travel expenses which may amount at the maximum to £161. Secondly, there are domiciliary visits; £840 can be earned from this source.

While whole-timers cannot undertake private practice and are expected to undertake domiciliary visits for no extra remuneration, the part-timer can

[1] Between home and main hospital. The maximum possible travel expenses is £364.

[2] Seven-elevenths of £2750.

[3] In certain cases the *British Medical Journal* has failed to publish advertisements for whole-time consultants when they are sent in by regional hospital boards in this form. In one such case the British Medical Association wrote to a Board: 'I note your explanation why the appointment was advertised on a whole-time basis but in view of the strong local objections we have received we have...referred the matter to the Ministry before publishing the advertisement.'

have a private practice and undertake domiciliary consultations at a charge of usually £4. 4*s*. 0*d*. each to public funds. In the South West Metropolitan Region whole-timers report an average of about five domiciliary visits per year. The option of whole-time or maximum part-time appointment appears to occur much more frequently in those specialities where proportionately more domiciliary visits are undertaken.[1]

For all these reasons[2] it is apparent that the maximum part-timer is not necessarily cheaper to public funds than the whole-timer. If he undertakes the same duties as a whole-timer and engages in private practice, his working week is presumably longer than that of the whole-timer. He may, however, delegate some of his duties to his juniors.

To provide some indication of the order of magnitude of the greater cost of part-time specialists[3] we give in Table 73 an analysis of cost figures supplied by the South West Metropolitan Board.

Table 73. *The cost per session of whole-time and part-time specialists (South West Metropolitan Region, 1 October 1952–30 September 1953)*

Remuneration	Whole-time	Part-time	Part-time as percentage of whole-time
Salaries (excluding merit awards*)	£792,416	£768,108	—
Travelling expenses	£24,285	£57,968	—
Superannuation (employers' contributions)	£63,393	£61,449	—
National Insurance (employers' contributions)	£4,652	£1,948	—
Total	£884,746	£889,473	
Sessions	216,216†	169,936	
Cost per session paid for	£4. 1*s*. 10*d*.	£5. 4*s*. 8*d*.	128
Estimated cost per session of actual work	£4. 1*s*. 10*d*.	£5. 17*s*. 9*d*.	144

* The fact that part-timers tend as a whole to receive more per head in merit awards should be excluded from the comparison, since if these same part-timers were transferred to whole-time contracts they would presumably have the same merit awards.

† On the assumption that whole-timers do eleven sessions per week.

The cost per session is £4. 1*s*. 10*d*. for the whole-timer and £5. 4*s*. 8*d*. for the part-timer. The part-timer is thus paid 28 % more.

It is not possible to estimate the cost of travelling time in the total number of sessions given to part-timers. In the figures quoted in Table 73 each part-timer averaged 4½ sessions. If we assume that half a session was devoted to travelling, the cost per session of actual work from the part-timer rises to £5. 17*s*. 9*d*., excluding merit award. This is 44 % greater than the cost of the whole-timer per notional hour of work.

[1] Of 21,276 domiciliary visits reported in the South West Metropolitan Region in 1953/4, 12,799 (60 %) were in general medicine and general surgery. Out of thirteen transfers to part-time appointment, twelve were made by consultants in these specialities.

[2] There are other tax advantages of the part-timer which we have not taken into consideration.

[3] The term specialists is used to cover both consultants and senior hospital medical officers.

This conclusion would only be valid if both part-timers and whole-timers were on average at the same point of their salary scale. In the South West Metropolitan Region, part-timers were on higher positions in their salary scales than whole-timers. This means that the figures we have quoted overstate the difference in remuneration. By averaging we are not comparing like with like. We have, therefore, made calculations from the number of part-time and whole-time specialists at each of the eighteen different points of their salary scale to estimate the amount of the overstatement. After making the necessary adjustment, we conclude that in the South West Metropolitan Region the part-timer is on the average paid 33 % more per notional unit of work.

It should not be forgotten that these are average figures and conceal wide variations between the positions of different specialists. Also, they omit any calculation of the advantages the part-timer derives from special tax treatment.[1] We do not know how far this region is typical of the country as a whole in its specialist services. But there is evidence to suggest that the expenditure of this region on specialists is close to the average of all regions, whether estimated on all hospital beds or all beds excluding mental and mental deficiency. The subject would obviously repay close study in all regions.

3. DOMICILIARY VISITS

In considering the rise in the cost of medical and dental staff in the hospital service since 1949, the question of domiciliary visits, referred to earlier, requires further consideration.

The domiciliary specialist service has been growing rapidly. The number of patients reported as visited has increased by 58 % from 129,538 in 1949 to 205,120 in 1953.[2] The proportion of visits in these totals made by part-timers is not known nationally. Table 74 gives estimates of the number of visits made by whole-time and part-time specialists in the South West Metropolitan Region between 1950/1 and 1953/4.

These figures show that only about 10 % of the visits were made by whole-timers, and that visits by part-timers increased at a greater rate both absolutely and relatively. If the proportion of visits done by whole-timers is about 10 % nationally, the growth of the domiciliary specialist service has contributed about £300,000 to the growth in the cost of the hospital service between 1949 and 1953.

In considering this trend and its potentialities for future expansion, it is

[1] Certain expenses incurred both by whole-timers and part-timers are allowable for taxation purposes in the case of the part-timer and are not allowable in the case of the whole-timer. The scope and value of these allowances was stressed by the President of the Association of Whole-time Salaried Specialists in a letter to the *British Medical Journal* on 10 January 1953 (*Supplement to the British Medical Journal*, 10 January 1953, p. 12). They include subscriptions to learned societies; purchase of medical books, periodicals and instruments; expenses of attendance at congresses and clinical meetings; car and telephone expenses; house and garden expenses.

[2] These figures (taken from the *Annual Reports of the Ministry of Health*) are not accurate. The return is made soon after the end of the year, and visits which have taken place in the year may be reported long afterwards.

significant that the use made of this service varies greatly in different areas. During the year 1952/3, 19,663 visits were carried out at public cost in the South West Metropolitan Region, of which 10,464 were made in the Western Area and 9199 in the Eastern Area. Converting these figures to a ratio per 10,000 of the population for the calendar year 1952, we get the following indices: Western Area 65·5 and Eastern Area 30·8. More than twice as many visits were made per head in the Western Area as in the Eastern Area. If the use made of the service were the same all over the country as in the Western Area of this Region, there would be a substantial increase in the cost of the service.

Table 74. *Estimates of domiciliary visits made in the South West Metropolitan Region (1950/1–1953/4)*

	1950/1	1951/2	1952/3	1953/4
By whole-time specialists	2,000	2,100	2,200	2,200
By part-time specialists	17,986	18,841	19,663	21,074
Total*	20,000	21,000	21,900	23,300

* The figures for part-time specialists are derived from statistics of payments made for visits carried out during the year even though they are reported long after the end of the year. The total figures are taken from returns made immediately after the year has ended and are therefore less accurate; this explains why they are rounded in the table. The figures for whole-time specialists are obtained by subtracting the figures for part-time specialists from the total and are therefore also shown rounded in the table.

Five factors can be suggested to account for the difference in the use made of the service between these two areas. First it may be that older people made proportionately greater demands for domiciliary consultations. The 1951 Census (one per cent samples) showed that the proportion of the population of England and Wales over age 65 was 10·9 %. The proportion over age 65 is probably higher in the Western Area. In Bournemouth the proportion was 15·6 %, in Worthing 23·8 % and in the Isle of Wight 15·8 %. Secondly, the proportion of the population classified by the Registrar General as in social class I may also be higher in the Western Area. In England and Wales this proportion was 3·3 %, in Bournemouth it was 5·4 %, in Worthing 9·7 % and in the Isle of Wight 3·4 %. This may mean that the higher social classes are making more use of this service. The third factor which might be relevant is that more part-time specialist work is done in the Western Area. In the Eastern Area there was one whole-time equivalent part-timer to every 16,000 of the population, and in the Western Area one to every 12,000 of the population.[1] The initiative for a domiciliary visit normally comes from outside the hospital service—from a general practitioner. It is the general practitioner's responsibility to exercise discretion as to whether the patient can visit a specialist at hospital or whether the circumstances of the case require that a specialist should visit the patient at home. The general practitioner may be more willing to ask for a domiciliary visit when he knows that a particular specialist is available and that he will be paid for a visit.[2] The

[1] This calculation is based on returns of hours of work.

[2] On this point see the leading article 'Full-time—part-time', *The Lancet*, 13 March 1954, p. 555.

cost to public funds of a domiciliary visit is normally £4. 4*s*. 0*d*. plus travel expenses, making about £4. 10*s*. 0*d*. if the journey is five miles each way.

A fourth factor which may be relevant is that there is a shortage of medical and surgical beds in the Western Area. Fifthly, as the Western Area is more rural in character, more patients may on average be farther from the nearest out-patient department.

Information is not available to determine for the country as a whole the part which these and other factors may be playing in causing the different use of the domiciliary specialist service in different areas. Nor can any estimate be made of the extent to which the growth of the service is effectively reducing the demand for more costly hospital beds.

4. SUMMARY AND CONCLUSIONS

(1) The role of part-time service at the consultant grade has been increasing. This is particularly true if mental and mental deficiency hospitals are excluded. There has probably been a net transfer of consultants from whole-time to part-time service. Service below the consultant grade is generally on a whole-time basis; this is becoming more frequent.

(2) It appears from evidence in one region that on the average the part-time specialist is paid 33 % more than the whole-timer per notional unit of work. In cases where specialists contribute only a few half-days to the hospital service part-time service can cost as much as 80 % more than whole-time service. When the maximum part-timer only does the number of hours for which he is paid, part-time service is still substantially more expensive. But when the maximum part-timer undertakes the same duties as a whole-timer there is little difference between the costs to the National Health Service.

(3) The domiciliary specialist service has been expanding rapidly. It may have cost £300,000 more in 1953 than in 1949. The use made of this service varies greatly in different areas. The reasons for this include the possibility that larger demands are made in areas with older populations, with greater proportions of the higher social classes, and with more part-time specialists available in such areas.

(4) The rise in the cost of medical and dental staff in the hospital service between 1949/50 and 1953/4 is attributable to a substantial increase in the number of staff employed, both part-time and whole-time; to the additional costs of more part-time consultant work and to the growth of the domiciliary specialist service.

APPENDIX E

AN ANALYSIS OF THE RISE IN THE COST OF THE PHARMACEUTICAL SERVICE

1. OUTLINE OF THE ANALYSIS

The attempt in Appendix B to effect a price deflation of the pharmaceutical service represents, for several reasons, an incomplete and unsatisfactory analysis of the rise in costs since 1948/9. The index we have applied is based on (*a*) the index used by the Ministry of Health of the prices of basic drugs and (*b*) changes in the remuneration of chemists, i.e. the percentage addition for overheads (oncost) and the container allowance. The basic drug index is so constructed as to give little more than a general indication of price trends. A second reason why it is unsatisfactory for our purposes is that ingredients in a prescription other than basic drugs are not represented in the index. Thirdly, the composition of the national prescription bill has changed so much since 1948 as to make the pharmaceutical service unsuitable for standard index number treatment. One illustration of this change has been the rise in the use of proprietaries as a percentage of total prescriptions from 11 % in January 1949 to 29 % in February 1954.

The purpose of this appendix is to analyse—though admittedly in somewhat crude terms—the rise in the cost of the pharmaceutical service in market prices from an annual rate of £31·7 million in 1949/50 to £43·5 million in 1953/4—a rise of £11·8 million.[1] The form of analysis which we follow here has not been chosen as that most suited to the task. It has been imposed by the limitations of the available data. We have used the 1 % prescription samples taken by the Ministry of Health two to three times a year which ascertain the percentage of prescriptions involving proprietary and non-

Table 75. *Break-down of the rise in the cost of the pharmaceutical service (England and Wales, 1949/50 and 1953/4)*

(£ m. in actual prices)

	1949/50*	1953/4	Increase of 1953/4 over 1949/50
A. Ingredient cost (including oncost)	19·9	31·4	11·5
B. Fees	10·3	11·0	0·7
C. Container allowance	1·5	1·1	−0·4
Total	31·7	43·5	11·8

* Annual rate—interpolated from the 270 days for which the National Health Service operated.

[1] These figures do not correspond to those given in Appendix B (Table 48, item 48), first, because receipts from prescription charges are not subtracted and, secondly, because they exclude costs other than payments to pharmacists.

proprietary preparations and the average cost of proprietary and non-proprietary prescriptions.[1]

In Table 75 the rise in cost of £11·8 million in current prices is broken down into ingredient costs (including oncost), fees to pharmacists and container allowance.

2. FACTORS PRODUCING THE RISE IN COST

Various factors have operated differentially to produce this increase; for example, changes in the ratio of proprietaries to non-proprietaries, changes in fees and so forth. From the meagre information available it is difficult to estimate the effects of these various factors. The difficulties concern items A and B; for item C (container allowance) changes in cost may be estimated, as the allowance can be related directly to the number of prescriptions dispensed. Accordingly, our first step is to set out the different factors which have operated on ingredient cost, fees and container allowance, and make estimates of the role of these factors for which no exact information is available. From this it will be possible to estimate the part played by residual factors.

(*a*) *Ingredient cost (including oncost)*

(1) *Changes in rates of payment.* Oncost was reduced from 33 to 25 % in 1950.

(2*a*) *The number of prescriptions.* The annual rate of prescriptions was 212·9 million in 1953/4 and 206·4 million in 1949/50.

(2*b*) *The quantity in prescriptions.* This estimate must be largely guesswork. We have, however, three scraps of evidence. The average fluid ounces in a mixture (8·6 % of ingredient cost in October 1950) rose during the five years from about 9½ to nearly 11 in 1952. The average number of tablets increased from 35 in 1949 to 47 in 1953. Between 1949 and 1952 the average fee (unweighted) for dispensing rose from 11·66*d.* to 11·99*d.* in constant prices. This increase in the average fee (which is only slightly related to quantity) operated for all types of prescriptions, thus suggesting that increases in quantity were not restricted to tablets and mixtures alone. A given increase in the quantity of a prescription does not, of course, imply a proportionate increase in price. From these pieces of evidence we have arbitrarily assumed an increase in cost of 15 % over the period attributable to increase in quantity.

(3) *Changes in proportion of proprietaries and non-proprietaries.* By averaging the results of the 1 % samples taken in the years 1949/50 and 1953/4 we estimate that the proportion of proprietaries increased from 16·3 to 28·3 %.

(4) *The residual.* We can calculate that the effect of residual factors was to increase ingredient cost by 22 % between 1949/50 and 1953/4.[2]

[1] An average of the samples taken in each financial year has been used as a rough correction for seasonal differences.

[2] We assume that

$$I_1 = I_0 \frac{q_1}{q_0} \frac{c_1}{c_0} \frac{r_1}{r_0} \frac{f_1}{f_0} \frac{n_1}{n_0},$$

where subscript 0 represents 1949/50; subscript 1 represents 1953/4; I represents the total ingredient cost; q represents quantities within each prescription; c represents oncost; r repre-

(*b*) *Fees*

(1) *Changes in rates of payment.* We estimate that changes in fees increased the cost by 3 %.

(2*a*) *The number of prescriptions.* As for ingredient cost.

(2*b*) *The quantity in prescriptions.* Increases in quantity led to increases in the average fee paid from 11·66*d.* to 11·99*d.* between 1949/50 and 1952/3.

(3) *Changes in proportions of proprietaries and non-proprietaries.* The increased proportion of proprietary drugs reduced the average fee because non-proprietaries have a higher average fee than proprietaries. The reduction was about 4 %.

(4) *The residual.* By the same method as that used for ingredient cost, we estimate that the effect of residual factors was to increase fees by 3 %.

(*c*) *Container allowances*

(1) *Changes in rates of payment.* The container allowance per prescription was reduced from 2½*d.* to 1¼*d.* on 1 September 1949.

(*d*) *Conclusion*

Although these results can only be brought together consistently in percentage terms, in Table 76 we bring them together arithmetically for the sake of clarity of exposition. Moreover, the number of estimated factors has already made precision impossible.

Table 76. *Factors accounting for the rise in the cost of the pharmaceutical service (England and Wales, 1949/50 and 1953/4)*

(£ m. in actual prices)

Factor	Change in cost between 1953/4 and 1949/50				
	Ingredient cost	Fees	Container allowance	Total	Percentage change in total cost
1. Changes in rates of payment	−1·2	0·3	−0·4	−1·3	−11
2. Increased quantity:					
(*a*) of prescriptions	0·6	0·3	—	0·9	8
(*b*) in prescriptions	3·1	0·2	—	3·3	28
3. Changes in proportions of proprietaries and non-proprietaries	4·5	−0·4	—	4·1	35
4. Other (including price changes)	4·5	0·3	—	4·8	40
Totals	11·5	0·7	−0·4	11·8	100

About a third of the increased cost of the pharmaceutical service was due to increased quantity, and a further third was attributable to the increased

sents proportion of proprietaries to non-proprietaries within ingredient cost; the relative costs of the average proprietary and non-proprietary prescriptions are assumed to be as in the September 1953 1 % sample; *f* represents residual factors; *n* represents the number of prescriptions.

use of proprietaries. In total, however, the introduction of new products played a considerable part in the changes that took place between 1949/50 and 1953/4. The payment of remuneration to chemists per prescription declined during this period. After account is taken of these trends it appears that the element attributable to changes in basic drug prices may be small. This is supported by the fact that the Ministry of Health's basic drug index fell by only about 3 % between 1949/50 and 1953/4.

The broad results of this study have been compressed in Table 17 of the main text (Chaper IV); because of the unsatisfactory nature of the statistical material we have had to use, these results are presented in round figures.

APPENDIX F

THE USE OF CAPITAL EXPENDITURE TO SAVE CURRENT EXPENDITURE

There are sound economic and social arguments for capital expenditure that is likely to yield net savings in the current costs of the National Health Service after making due allowance for depreciation and interest charges. They are particularly relevant in the case of the hospital services when we recall the age, structural lay-out, condition and general social inadequacy of Britain's existing stock of hospitals.[1] Most of them were built for another age; for a 'primitive' kind of medicine; for a society with abundant reserves of cheap labour; and, above all, for custodial care.

The attempt to enclose within this out-of-date structure the functions of modern medicine inevitably increases the costs of diagnosis, treatment and care. The gross inadequacies of out-patient departments—which many authorities see as the focus of hospital work in the future rather than the in-patient ward—probably result in many people being admitted unnecessarily as in-patients. Better out-patient facilities would also have important effects in lightening and improving the work of the general practitioner. Better hospital lay-out and design might well lead to substantial economies in staffing and to a reduction in the present extravagantly high wastage rate among trained nurses and student nurses.[2]

It is not the purpose of this appendix to discuss at length these complex issues of the future of the hospital in relation to the costs of medical care. These general observations are no more than an introduction to some practical illustrations of cost-saving schemes generously provided for us by the Treasurer of the South West Metropolitan Regional Hospital Board. We considered them to be relevant to this study and worth attention as examples of the interrelationship of current and capital expenditure.[3]

The schemes discussed below relate to the ancillary departments of hospitals—boiler houses, kitchens, laundries and so forth. The scope for economies in these departments is potentially very substantial. Much of the equipment is of ancient design, and it is known that modern equivalents can give the same output for lower current input; for example, the same amount of steam for less fuel and labour. The value of fuel-saving schemes in general needs no emphasis here. Moreover, much of the old equipment in boiler houses, laundries and kitchens is not now producing as high an output as when it was first installed owing to deterioration with age. These and many other considerations were taken into account in the following estimates.

[1] See Chapter v, pp. 54–6.

[2] See Ministry of Health, *Report of the Working Party on the Recruitment and Training of Nurses* (H.M.S.O. 1947), pp. 41–2, and Nuffield Provincial Hospitals Trust, *The Work of Nurses in Hospital Wards* (London, 1953).

[3] Some general observations on this matter are made in the *Survey Report 1951–4*, published by the North West Metropolitan Regional Hospital Board (London, 1954).

The data summarized in Table 77 are derived from a special inquiry undertaken by the Finance Officers of twenty-two hospital management committees in the area of the South West Metropolitan Regional Hospital Board. They show the estimated annual saving in current expenditure which, in the judgement of the officers concerned, might accrue from a given amount of capital expenditure.

Table 77. *Cost-saving capital schemes estimated for twenty-two hospital management committees in the South West Metropolitan Region*

(Capital cost in £000)

Percentage annual saving	Type of scheme				
	Boiler	Laundry	Catering	Miscellaneous	Total
10–19	58·1	6·8	3·8	11·1	79·8
20–29	25·5	4·6	0·6	7·5	38·2
30–49	12·8	3·0	0·5	0·3	16·6
Over 50	6·1	1·5	—	—	7·6
Total	102·5	15·9	4·9	18·9	142·2

The bulk of the schemes included in these returns are concerned with the installation of new boilers; nearly half are estimated to yield returns of over 20 % in running costs. In total, the schemes involve an approximate capital cost of £140,000. It is estimated that this expenditure might save around £34,000 a year.

If the returns for these twenty-two hospital groups (out of a total of fifty-three in the region) are at all representative of the situation in the region as a whole, the total capital expenditure would amount to approximately £300,000. The annual saving in current costs would run to about £70,000.

To supplement this information we were provided with details of particular cost-saving schemes submitted by the Chief Engineer and other officers of the Regional Board. Some examples are given below.

Conversion of hand-fired boilers to mechanical stoking. There are 160 hand-fired boilers in the region's hospitals which need to be converted at a cost of £1200 each = £192,000. The Engineer is of the opinion that conversion would show a saving of 10 % on the present cost of fuel consumed (£715,000) —an annual saving of £71,500.

Capital cost	£192,000
Revenue saving	£71,500 per annum
Percentage	37

Economizers. Approximately twenty economizers are required for forty-eight boilers. The Engineer estimates that the cost of fitting these would be £3500 each, making a capital cost of £70,000. He states that the cost of fuel consumed by these boilers lacking economizers is £226,000 per annum, and estimates that economizers would show a 10 % saving:

Capital cost	£70,000
Revenue saving	£22,600 per annum
Percentage	32

Steam and gas sterilizers. The total in use in the region lacking thermostatic control and insulating is estimated at 1200. The Engineer is of the opinion that the cost of fuel consumption is £32. 17*s.* 0*d.* each per annum, or £39,500. With controls and insulators fitted he thinks the fuel cost would be reduced to £4. 9*s.* 0*d.* per annum, or £5,340. The cost of fitting controls and insulating would amount to £18 per sterilizer showing:

Capital cost	£21,600
Revenue saving	£34,000 per annum
Percentage	157

Central linen rooms. Linen losses are partly attributed to lack of adequate centralized control. It would cost on the average about £750 to provide new linen rooms or to adapt rooms used for other purposes. It is thought that there are about 100 hospital units where a central linen room would reduce losses. This potential saving is of course more speculative than in the examples we have given above. On this basis:

Capital cost	£75,000
Annual saving	£15,000
Percentage	20

Table 78 brings together the foregoing estimates and the information summarized in Table 77.

Table 78. *Cost-saving capital schemes in the South West Metropolitan Region*

(Estimated in 1954)

(£)

	Capital cost	Annual revenue saving
Schemes from twenty-two hospital management committees (summarized in Table 77) rated up for the whole of the region	300,000	70,000
Regional schemes:		
(1) Mechanical stoking	192,000	71,500
(2) Fuel economizers	70,000	22,600
(3) Gas and steam sterilizers	21,600	34,000
(4) Central linen rooms	75,000	15,000
Total	658,600	213,100

Table 79. *Cost-saving schemes in the South West Metropolitan Region showing the percentage saving on current expenditure*

(£000)

Percentage of saving	Capital cost
10–19	168·6
20–29	155·6
30–49	296·8
Over 50	37·6
Total	658·6

On the basis of this information, which represents only certain types of cost-saving capital schemes applicable to hospital equipment, it is shown that a saving of £213,000 annually in current expenditure is thought likely to accrue from a capital expenditure of around £650,000. The total hospital beds in this region amount to nearly one-eighth of all the beds in England and Wales. It would thus appear that, if the situation in the hospital service as a whole is anything like that obtaining in this particular region, the scope for economy in even this limited sector of hospital equipment is very substantial indeed. Similar and more detailed studies in other fields of hospital function would seem to merit more attention than they have hitherto received.

APPENDIX G

A COMPARISON OF HOSPITAL CAPITAL EXPENDITURE IN 1938/9 AND 1952/3

Table 80 shows in summary form the statistics that have been collected on hospital capital expenditure in 1938/9.

Table 80. *Hospital capital expenditure in 1938/9 (England and Wales)*

(£000)

Type of hospital	Expenditure
By local authorities:*	
Tuberculosis hospitals	518
Venereal disease hospitals	6
Infectious disease hospitals	1070
General hospitals	1703
Mental hospitals	1465
Mental deficiency institutions	1150
By voluntary hospitals reporting to the British Hospitals Association†	3285
Total	9197

* Ministry of Health, *Local Government Financial Statistics, England and Wales, Summary, 1938/9* (printed for official use, 1942).

† *The Hospitals Year-Book, 1940* and *1941*, published by the Central Bureau of Hospital Information. The figures given in the year books have been converted from calendar to financial years.

These figures are not comparable with those for the National Health Service owing to differences in the number and proportions of hospitals included in the two sets of figures and to differences in the definition of capital expenditure.

1. ADJUSTMENTS FOR DIFFERENCES IN THE HOSPITALS COVERED

Neither the pre-war nor the post-war figures cover all hospitals in England and Wales. In both cases institutions run for profit are omitted. The pre-war figures also omit those hospitals that did not report to the British Hospitals Association. The post-war figures omit certain voluntary hospitals which were disclaimed by the Minister, or which have been established since 1948. In the 1952 *Hospitals Year-Book* the voluntary hospitals are shown as providing 8368 available beds in England and Wales. This figure may be compared with the 468,255 available beds under the National Health Service at the end of 1952. Those voluntary hospitals in England and Wales failing to make returns to the British Hospitals Association before the war represented 6539 beds in 1938 and 7479 in 1939. The omissions are not however large, and they can be regarded as roughly balancing each other.

Some addition to the figures in Table 80 has, however, to be made in respect to capital expenditure on poor law institutions (not allocated to local authority public health expenditure) which provided medical services. From an examination of unpublished material in the Ministry of Health and other sources we estimate a figure of £750,000 for capital expenditure in 1938/9 on these particular institutions. This raises the total of Table 80 to approximately £10 million.

2. DEFINITIONS OF CAPITAL EXPENDITURE

The standard system of accounts[1] introduced before the war by the King Edward VII Fund in the voluntary hospitals of London was broadly, though not completely, followed by voluntary hospitals in the provinces. Many local authority hospitals also used the same definition. In a number of cases, however, both voluntary and local authority, the question as to whether an item was classified as capital depended on whether it was or could be financed from loan funds rather than on the nature of the expenditure itself. In addition to these pre-war differences in the definitions actually employed there are more important differences between the definition of capital expenditure in the National Health Service accounts and the 'commercial' accounting definition of the King Edward VII Hospital Fund.

In Table 81 we summarize the laborious results of an estimate of capital expenditure for 1952/3 based on a definition approximating to that laid down by the King Edward VII Hospital Fund.

Table 81. *Capital expenditure in 1952/3 approximating to the King Edward VII Hospital Fund definition (England and Wales)**

(£000)

	Expenditure
1. Capital expenditure by hospital authorities	9,140
2. Capital expenditure by the Ministry of Works	306
3. Expenditure on additional X-ray equipment	248
4. Net expenditure on land, hospitals and equipment	470
Total	10,164

* Items 1, 2 and 3 come from Appendix A, Table 47 (items 1, 2 and 5). Item 4 can be found in Appendix A, Table 45 (items 45 and 46). Such transactions in existing assets covered by item 4 do not fall within our definition of capital although they would have been treated as capital expenditure under the Fund's definition.

From this table we see that capital expenditure in 1952/3 on a roughly comparable basis to that used in 1938/9 was £10·2 million at current prices. The expenditure in 1938/9 of £10 million would be equivalent to about £32 million in 1952/3 prices.[2] We conclude, therefore, that capital expenditure in 1952/3 was at a third of the rate of 1938/9.

[1] See King Edward's Hospital Fund for London, *The Revised Uniform System of Hospital Accounts*, 4th ed. (London, 1926).

[2] Based on information supplied by the Ministry of Health.

APPENDIX H

THE HOSPITAL POPULATION

During the course of this study we found ourselves continually asking questions about the hospital population. Because of the wide differences in cost and for other reasons we wanted to know the age and sex structure of the patient population in different types of hospital. We wanted to know if there was any evidence for the assertion that a high proportion of hospital beds are occupied by old people. We wanted to know the character of demand from different social groups. We wanted to know what proportion of beds in hospitals are occupied by resident staff. These and other questions bearing on present and future demand for hospital in-patient care could not, however, be answered from available data. Such studies as have been made of hospital demand are either incomplete in the sense of not covering all hospitals or are cast in such a form as not to yield the information we required.[1]

Accordingly, we sought the assistance of the General Register Office who generously undertook for us a special tabulation of the 1951 Census schedules for all hospitals and certain other specified institutions in England and Wales. We present below some of the provisional results of an analysis of this material. In any attempt to interpret these facts it should be borne in mind that they do not accurately depict the total demand for in-patient care during the year in question (1951); they relate only to the number of people in hospital on the census night, 8 April 1951. Length of stay, the incidence of re-admission, transfers of patients from one to another hospital or institution and other factors are not, therefore, considered separately in this analysis. The tables relating to National Health Service hospitals also exclude the population of hospitals for whom the Ministry of Pensions and the Service Departments were responsible in 1951.[2] Many of these problems of definition and of measuring the hospital load (including the question of selection in its effect on the age and sex structure of the hospital population) are carefully discussed by Dr MacKay and in other publications of the General Register Office.[3] Valuable information on mental and mental deficiency hospitals is also contained in the 1949 Supplement to the Registrar General's *Review*.[4]

Table 82 shows the position for all hospitals in England and Wales covering a total of 421,096 patients.

1 See below and Nuffield Provincial Hospitals Trust, *Hospital and Community*, 2 vols. (London, 1948).

2 Newly born infants are included although they are not counted in the hospital bed complement (*Report of the Ministry of Health for the year ended 31st December, 1953, Part I*, Cmd. 9321 (H.M.S.O. 1954), p. 202).

3 D. MacKay, *Hospital Morbidity Statistics*, General Register Office Studies on Medical and Population Subjects, no. 4 (H.M.S.O. 1951) and General Register Office, *The Registrar General's Statistical Review of England and Wales for the year 1949, Supplement on Hospital In-patient Statistics* (H.M.S.O. 1954).

4 General Register Office, *The Registrar General's Statistical Review of England and Wales for the year 1949, Supplement on General Morbidity, Cancer and Mental Health* (H.M.S.O. 1953).

Table 82. *The percentage of the census population (1951)* in England and Wales in all National Health Service hospitals† by age, sex and civil state*

Age group	Single		Married		Widowed and divorced	
	Number	%	Number	%	Number	%
			Males			
0–14	27,465	0·6	—	—	—	—
15–44	50,483	1·4	17,104	0·3	601	0·7
45–64	25,266	5·9	25,680	0·6	2,959	1·3
65–74	7,639	6·6	10,131	1·0	4,616	1·8
75+	4,093	8·5	4,631	1·5	7,792	3·2
Total	114,946	—	57,546	—	15,968	—
			Females			
0–14	22,904	0·5	—	—	—	—
15–44	42,457	1·4	37,672	0·6	1,525	0·7
45–64	30,204	3·5	26,602	0·7	7,919	0·9
65–74	11,472	3·8	9,878	1·2	11,011	1·4
75+	9,117	5·9	4,510	2·4	17,365	2·9
Total	116,154	—	78,662	—	37,820	—

* Based on General Register Office, *Census 1951 Great Britain One Per Cent Sample Tables, Part I* (H.M.S.O. 1952).

† Including contracted institutions.

There are several conclusions to be drawn from this table:

(1) With advancing age among both sexes the proportion in hospital rises most sharply for the single, less so for the widowed and divorced, and even less so for the married.

(2) Among married people, the proportion in hospital even at the advanced age of 75 and over is only about 2 % of the population at risk.

(3) At all ages, the proportion of single, widowed and divorced men in hospital is higher, and rises more sharply, than the corresponding rates for women.

These figures cover all reasons for admission and all types of hospitals. Because of the variations in age and sex and also because of the different considerations which obtain we have subtracted, in Table 83, the data for all hospitals classified as mental, and mental deficiency.

Although the rates are all lower, much the same conclusions can be drawn from this table as from Table 82. It is seen that with the exclusion of mental and mental deficiency hospitals, the proportion of married men and women aged 75 and over in all other types of hospital falls to the remarkably low figure of 1·1 %. It is also noteworthy that among married men and women aged between 15 and 64 there is little variation in the proportions in hospital.

After age 45—and only after that age—the proportions of single people and, to a lesser extent, of the widowed and divorced, diverge more and more sharply with advancing age from those of married people.[1] The fact that this divergence does not show itself until after the age of 45 for the general hospital

[1] This may be owing to more frequent admission or longer stay.

Table 83. *The percentage of the census population (1951)* in England and Wales in all National Health Service hospitals† (excluding mental and mental deficiency) by age, sex and civil state*

Age group	Single		Married		Widowed and divorced	
	Number	%	Number	%	Number	%
			Males			
0–14	23,502	0·5	—	—	—	—
15–44	14,815	0·4	13,909	0·3	351	0·4
45–64	4,939	1·2	17,124	0·4	1,803	0·8
65–74	2,894	2·5	6,478	0·7	3,387	1·3
75+	2,528	5·2	3,245	1·1	6,603	2·7
Total	48,678	—	40,756	—	12,144	—
			Females			
0–14	20,459	0·4	—	—	—	—
15–44	14,641	0·5	32,431	0·5	928	0·4
45–64	6,551	0·8	13,871	0·3	4,066	0·5
65–74	3,971	1·3	4,372	0·5	6,711	0·9
75+	5,118	3·3	2,161	1·1	13,018	2·2
Total	50,740	—	52,835	—	24,723	—

* Based on General Register Office, *Census 1951 Great Britain One Per Cent Sample Tables, Part I* (H.M.S.O. 1952).

† Including contracted institutions.

Table 84. *The percentage of the census population (1951) in England and Wales in all National Health Service hospitals classified as mental hospitals by age, sex and civil state*

Age group	Single		Married		Widowed and divorced	
	Number	%	Number	%	Number	%
			Males			
0–14	307	0·0	—	—	—	—
15–44	18,054	0·5	3,028	0·1	243	0·3
45–64	15,998	3·7	8,446	0·2	1,147	0·5
65–74	4,395	3·8	3,623	0·4	1,204	0·5
75+	1,491	3·1	1,369	0·4	1,155	0·5
Total	40,245	—	16,466	—	3,749	—
			Females			
0–14	174	—	—	—	—	—
15–44	13,277	0·4	5,084	0·1	574	0·3
45–64	18,229	2·1	12,578	0·3	3,792	0·5
65–74	6,898	2·3	5,461	0·7	4,254	0·5
75+	3,781	2·5	2,300	1·2	4,200	0·7
Total	42,359	—	25,423	—	12,820	—

population does not suggest that genetic or constitutional factors are playing a dominating role.

In Tables 84 and 85 we give separate figures for mental and mental deficiency hospitals.

There is ample scope for speculation about the biological and social meaning of these tables, but here we restrict ourselves to the more obvious deductions. To deal first with Table 85, we note that the population of mental deficiency hospitals is almost wholly made up of single people; that most of them are admitted between the ages of 15 and 44;[1] and that their expectation of life appears to be relatively short.

Table 85. *The percentage of the census population (1951) in England and Wales in all National Health Service hospitals classified as mental deficiency hospitals by age, sex and civil state*

Age group	Single		Married		Widowed and divorced	
	Number	%	Number	%	Number	%
			Males			
0–14	3,656	0·1	—	—	—	—
15–44	17,614	0·5	167	0·0	7	0·0
45–64	4,329	1·0	110	0·0	9	0·0
65–74	350	0·3	30	0·0	25	0·0
75+	74	0·2	17	0·0	34	0·0
Total	26,023	—	324	—	75	—
			Females			
0–14	2,271	0·0	—	—	—	—
15–44	14,539	0·5	157	0·0	23	0·0
45–64	5,424	0·6	153	0·0	61	0·0
65–74	603	0·2	45	0·0	46	0·0
75+	218	0·1	49	0·0	147	0·0
Total	23,055	—	404	—	277	—

As regards the mentally ill, the bulk of the hospital population are single people, their proportions being many times greater than for the married, widowed and divorced. This difference is most striking after the age of 45 for both men and women. Among men, and contrary to the general hospital figures, there is no noticeable tendency for the proportion to rise with advancing age after age 45. Among women, the proportions do increase somewhat, particularly for married women, where the age rates are of much the same order as those for the general hospital population of married women (Table 83).

In some respects, a roughly comparable picture is retained for mental hospitals when admissions (instead of residents) are related to the national population at risk. This was done in an interesting analysis by the General Register Office and we reproduce the salient points in Table 86.

For single persons there is no suggestion here of a rising admission rate with

[1] According to the General Register Office's analysis of admissions in 1949, the peak age of admission for both sexes is 16–20 (General Register Office, *The Registrar General's Statistical Review of England and Wales for the year 1949, Supplement on General Morbidity, Cancer and Mental Health* (H.M.S.O. 1953), Table M. 30).

Table 86. *Admissions to mental hospitals in 1949*. Ratio of single and of married, widowed, separated or divorced persons† among 1949 admissions to corresponding numbers in 1951 census*

	Single			Married, widowed, separated and divorced		
Age group	Census 1951‡ from 1 % sample	Mental hospitals 1949	Ratio per 10,000	Census 1951‡ from 1 % sample	Mental hospitals 1949	Ratio per 10,000
			Males			
16–	1,030,4	712	7	7,8	3	4
20–	1,071,9	1,914	18	340,7	213	6
25–	839,1	3,126	37	2,282,7	1,846	8
35–	395,0	1,455	37	2,919,3	2,856	10
45–	259,6	816	31	2,600,5	2,858	11
55–	169,0	513	30	1,867,7	2,784	15
65–	116,6	320	27	1,243,1	2,373	19
75 and over	48,4	126	26	548,9	1,390	25
16 and over	3,930,0	8,982	23	11,810,7	14,323	12
			Females			
16–	1,037,8	749	7	61,5	59	10
20–	775,4	1,165	15	726,8	590	8
25–	578,8	2,012	35	2,625,8	3,371	13
35–	458,6	1,652	36	2,953,0	4,399	15
45–	469,3	1,564	33	2,657,8	4,675	18
55–	392,3	1,115	28	2,143,5	4,078	19
65–	301,7	826	27	1,584,2	3,269	21
75 and over	154,3	466	30	791,2	1,932	24
16 and over	4,168,2	9,549	23	13,543,8	22,373	17

* General Register Office, *The Registrar General's Statistical Review of England and Wales for the year 1949, Supplement on General Morbidity, Cancer and Mental Health* (H.M.S.O. 1953), Table M. 8.

† Seventy-eight males and thirty-one females whose status was unknown were excluded from the admissions total.

‡ To the nearest hundred.

advancing age. The peak admission age for both men and women comes at 25–45—a fact which is not shown in Table 84. One reason for this may be a higher recovery rate and the greater possibilities of returning these younger single patients to their families and the community at large. Treatment may also be more active, whereas with the older mentally ill patient a more pessimistic or negative attitude may prevail. Apart, however, from such questions of differential standards of treatment and severity of illness it will also be more difficult to discharge older patients who may no longer have families who can help them adjust to the demands of the outside world. Little can be said on these particular aspects in regard to the married, widowed and divorced because separate figures are not given.

In Table 87 we give only the rates for other classified types of hospitals and institutions.[1]

[1] The complete data for these break-downs may be obtained on application to the authors.

Table 87. *The percentage of the census population (1951) in England and Wales in certain classified types of hospitals and institutions by age, sex and civil state*

(Percentages)

Age group	Males: Single	Males: Married	Males: Widowed and divorced	Females: Single	Females: Married	Females: Widowed and divorced
(a) All National Health Service teaching hospitals						
	(4,159)	(4,959)	(604)	(4,517)	(6,465)	(1,604)
0–14	0·05	—	—	0·05	—	—
15–44	0·03	0·03	0·02	0·05	0·06	0·07
45–64	0·07	0·06	0·07	0·06	0·05	0·06
65–74	0·10	0·07	0·08	0·07	0·06	0·06
75+	0·15	0·07	0·09	0·10	0·06	0·08
(b) All National Health Service hospitals classified as wholly general and mainly general						
	(20,682)	(25,434)	(6,053)	(20,876)	(30,936)	(12,345)
0–14	0·21	—	—	0·18	—	—
15–44	0·16	0·13	0·19	0·17	0·29	0·20
45–64	0·52	0·27	0·47	0·34	0·23	0·30
65–74	0·99	0·45	0·74	0·59	0·37	0·48
75+	1·77	0·63	1·21	1·32	0·64	0·94
(c) All National Health Service hospitals classified as chronic and mainly chronic						
	(5,667)	(2,858)	(4,477)	(7,680)	(3,271)	(8,509)
0–14	0·01	—	—	0·01	—	—
15–44	0·02	0·00	0·02	0·03	0·02	0·02
45–64	0·33	0·02	0·13	0·23	0·02	0·07
65–74	1·14	0·08	0·43	0·52	0·08	0·24
75+	2·90	0·29	1·26	1·63	0·35	1·01
(d) All National Health Service hospitals classified as tuberculosis, tuberculosis and isolation, and isolation						
	(7,938)	(5,220)	(359)	(7,263)	(4,429)	(408)
0–14	0·06	—	—	0·06	—	—
15–44	0·13	0·07	0·15	0·14	0·06	0·10
45–64	0·08	0·03	0·06	0·02	0·01	0·01
65–74	0·04	0·01	0·01	0·01	0·00	0·01
75+	0·04	0·01	0·01	0·01	0·00	0·01
(e) All National Health Service hospitals classified as all other (including contracted institutions)						
	(10,232)	(2,785)	(651)	(10,404)	(7,734)	(1,857)
0–14	0·14	—	—	0·13	—	—
15–44	0·06	0·02	0·04	0·07	0·10	0·06
45–64	0·15	0·03	0·05	0·12	0·03	0·05
65–74	0·22	0·04	0·07	0·14	0·04	0·07
75+	0·36	0·06	0·13	0·26	0·07	0·13

In comparing the figures in the various sections of this table with those in Tables 84, 85 and 86 certain differences stand out clearly. In respect to certain characteristics, the population of teaching hospitals (and to a somewhat lesser extent general hospitals) is different from that of all hospitals. The majority of their patients are married (and presumably, therefore, easier to discharge); they have a younger population; a much less noticeable progression with age; and they apparently admit only a small fraction of elderly people. They are obviously selective to a high degree.

The picture presented by the population structure of the general hospitals is somewhat similar, though drawn on a smaller scale, to that given in Table 83. The same progression with age and the same divergence after age 45 in the rates for the single, widowed and divorced in contrast to those for married people are prominent features here as they are in Table 83.

The most striking fact about the population structure of the so-called 'chronic' hospitals is that among those aged over 15, 38 % are single and 42 % are widowed and divorced. Unlike the rates for married people, the proportions for both sexes in these three groups rise very steeply with advancing age—particularly among men. For all persons aged over 65 in the country as a whole, it would seem that the single and the widowed needing hospital care are most likely to be found in the 'chronic' and mental hospitals. The distribution is quite different for married people of these ages. Marriage and its survival into old age would seem to be a powerful safeguard against admission to hospitals in general and to 'chronic' and mental hospitals in particular. Obviously, the physical and psychological factors that play a part in determining selection for marriage are important in this connexion, but we cannot discuss them here.

The statistics for hospitals classified as tuberculosis and isolation reflect to a large extent the current incidence by age and sex of tuberculosis and other infectious diseases. The majority of the patients are single people and 89 % are aged under 45.

About 40 % of 33,663 patients in 'all other' hospitals (sub-table (*e*)) are children; 60 % of the total population are single.

To show the importance of the social factors in relation to demand for hospital care which this analysis has brought out we give below certain significant proportions derived from the foregoing tables (the figures in brackets refer to the corresponding proportions for the total population of England and Wales). Of all males and females in all National Health Service hospitals[1] in England and Wales in April 1951:

Males		Females	
15 % were aged under 15	(23 %)	10 %	(21 %)
47 % were single aged 15 and over	(21 %)	40 %	(19 %)
8 % were widowed and divorced aged 15 and over	(4 %)	16 %	(11 %)
30 % were married aged 15 and over	(52 %)	34 %	(49 %)

In relation to their numbers in the total adult population of the country, the single, widowed and divorced make about double the demand on hospital

[1] Including contracted institutions.

accommodation. Children and married people make proportionately smaller demands.

Separate figures are given below for persons aged 65 and over, together with the corresponding percentages for the more important hospital groups:

Males aged 65 and over

	Single (%)		Married (%)		Widowed and divorced (%)	
All hospitals	30	(9%)	38	(66%)	32	(25%)
(*a*) Teaching	13		60		27	
(*b*) General	15		49		36	
(*c*) Chronic	32		20		48	
(*d*) Mental	44		38		18	
(*e*) Mental deficiency	80		9		11	

Females aged 65 and over

	Single (%)		Married (%)		Widowed and divorced (%)	
All hospitals	32	(16%)	23	(35%)	45	(49%)
(*a*) Teaching	20		30		50	
(*b*) General	22		24		54	
(*c*) Chronic	31		10		59	
(*d*) Mental	40		29		31	
(*e*) Mental deficiency	74		9		17	

About two-thirds of all the hospital accommodation in the country for those aged over 65 is taken by the single, the widowed and divorced. In other words, it is taken by those who have either never married or by those whose marriages have been broken—chiefly by death. The largest proportion of people in these 'dependent' situations are to be found in the population of chronic and mental hospitals.

In any attempt to interpret these statistics in relation to the role of the family (and particularly the part played by surviving children of elderly hospital patients) it has to be borne in mind that no information whatever is available to show what proportion of married, widowed and divorced people have children to whom they can turn for support. Judged by such evidence as can be derived from the Registrar General's analysis of childlessness among deceased women it would not be unreasonable to suppose that approximately 15% of married and widowed men and women aged 65 and over have no children to assist them.[1] It is, moreover, conceivable that the proportion may be twice as high for the hospital population of married and widowed if the higher ratio of demand on hospital accommodation made by 'dependent' single people is applicable also to the 'dependent' married and widowed. In short, this would imply that well over half all the adults in all hospitals are either childless or have no surviving children.

What is also significant is that the existence or otherwise of surviving

[1] See General Register Office, *The Registrar General's Statistical Review of England and Wales, 1946–1950 Text, Civil* (H.M.S.O. 1954). A later study indicates that this is probably a conservative estimate (see Papers of the Royal Commission on Population, vol. VI, *The Trend and Pattern of Fertility in Great Britain*, 2 parts (H.M.S.O. 1954)).

husbands, wives and children is perhaps the most important single social factor governing the amount and distribution by age and sex of demand for hospital care—particularly from the older age groups in the population. This being so, it would follow that the past social structure of the population determines in some measure current demands for hospital care. The low marriage rates of forty and fifty years ago represent one important factor.[1] A second is the relatively high mortality rates which operated in the past among married couples in the working classes which, in addition to the losses caused by the First World War, led to a higher incidence of broken marriages. One long run effect of the First World War which has an obvious bearing on hospital demand today is the present 'abnormally' high proportion of elderly widows.[2] A third factor is the decline in family size and the survival into old age of a larger proportion of childless married men and women.

It would be an exceedingly hazardous task to attempt to estimate the influence of these important social factors in shaping the future course of hospital demand. Clearly, they will continue to be important, but the substantially higher rate of marriage which has now prevailed for several decades and the equally substantial fall in the proportion of marriages broken by death are two encouraging features. Indeed, if the Government Actuary's estimates of the population of Great Britain in 1979 are accepted there will be no significant change in the actual number of single people of pensionable ages. There will in fact be 22,000 *fewer* single women, and only 47,000 more single men. The number of widowed and divorced women rises by 597,000; the corresponding figure for men is only 85,000. According to the assumptions adopted by the Government Actuary, the great bulk of the increase in the population of pensionable ages by 1979 (a total of 2,510,000) is attributed to married men and women (1,902,000). These estimates, it should be noted, are based on the somewhat optimistic assumption of a decline in mortality at advanced ages at the average rate experienced during the first half of this century. If the alternative assumption is adopted of a continuance of mortality rates at their 1954 level the estimated additional pensionable population would be lower by nearly 700,000.[3]

So far as hospital demand is concerned, it can thus be seen that among the group of old people who make the largest demands for in-patient care (single men and women) there is not likely to be any material increase in the population at risk during the next twenty-five years. The number of widowed and divorced, who make fewer demands than the single but more than the married, rises by about 27 %, while the increase among married persons is about 56 %. To look at the facts of population change from this particular aspect of 'dependency' and the need for institutional care obviously puts a different complexion on the pattern of future demands.

[1] In 1911 13 % of women aged 65 or over in Great Britain were single and 31 % were widowed. By 1951 these proportions had risen to 17 and 49 % respectively. Divorce accounted for 1 % in 1951.

[2] *National Insurance Act, 1946. Report by the Government Actuary on the First Quinquennial Review* (H.M.S.O. 1954), p. 39.

[3] Even this assumes, for men, a reversal of the recent tendency for mortality rates to increase at ages 65 and over.

This study has been mainly concerned with an analysis of the structure of the hospital population at the time of the 1951 Census. Little can be added here about length of stay and the 'turnover' rate in respect to the factors that have been discussed. From a certain amount of scattered information, however, it would seem that there is—particularly in the 'chronic' and mental hospitals—a relatively small proportion of patients who stay for exceptionally long periods and who therefore make disproportionately heavy claims on hospital resources. It is not possible to say, however, to what extent these long-stay demands are wholly or partly explicable in terms of the social factors under discussion.

With the publication of two reports on the 1949 hospital in-patient statistics,[1] the General Register Office has begun to make what promises to be an important contribution to many aspects of the character and amount of demand for hospital care. In time, not only should we know more about the complex relationships of the social factors, the incidence of hospital treated disease and the work of different types of hospital departments, but it should become less hazardous to assess the character of future demand. We would also hope that these studies will throw more light on another question of importance to social and budgetary policy: what is the pattern of demand (and use) of hospital resources by different occupational and social groups in the population?

The 1949 statistics relating to hospital discharges, incomplete and inadequate as they admittedly are, do furnish some indication of the pattern of demand. In Table 88 we confine the analysis to men aged 25–64 for the reason that the information about occupation and social class is much more complete for this group than for the retired, for children and for women. The percentage of 'not stated' for occupation ranges from only 4 to 8 %, whereas it is several times higher for other groups. We have also omitted all discharges attributable to 'accidents'. Among males of all ages these are an important element in hospital demand; even among the teaching hospitals contributing to the General Register Office's 1949 study 10 % of all male discharges (totalling 105,114) were discharges of 'accident' cases.[2] This fact alone points to the difficulty of estimating future demands on the hospitals, for few students of the subject would care to predict the future trend of road accidents. A steadily rising accident rate (with all its consequential effects on out-patient as well as in-patient resources) might well be a more influential factor in the immediate future than any effects of age changes in the national population. A second reason for omitting accidents from Table 88 is that the working classes (social classes III–V) experience a heavier accident rate than social classes I–II. We thus obtain a more faithful picture of demand resulting from physical and mental illness requiring in-patient hospital care.

[1] D. MacKay, *Hospital Morbidity Statistics*, General Register Office Studies on Medical and Population Subjects, no. 4 (H.M.S.O. 1951) and General Register Office, *The Registrar General's Statistical Review of England and Wales for the year 1949, Supplement on Hospital In-Patient Statistics* (H.M.S.O. 1954).

[2] Among men aged 16–64, 15 % of *all medical consultations* were attributable to injuries in 1949 (General Register Office, *The Registrar General's Statistical Review of England and Wales for the year 1949, Supplement on General Morbidity, Cancer and Mental Health* (H.M.S.O. 1953), part 1, *Survey of Sickness*, Table S.S. 11, p. 43).

Table 88. *The proportionate distribution by social class of discharges in 1949 from three groups of hospitals participating in the General Register Office's study of hospital morbidity in England and Wales. Males only aged 25–64. All diagnostic conditions excluding injuries**

Social class (as grouped by the General Register Office) (1)	London teaching hospitals (%) (2)	Provincial teaching hospitals (%) (3)	Regional board hospitals (%) (4)	England and Wales 1951† (%) (5)	Greater London 1951‡ (%) (6)
I and II	21	16	15	20	21
III	56	55	58	51	55
IV and V	23	29	27	29	24

* See General Register Office, *The Registrar General's Statistical Review of England and Wales for the year 1949, Supplement on Hospital In-patient Statistics* (H.M.S.O. 1954), Table H. 3. The numbers 'Not stated' (col. 2, 8%; col. 3, 6%; col. 4, 4%) have been distributed rateably.

† Percentage distribution for all males ages 25–64 occupied and retired (General Register Office, *Census 1951 Great Britain One Per Cent Sample Tables, Part I* (H.M.S.O. 1952)).

‡ Percentage distribution for all males aged 15 and over occupied and retired (General Register Office, *Census 1951 Great Britain One Per Cent Sample Tables, Part I* (H.M.S.O. 1952)).

As a whole there is not much difference between the hospital proportions and the social class proportions for England and Wales. For the London teaching hospitals, social classes I, II and III are well represented while the semi-skilled and unskilled classes (IV and V) are slightly under-represented. For the provincial teaching hospitals and regional board hospitals tentative comparisons with the population at risk indicate that, in general, there is little difference in the social class proportions. In this connexion, it should, however, be remembered that social classes IV–V in the aggregate experience substantially higher death-rates between the ages of 25 and 64 and possibly more sickness than do classes I and II.[1] It might therefore be said on the basis of these data that professional and middle-class men of these ages are making full use of National Health Service hospitals, whereas the semi-skilled and unskilled groups are making fewer demands than might have been expected from their relatively higher mortality experience.

As an illustration of the information that can be extracted from these hospital data we list in Table 89 some of the diagnostic groups (based on the principal cause of admission) which contribute, first, to excess representation of social classes I and II and, secondly, to excess representation of classes IV and V.[2]

In no sense does this list depict the social class incidence of particular diseases among men aged 25–64. A great many selective factors operate in determining the frequency with which cases of a particular condition among different groups in the population are admitted to hospital instead of being treated at home. 'Hospitalized illness', as the Registrar General remarks, 'is

[1] See Table 1 of General Register Office, *The Registrar General's Decennial Supplement England and Wales 1951, Occupational Mortality, Part I* (H.M.S.O. 1954).

[2] Only a selection of the more obvious examples are given here; the *Registrar General's Statistical Review of England and Wales for the year 1949, Supplement on Hospital In-patient Statistics* (H.M.S.O. 1954), Table H. 3 should be consulted for further information.

thus not only a relatively small but a highly selected fraction of all medically treated illnesses, the selection depending on one or other of several criteria according to the nature of the disease.'[1]

Table 89. *The proportionate distribution by social class of discharges in 1949 for selected diagnostic groups from all hospitals participating in the General Register Office's study of hospital morbidity in England and Wales. Males only aged 25–64**

Number in Condensed International List of Classification of Diseases	Final diagnosis of principal cause of admission	Social classes: I and II (%)	III (%)	IV and V (%)	Total discharges in group
	(*a*) Relatively high proportion social classes I and II				
86	Disorders of character, behaviour and intelligence	43	38	19	90
165	Cirrhosis of liver	35	35	30	153
25	Infectious hepatitis	33	44	23	97
15	Dysentery, all forms	28	58	14	93
20/1	Acute poliomyelitis and late effects	27	56	17	63
78/80	Schizophrenic disorders, manic-depressive reaction and other psychoses	25	54	21	264
109	Coronary heart disease and angina pectoris	24	51	25	688
65	Asthma	23	55	22	262
81/5	Anxiety, hysterical and neurotic-depressive reactions, psychoneuroses with somatic symptoms and other psychoneuroses	22	57	21	615
129	Chronic sinusitis	20	59	21	385
146	Disorders of teeth	20	57	23	447
	(*b*) Relatively high proportion social classes IV and V				
120	Haemorrhoids	13	57	30	1108
134/9	Bronchitis and pneumonia	13	48	39	1627
148	Ulcer of the stomach	10	56	34	1911
149	Ulcer of the duodenum	13	57	30	3932
152/4	Hernia	13	58	29	3774
Section XVII	Accidents, poisonings and violence	10	56	34	6141

* Excluding the number for whom social class was not specified.

Table 89 indicates that psychiatric cases play a part in the relative excess representation of social classes I and II and deficient representation of classes IV and V. Further information on this subject is available from a study by Moya Woodside.[2] This study shows that in York Clinic, a psychiatric unit attached to Guy's Hospital, the number of men in social classes I and II admitted as National Health Service patients rose between 1949/50 and 1951/2, and that for the whole period studied (1949/52) only 10% of Health

[1] *The Registrar General's Statistical Review of England and Wales for the year 1949, Supplement on Hospital In-Patient Statistics* (H.M.S.O. 1954), p. 3.

[2] M. Woodside, 'Social class in a psychiatric clinic', *Guy's Hospital Reports*, vol. 103, 1954, no. 4, p. 337.

Service admissions were men in classes IV and V and only 1 % of private patients were men in these classes. In Table 90 the proportions in different social classes admitted to the clinic as Health Service patients are compared with similar figures for in-patients at the Bethlem-Maudsley Hospital, and with the population of Greater London.

Table 90. *Admissions by social class of psychiatric cases: National Health Service patients (men only)*

Social class	1951* Greater London	1950† Bethlem-Maudsley	1949/52‡ York Clinic
I	5	9·5	32·9
II	16	17·4	18·4
III	55	53·0	29·1
IV	11	10·6	7·6
V	13	9·5	2·5
Retired or not gainfully occupied	—	—	9·5

* General Register Office, *Census 1951 Great Britain, One Per Cent Sample Tables*, Part 1 (H.M.S.O. 1952), p. 83.

† Total of men in-patients 514.

‡ Total of men in-patients 312.

A number of other studies, undertaken for different reasons, have thrown up since 1948 pieces of evidence concerning the use made of the National Health Service which seem to point in the same direction as Miss Woodside's results. Douglas, for example, has shown that in a national sample of 2428 4-year-old children the operation of circumcision was more often performed among the well-to-do than among manual workers.[1] In the former classes, 39 % of the children had been circumcised by the age of 4 years 3 months; among manual workers, the proportion was 22 %.[2] Somewhat similar results have emerged from studies of the incidence of tonsillectomy among children in different social groups.[3]

When all these scattered pieces of evidence are put together along with the figures in Tables 88 and 89, it would seem that, in general and for many particular conditions which do not constitute a grave threat to life, the

[1] D. MacCarthy, J. W. B. Douglas and C. Mogford, 'Circumcision in a national sample of 4-year-old children', *British Medical Journal*, 4 October 1952, p. 755. It is estimated that about 100,000 such operations are performed annually, most of them as a matter of routine or, as the *British Medical Journal* remarked, as 'an anthropological rite'. 'The offending foreskin', *British Medical Journal*, 4 October 1952, p. 766.

[2] Gairdner has demonstrated much the same social class difference. He found that while about half the boys in the primary and secondary schools of Cambridgeshire had been circumcised, the proportion was 84 % among Cambridge undergraduates 'coming from the best public schools' (D. Gairdner, 'The fate of the foreskin: a study of circumcision', *British Medical Journal*, 24 December 1949, p. 1433).

[3] Studies by Glover and others in the past have shown that whereas, for example, about 20 % of children in elementary schools had been operated on by the age of 14, over 80 % of new entrants to Eton had had their tonsils removed. About 200,000 tonsillectomies are performed annually (J. A. Glover, 'Tonsillectomy in the school medical service. IV. Increased evidence in 1948', *Monthly Bulletin of the Ministry of Health*, March 1950, p. 62, and R. S. Illingworth, 'Discussion on the tonsil and adenoid problem', *Proceedings of the Royal Society of Medicine*, vol. 43, 1950, p. 317).

professional and middle classes are keener to go to their doctors and to hospital in the early or premonitory stages of disease; are more disposed to have vague symptoms investigated in hospital, and adopt a more positive attitude to elective surgery or other treatment for relatively minor conditions such as sinusitis.

To what extent such evidence reflects a higher incidence of certain conditions among social classes I and II it is impossible to say. Obviously, these are only hints of what may be happening in terms of demand on the National Health Service; much more research needs to be done before any definite conclusions could be drawn.

It cannot, therefore, be claimed that the material assembled in this appendix has done more than to throw a little light on some of the characteristics of the hospital population. This population is clearly a highly selected one, and it may change substantially in its characteristics from year to year. Nevertheless, it would seem that the social situation of the sick person—and particularly the older sick person—is playing a critical role in determining the pattern of demand for hospital treatment. The factor of age, by itself, is only one of many interrelated factors. The general conclusions of this study should, therefore, be borne in mind throughout in assessing the results of Appendix I in which, paradoxically, we attempt to study in isolation the implications for the National Health Service of an 'ageing population'.

APPENDIX I

POPULATION CHANGE AND THE FUTURE COST OF THE NATIONAL HEALTH SERVICE

1. INTRODUCTION

The purpose of this appendix is to examine the effects of certain projected changes in the size and age structure of the population of England and Wales on the current cost of the National Health Service. It is an extremely risky enterprise undertaken, with many misgivings, at the request of the Guillebaud Committee. As we saw from Appendix H, population change is only one of an immense number of variables affecting demand for medical care. The future course of many of these variables is quite incalculable. They become increasingly so as the speed and extent of scientific and technological change in medicine advance. The accumulating effect of these advances in knowledge—psychological and physical—on the practice of medicine is leading us to question the efficacy of many existing systems of organized medical care. The impact of science on medicine is giving rise to new ideas and new policies concerning the most fruitful ways of arranging medical care systems. At present, it would seem to many that we are attempting to fit these new ideas and policies into an outmoded organizational structure. At the centre of this is the crucial unanswered question of the future role of the hospital and, in particular, of in-patient care. The phase of reaction through which we now seem to be passing takes the form of: 'keep people out of hospital and other institutions—especially old people.' This is being said not only in relation to the elderly but in relation to mental illness, mental defect, maternity, tuberculosis, and other conditions. It is in some respects an expression of negativism in the face of the deeply disturbing implications of scientific and technical change. And it is often supported on the debatable grounds that the cost of institutional care has been rising steeply and will continue to do so.

Though this is not the place to discuss the future of institutional care in relation to medical needs it does not seem to us that the problem of applied scientific medicine is likely to be solved by putting up more barriers round the hospital—by isolating it still further from the community. What we have to seek out is the most appropriate and co-operative role for the hospital to play in the total process of preventing and treating ill-health. Approached in this light and not simply in terms of institutional and custodial care as an end in itself, it is possible to see the centre of gravity in hospital work shifting from in-patient treatment to community service. With the out-patient department becoming (in the words of the United States Magnuson Report) 'the focus of health services which promote health',[1] and thus helping to mobilize diag-

[1] United States President's Commission on the Health Needs of the Nation (Magnuson Commission), *Building America's Health*, vol. 1, *Findings and Recommendations* (Washington, Superintendent of Documents, 1953), p. 25.

nostic facilities, observation units, specialized therapeutic services, domiciliary consultant work and much else besides, the hospital will, in effect, be *servicing* the community's health and welfare agencies—and not least the family and the general practitioner—with a battery of scientific and technological aids. It will no longer be predominantly and primarily a hospital in the traditional sense.[1] Already it is possible to discern trends in this direction—in practice as well as in theory. The growing use and importance of out-patient departments; of diagnostic clinics; of the direct linking of general practitioners to diagnostic and hospital therapeutic facilities; of shorter periods of institutional care (dramatically illustrated in the case of mental illness); of day hospital and rehabilitation services (for example, the work of Dr Cosin at Oxford); of observation wards, home nursing units and other developments all bear witness to the need to reformulate the role and functions of the hospital.[2] The continuation and expansion of these trends may in time provide a solution to two of our most pressing contemporary problems; the shortage of nurses and other staff in mental and mental deficiency hospitals, and the shortage of hospital beds in general. But in the process of solving these problems we may create new problems or accentuate existing ones in the field of community care. The corollary of fewer hospital nurses and hospital beds may be more domiciliary nurses, more social and welfare workers of all kinds, more socially minded doctors at work in the community, more and better out-patient departments and so forth. In brief, less hospitalized sickness and shorter periods of institutional care mean more social service to support the family and the community.

These cursory generalizations concerning the future role of the hospital are offered simply as *one selected illustration*—selected because of the dominance of the hospital in National Health Service expenditure—of the difficulty of estimating the future effects of population change. The analysis in Appendix H provides a second illustration of the difficulty; it also serves to underline again the social elements—as distinct from the purely medical ones—in the problem of assessing hospital bed demand in relation to the size and structure of the population at risk for medical care.

In the following exercise, therefore, we assume throughout that certain estimated population changes are the only changes which will affect the current cost of the National Health Service. Everything else remains unchanged: the incidence and character of sickness and injury; standards of diagnosis; quantity and quality of treatment; the provision of resources in goods and services; the present level of unsatisfied demand; and the present proportionate distribution of consumer use of the Service by age, sex and many other factors.

[1] As discussed, for example, by Dr E. D. Churchill in N. W. Faxon (ed.), *The Hospital in Contemporary Life* (Harvard University Press, 1949).

[2] Some of these developments are referred to in the following: L. Z. Cosin, 'Statistical analysis of geriatric rehabilitation', *Journal of Gerontology*, vol. 7, 1952, no. 4, p. 570; Royal Society of Medicine, 'Function of the hospital outpatient department', *The Lancet*, 7 February 1953, p. 275; J. A. R. Bickford, 'Treatment of the chronic mental patient', *The Lancet*, 1 May 1954, p. 924; J. A. Gillet, 'Children's nursing unit', *British Medical Journal*, 20 March 1954, p. 684; J. Tizard and N. O'Connor, 'The occupational adaptation of high-grade mental defectives', *The Lancet*, 27 September 1952, p. 620.

There should be no need for us to emphasize the unreality of these assumptions nor the frailty of the statistical material on which we have based our calculations. We are not attempting to estimate what the future cost of the National Health Service is likely to be. With the limited facts at our disposal we are simply trying to gain some idea of the order of magnitude of additional cost which might result from these particular changes in population if nothing else changed.

The population projection which we use is the one made by the Government Actuary's Department in 1953.[1] The main assumptions adopted in this projection are:

Mortality. At ages under 45 death-rates decline steadily at such a rate that by 1978 they will be about one-half the rates experienced in 1953. At ages over 45 the assumed ratio of decline becomes progressively smaller as the age advances.

Natality. Annual births averaging 640,000.

Migration. Nil.

This is not the place to comment on the validity of these assumptions. There are reasons for believing that the assumption of declining mortality may be too optimistic.[2] We employ this projection not because we consider that it is more or less likely to be borne out in the future but because it is the most appropriate official calculation for our purposes. The figures are given in Table 91.

Table 91. *Projected civilian population of England and Wales*

(Million persons)

Age group	1951/2	1956/7	1961/2	1971/2	1971/2 less 1951/2
		Males			
0–14	4·98	5·14	5·11	4·75	−0·23
15–44	8·64	8·39	8·40	8·65	0·01
45–64	4·95	5·34	5·57	5·71	0·76
65–74	1·37	1·40	1·46	1·85	0·48
75 and over	0·61	0·66	0·68	0·77	0·16
		Females			
0–14	4·77	4·91	4·87	4·51	−0·26
15–44	9·44	9·09	9·00	9·08	−0·36
45–64	5·69	5·95	6·07	6·10	0·41
65–74	1·89	1·97	2·07	2·40	0·51
75 and over	0·97	1·13	1·23	1·43	0·46
Totals	43·31	43·98	44·46	45·25	1·94

This projection shows for the period of twenty years an increase of a million women and two-thirds of a million men aged 65 and over, and a decrease of half a million children aged under 15. The age group 15–64 increases by about 800,000—nearly all of them being men in the group 45–64. The total population increases by nearly two million or $4\frac{1}{2}$ %.

[1] General Register Office, *The Registrar General's Quarterly Return for England and Wales*, 4th qtr. 1953, no. 420, p. 29.

[2] R. M. Titmuss, 'Pension systems and population change', *Political Quarterly*, vol. 26, 1955, no. 2, p. 154.

2. THE HOSPITAL SERVICE

In the analysis undertaken for us by the General Register Office (Appendix H) the hospital population on census night 1951 was shown in certain age and sex groups. Children aged under one month were separately recorded. This was done to allow separate calculations to be made of future hospital confinements (see p. 159 below). In Table 92 we have, therefore, excluded all children aged under one month and, for each child, a woman aged 15–44. This rough correction means that we have removed the mothers and babies of confinement cases from the hospital population.[1] With this correction, the table shows the percentage of the civilian population in hospital on census night 1951 by age and sex.

Table 92. *Population in National Health Service hospitals on census night 1951 for reasons other than confinement as a proportion of the estimated average civilian population in 1951/2 (England and Wales)*

(Thousand persons)

Age group	Males			Females		
	Hospital population (i)	Civilian population (ii)	% (iii) (i) as percentage of (ii)	Hospital population (iv)	Civilian population (v)	% (vi) (iv) as percentage of (v)
1 month–14 years	20·608	4,980	0·4	16·168	4,770	0·3
15–44 years	66·772	8,640	0·8	67·091	9,440	0·7
45–64 years	52·916	4,950	1·1	64·209	5,690	1·1
65–74 years	22·105	1,370	1·6	32·085	1,890	1·7
75 years and over	16·372	610	2·7	30·715	970	3·2
Total	178·773	20,550	0·9	210·268	22,760	0·9

* Excluding contracted institutions.

As was depicted in Appendix H, the chances of being in any National Health Service hospital increases with age for both sexes. The increase for women is greater than that for men only after the age of 75. In this age group the proportion of persons in hospital is four times higher than at ages 15–44. In Table 93 we apply these proportions to the projected civilian population in Table 91.

On these estimates, the number of patients in hospital on any one day increases by 44,000 or 11 % in the twenty years. One-half this increase is accounted for by women aged over 65.

The present cost per day of a patient in hospital varies substantially and for a great many reasons. Even if it were possible to estimate approximately variations in cost according to the treatment provided, age and sex of patient and other factors, no data are available for such 'guesswork' purposes. However, we attempt here a tentative approach by applying the age and sex distribution of the population in seventeen different types of hospital to the

[1] It is only a very rough correction for it makes no allowance for mothers in hospital awaiting birth, multiple births, babies admitted to hospital for treatment and other factors.

cost per patient figures published in the Ministry of Health's Annual *Costing Returns*.[1] For the calculations shown in Table 94 we have used the 'total inclusive net cost per week of maintaining a patient'. These cost figures include out-patient as well as in-patient expenditure. We have, therefore, to assume that the age and sex demand on out-patient departments is the same as the age and sex structure of hospital in-patients. This is most unlikely to be so if only because of (to take one example) the differential demand on out-patient departments arising from industrial and road accidents. A further assumption we have to make is that there will be no change in the present variations of the 'vacant bed factor' as between different types of hospital throughout the period we are considering.

Table 93. *A projection of the National Health Service hospital population by age and sex (England and Wales)*

(Thousand persons)

Age group	1951/2	1956/7	1961/2	1971/2
	Males			
0–14	20·6	21·3	21·1	19·7
15–44	66·8	64·8	64·9	66·8
45–64	52·9	57·1	59·5	61·0
65–74	22·1	22·6	23·6	29·8
75 and over	16·4	17·7	18·3	20·7
	Females			
0–14	16·2	16·6	16·5	15·3
15–44	67·1	64·6	64·0	64·5
45–64	64·2	67·1	68·5	68·8
65–74	32·1	33·4	35·1	40·7
75 and over	30·7	35·8	38·9	45·3
Total	389·0	401·1	410·5	432·7
Percentage of 1951/2	100·0	103·1	105·5	111·2

The 1953 *Costing Returns* show that there are considerable variations in cost per week in different hospitals. In approximate weekly figures, the costs for some of the main types of hospital are: teaching hospitals £28, general hospitals £20 and, at the other end of the expenditure scale, mental and mental deficiency hospitals £4 and chronic sick hospitals £6. 10*s*. By applying these differential cost figures to the population by age and sex of different types of hospital we derive a rough average cost per week of patients in each age and sex group for all hospitals. The results are shown in Table 94.

In addition to those already stated, two further assumptions in these calculations need to be made explicit. The first is that, in terms of the age and sex structure of the hospital population, census night 1951 was representative of the financial year 1951/2. The second is that for each individual hospital of a particular type the weekly cost does not vary with the age and sex of the patient. Both assumptions are dubious; both could only be checked with the aid of extensive research.

[1] Ministry of Health, *Hospital Costing Returns year ended 31st March, 1953* (H.M.S.O. 1954). This return has been used as it contains more information than the return for 1951. We are concerned with the relative differences rather than with the absolute cost figures.

Table 94. *Estimated average cost per week of patients by age and sex in all types of hospital (England and Wales 1951/2)*

Age	Males	Females
1 month–14 years*	£14. 12s.	£15. 0s.
15–44 years	£9. 5s.	£10. 7s.
45–64 years	£10. 0s.	£9. 2s.
65–74 years	£10. 13s.	£9. 6s.
75 years and over	£10. 15s.	£9. 12s.

* Excluding confinement costs (see p. 156).

However, on the basis of these questionable assumptions, Table 94 shows that a child patient costs on an average about 50% more than an adult. The main reason for this is that most child patients are not to be found in the cheaper type of hospital.[1] Among adults, there is a slight increase in costs with advancing age and there are slight differences between the sexes. Bearing in mind, however, the assumptions adopted it is doubtful whether these small differences can be accepted. It is arguable, for example, that patients in the working age groups receive on the average substantially more active (and thus more costly) treatment—especially surgical treatment —than older patients in general and teaching hospitals. If this is so then these estimates will have exaggerated the hospital cost effects of an ageing population.

Table 95 of projected hospital costs is based on the application of the average cost figures in Table 94 to the projected hospital population given in Table 93.

Table 95. *Projection of hospital costs to 1971/2 (excluding confinements)*

Year	Percentage of 1951/2
1951/2	100·0
1956/7	103·1
1961/2	105·3
1971/2	110·6

The increase in costs over the twenty years is shown to be of the order of 10%. It has worked out at a slightly lower percentage than the figure for increased hospital beds, mainly because of the effects of a declining child population.

These cost estimates only relate to the field of expenditure covered by the Ministry's *Costing Returns*.[2] The cost of specialists, goods bought centrally, and those items in the tables to Appendix B which do not come under the heading of hospital maintenance (items 32–41) are excluded. In the absence of any data about age and sex differences in the consumption of these items (which constitute about 10% of total hospital expenditure) we have allocated these costs in the same way as for the bulk of hospital expenditure. By so doing, we

[1] Whereas 36% of the total hospital population was in mental and mental deficiency hospitals in 1951 only about 1% of children in hospital were in such hospitals in the same year.

[2] Ministry of Health, *Hospital Costing Returns*, annual.

have again probably exaggerated the effects of an ageing population because it may be that, on the whole, specialists do not devote proportionately as much time to the care of the elderly as they do to younger patients.

In the official population projection it was assumed that births will average out at 640,000 a year throughout the twenty years. We have, therefore, assumed that there will be no change in the proportion of hospital confinements and that the cost of such confinements will remain constant. By multiplying the number of children aged under one month recorded in the census figures by the average weekly cost of maternity hospitals we derive a weekly confinement cost for 1951/2 of around £230,000. In annual terms, this gives a figure of about £12 million. This is added to the main hospital costs in Table 96.

Table 96. *The effects of estimated population changes on the current net cost to public funds of the hospital service (England and Wales)*

(£m. in 1951/2 prices)

Year	Net cost	Percentage of 1951/2
1951/2	228·9	100·0
1956/7	235·6	102·9
1961/2	240·4	105·0
1971/2	251·9	110·0

The order of magnitude in the additional costs to 1971/2 attributable to population changes thus works out at 10% for the hospital service.

3. THE EXECUTIVE COUNCIL SERVICE

(a) *General medical services*

Part of the expenditure under this heading is for the maternity medical services. This expenditure has to be related to the estimated number of future births and, therefore, remains constant up to 1971/2. The bulk of the remaining expenditure is represented by the central pool from which general practitioners are paid. On the assumption that, broadly speaking, a per capita system of payment operates in the future, the future cost will follow the trend of total population. There is a considerable body of evidence which suggests that older people (and especially women) make heavier demands on the general practitioner than people of working ages.[1] It is conceivable that

Table 97. *The effect of changes in the total population on the current cost of the general medical services (England and Wales)*

(£ m. in 1951/2 prices)

	1951/2	1956/7	1961/2	1971/2
Maternity medical services	2·3	2·3	2·3	2·3
Other, mainly central pool	48·2	48·9	49·5	50·4
Total	50·5	51·2	51·8	52·7

[1] See, for example, E. M. Backett, J. A. Heady and J. C. G. Evans, 'Studies of a general practice (II): the doctor's job in an urban area', *British Medical Journal*, 16 January 1954, p. 109.

these differences—if they continue—might lead to the institution of differential per capita payments. But we cannot allow for such a change in this exercise, and Table 97, therefore, shows the estimated cost of the general medical services on a total population basis.

The total cost rises by just over £2 million by 1971/2.

(*b*) *The pharmaceutical service*

An inquiry carried out by the Social Survey in February and March 1952 gave figures of medical consultations resulting in a prescription for different age groups.[1] These are shown in Table 98.

Table 98. *Rates of medical consultations resulting in a prescription (England and Wales, February/March 1952)*

(Weekly rate per 100 persons)

Sex	
Males aged 21 and over	6·3
Females aged 21 and over	8·4
Age group	
21–34	5·0
35–44	6·2
45–54	7·5
55–64	8·1
65 and over	11·7

For ages over 21, prescriptions were more frequent among women than men (separate age rates were not given). For both sexes combined the prescription rate increased with age.

For what it is worth and because no other information exists we use this material in the following calculations. We should, however, first make clear some of the more important inadequacies and sources of error. As regards this particular inquiry, the investigation covered only two unrepresentative months (it was suspended by the Government on grounds of economy). In consequence, therefore, the sample was smaller than had been planned. In more general terms, however, it is necessary to bear in mind that such crude prescribing data take no account of variations in the cost of prescriptions as between different age, sex and income groups; of other sources of obtaining drugs through the National Health Service, and of seasonal and yearly fluctuations according to the incidence of sickness. No data at all are available for children and young people. Because of these particular *lacunae* we have had to assume, in constructing Table 99, that the prescribing rate for those under the age of 21 is similar to that for adults aged 21–34. This assumption may introduce a substantial amount of error—possibly in the direction of exaggerating the effects of an ageing population. A number of studies of general practitioner consultation rates by Backett, Logan and others have shown that such rates are higher for the age group 0–14 than for 15–44 and,

[1] P. G. Gray and A. Cartwright, 'Who gets the medicine?', *Applied Statistics*, vol. 3, 1954, no. 1, p. 19.

in some respects, than for 45–64[1]. If, therefore, consultation and prescription rates are closely correlated (as seems likely) then it follows that a decline in the proportion of children in the population should, other things being equal, mean a decline in the average prescription rate. This would offset to a limited extent the effects of a higher proportion of old people.

A further assumption we have had to adopt for Table 99 is that the difference in the prescription rate for men and women is proportionately applicable to all ages over 21.

Table 99. *The effect of changes in population on the current net cost to public funds of the pharmaceutical service (England and Wales)*

(£ m. in 1951/2 prices)

Year	Net cost	Percentage of 1951/2
1951/2	44·1	100·0
1956/7	45·1	102·3
1961/2	45·8	103·9
1971/2	47·2	107·0

The estimate shows that the cost of the service increases by 7 % over the twenty years.

(c) *The dental service*

For our estimates under this heading we use certain data published by the Ministry of Health.[2] These show the distribution of fees paid by public funds in the first half of 1952 in respect of dental services for four age groups in the population. The work of the school dental service is excluded; as also are dental services provided at hospitals.

Table 100. *Proportion of fees paid by executive councils for the dental service by age groups (England and Wales, first half 1952)*

Age	%
0–14	7
15–20	12
21–44	57
45 and over	24

After applying these proportions of cost to the population in 1951/2 it appears that dental services for a child cost 4*s.* per head per year, for persons aged 15–44 23*s.* per head, and for persons aged 45 and over 9*s.* per head. It should be pointed out that this information is very crude. The age groups used are too broad; it is not known how much error is introduced by studying only six months' experience, and we have had to assume that there are no

[1] E. M. Backett, J. A. Heady and J. C. G. Evans, 'Studies of a general practice (II): the doctor's job in an urban area', *British Medical Journal*, 16 January 1954, p. 109, and W. P. D. Logan, *General Practioners' Records*, General Register Office Studies on Medical and Population Subjects, no. 7 (H.M.S.O. 1953).

[2] *Report of the Ministry of Health for the year ended 31st December, 1952, Part I*, Cmd. 8933 (H.M.S.O. 1953), p. 59.

differences in cost between the sexes.[1] However, from these data we have estimated in Table 101 the effect of changes in population.

The effect of changes in age structure is to decrease the cost of the dental service as the total increase in cost by 1971/2 ($2\frac{1}{2}$%) is less than the increase in the total population ($4\frac{1}{2}$%).

Table 101. *The effect of changes in population on the current net cost to public funds of the dental service (England and Wales)*

(£ m. in 1951/2 prices)

Year	Net cost	Percentage of 1951/2
1951/2	29·9	100·0
1956/7	29·8	99·7
1961/2	29·9	100·0
1971/2	30·7	102·7

(*d*) *The supplementary ophthalmic service*

An inquiry carried out by the Social Survey in June 1951 showed the percentage of the population wearing spectacles.[2] From these figures we have constructed Table 102.

Table 102. *Proportion of the population by age and sex wearing spectacles (England and Wales, June 1951)*

Age	Males	Females
0–14	5·6	6·1
15–44	22·4	39·5
45–64	73·0	85·6
65–74	93·6	93·1
75 and over	90·1	91·0

The proportion of spectacle wearers increases sharply with age—especially for women in the younger age groups. After applying these proportions to the projected population we proceed, in Table 103, to estimate future costs[3] using as a basis the current cost to public funds of the supplementary ophthalmic service.

[1] So far as dental consultations are concerned, this assumption appears to be incorrect. According to Social Survey data for 1947/9, women aged 16–64 averaged more dental consultations than men, especially younger women (General Register Office, *The Registrar General's Statistical Review of England and Wales for the year 1949, Supplement on General Morbidity, Cancer and Mental Health* (H.M.S.O. 1953), p. 47).

[2] Either occasionally or all the time (P. G. Gray, 'Who wears spectacles?', *The Lancet*, 22 September 1951, p. 537). In general, these rates seem higher than might be expected. For example, the table shows that nearly 86% of women aged 45–64 wear spectacles occasionally. The proportion wearing spectacles all the time is, however, only about a third in this age group.

[3] An analysis by age of pairs of glasses authorized under the Service is published in the *Report of the Ministry of Health for the year ended 31st December, 1953, Part I*, Cmd. 9321 (H.M.S.O. 1954), p. 94. We believe that the calculations we have made on the basis of estimates of wearers of spectacles are preferable to calculations that could be made from these figures. The demands on the Service in the first six years are unlikely to represent correctly the long term trend.

Table 103. *The effect of changes in population on the current net cost to public funds of the supplementary ophthalmic service (England and Wales)*

(£ m. in 1951/2 prices)

Year	Net cost	Percentage of 1951/2
1951/2	7·90	100·0
1956/7	8·15	103·2
1961/2	8·37	105·9
1971/2	8·82	111·6

On this estimate the cost increases by 11½% by 1971/2—or 7% more than the increase in the total population. The important assumptions that have had to be made here include the following: that the frequency of changing spectacles does not vary with age and sex; that the cost to public funds of eye testing, repairs and other services is proportionately distributed in the same way as in Table 102, and that there are no differences in the proportion of people requiring two pairs of spectacles at the same time.

(*e*) *Administrative costs*

These are assumed to follow the trend of total expenditure on the executive council services.

4. LOCAL AUTHORITY SERVICES

No comprehensive information is available which might be adopted as a detailed guide to the age and sex distribution of users of these services. The estimates we have framed are, therefore, exceedingly rough. In general, it would appear that a considerable part of the total cost is devoted to confinement and the care of mothers and young children. In estimating future costs we have therefore related the following to the estimated number of future annual births: the midwifery service (£4·5 million in 1951/2); other maternity and child welfare services (£7·7 million in 1951/2); 90% of the health visiting service[1] (£2·6 million in 1951/2); and some part of the home help and other services. In all, we have related a total of £15½ million in this way. The rest of the expenditure is concerned with the ambulance service, home nursing, home help and other domiciliary services. In the absence of any reliable information we have distributed the cost of these services by age and sex in accordance with the structure of the hospital population in 1951.

Table 104. *The effect of changes in population on the current net cost to public funds of the local authority services (England and Wales)*

(£ m. in 1951/2 prices)

Year	Net cost	Percentage of 1951/2
1951/2	35·1	100·0
1956/7	35·7	101·7
1961/2	36·2	103·1
1971/2	37·3	106·3

[1] In 1951/2, 90% of all visits were to mothers and children.

On these obviously insecure foundations we have estimated the future cost of the local authority services in Table 104.

The increase in cost by 1971/2 comes out at about 2% more than the increase in the total population.

5. CENTRAL AND MISCELLANEOUS EXPENDITURE

The small residual costs under this heading are assumed to increase in the same proportion as that for all expenditure on the National Health Service.

6. CONCLUSION

All the foregoing estimates are brought together in Table 105.

Table 105. *The effect of changes in population on the current net cost to public funds of the National Health Service (England and Wales)*

(£ m. in 1951/2 prices)

Service	1951/2	1956/7	1961/2	1971/2
Central and miscellaneous	3·1	3·2	3·2	3·4
Hospital services	228·9	235·6	240·4	251·9
Executive council services:				
(*a*) Administration	2·5	2·5	2·6	2·6
(*b*) General medical services	50·5	51·2	51·8	52·7
(*c*) Pharmaceutical service	44·1	45·1	45·8	47·2
(*d*) Dental service	29·9	29·8	29·9	30·7
(*e*) Supplementary ophthalmic service	7·9	8·2	8·4	8·8
Total executive council services	134·9	136·8	138·5	142·0
Local authority services	35·1	35·7	36·2	37·3
Grand total	402·1	411·3	418·3	434·6
Percentage of 1951/2	100·0	102·3	104·0	108·1

As a whole, the cost of the Service increases steadily by 8% after twenty years. About half this increase (4½%) is attributable to the projected rise in the total population of England and Wales (using the official projection figures). Changes in age structure account for the balance of the increase in cost of 3½% or an additional £14 million by 1971/2.

These changes may be demonstrated in another way. Table 106 shows the cost per head of the Service in certain age and sex groups.

Table 106. *The current net cost of the National Health Service to public funds per head in age and sex groups (England and Wales 1951/2)*

(£ in 1951/2 prices)

Age group	Males	Females
0–14	£8. 15*s*.	£8. 9*s*.
15–44	£7. 10*s*.	£7. 17*s*.
45–64	£9. 7*s*.	£9. 11*s*.
65–74	£13. 16*s*.	£13. 10*s*.
75 and over	£20. 16*s*.	£22. 7*s*.

The cost per head does in general increase with age, but the amount of the increase appears to be much less than has been supposed, and it is not significant until after the age of 65. Because of the high costs involved in the birth and care of children,[1] the cost per head of the under 15 age group is higher than that for the 15–44 group.

The really big increase with age does not occur until 75 and over. The cost per head of this group is about three times as high as that for the 15–44 group.

In Table 107 we have translated these figures into percentages of the total cost by age and sex of the National Health Service.

Table 107. *The current net cost of the National Health Service to public funds in age and sex groups (England and Wales 1951/2)*

(£ m. in 1951/2 prices)

	Males		Females		Total	
Age group	Cost	%	Cost	%	Cost	%
0–14	43·6	23	40·2	19	83·8	21
15–44	64·7	35	74·2	34	138·9	35
45–64	46·3	25	54·3	25	100·6	25
65–74	18·9	10	25·5	12	44·4	11
75 and over	12·7	7	21·7	10	34·4	9
Total	186·2	100	215·9	100	402·1	100

This table makes clear why, on the basis of all these estimates, the effects of the projected age changes in the population on the cost of the National Health Service are relatively insignificant. In 1951/2 the estimated cost of persons aged 65 and over was about £80 million. On a projected increase of some 1½ million persons in this age group by 1971/2 the additional cost works out at only another £30 million. Set against a total annual expenditure of some £400 million this represents a small proportionate increase.

At the present time, it should be noted, a higher proportion of the cost of the National Health Service is devoted to the medical care of the under 15 age group (including confinements) than on the medical care of persons aged 65 and over. A lower birth-rate during the next twenty years is thus likely to have a significant effect on the cost of the Service. But this, of course, is to ignore the profound importance of the social factors discussed in Appendix H—among which the role of the smaller family in relation to the care of sick people is perhaps crucial.

In all the estimates put forward in this appendix no account has been taken of possible changes in the proportions of the population who are married, single, widowed and divorced. The essential data are not available. It was concluded in Appendix H, however, that these factors are likely to exercise in the future an important effect on demand for hospital and institutional care—especially at the older ages. According to the assumptions adopted by the Government Actuary, the great bulk of the increase in the number of people of pensionable ages is made up of married men and women. So far as hospital

[1] It should be noted that, for reasons given earlier, the whole cost of confinement has been allocated to the age group 0–14.

demand is concerned, among the group of old people who now make by far the largest demands (single men and women) there is not likely to be any material increase in the population at risk during the next twenty years if the Government Actuary's projections turn out to be anywhere near the truth. To look at the facts of future population changes from these aspects of 'dependency' and the need for institutional care obviously puts a different—and perhaps even less gloomy—complexion on the pattern of future demand.

This appendix has been full of qualifications, reservations and guarded assumptions; and rightly so. The calculations we have made have been uneasily made. Where calculation has been impossible we have been obliged to employ little more than suggestion. We began with an acknowledgement of faults in material and method; we end on the same note.

SUMMARY

1. The main part of this study comprises an analysis of expenditure on the National Health Service during the period 1948–54. This analysis has raised a number of important questions of two kinds; one relating to changes in particular types of cost, the other to (what we broadly term) the social role of the National Health Service. These questions have been singled out for special attention in certain of the appendices. For this reason, this summary does not follow the plan of the book. The matters dealt with in the appendices have been summarized at the appropriate points in the main body of the book. Only the main conclusions of this study are briefly summarized here.

2. At the time this study was undertaken a general impression was abroad of a great and continuing rise in the cost of the Service. The view was also widely held that an 'ageing population' might eventually lead to a situation in which the cost of the Service might threaten to get completely out of control (p. 4). It is part of the purpose of this book to examine these beliefs.

3. The aim of our statistical analysis has been to throw light on the major factors responsible for changes in the rate of expenditure during the period under review, so far as possible in a form which may be of use in any attempt to assess possible future costs (p. 5).

4. Most of the material on which this study rests consists of the official records of expenditure (published and unpublished) by the central government, hospital authorities, executive councils and local authorities. These records have had to be extensively rearranged and reclassified to provide statistics in a form suitable for our purpose. They have been supplemented with records of prices, of quantities of goods and services purchased, of manpower, and with demographic statistics, the latter including a special tabulation of the hospital population in 1951 carried out from Census records by the General Register Office. (Pp. 18–19.)

5. Our main concern is with the cost of the National Health Service in terms of current productive resources to public authorities as a group, distinguishing current from capital costs so far as the records permit. This has involved (*a*) measuring the absorption of goods and services by the activities of the National Health Service in each period and, conversely, distinguishing these from expenditures which do not involve the absorption of current productive resources, or which involve their absorption in another period; (*b*) eliminating payments *between* different types of public authority, so as to arrive at a measure of transactions between public authorities as a whole and the rest of the economy; (*c*) deducting from gross expenditures the amounts recovered in charges from beneficiaries of the Service; and (*d*) distinguishing, at least in a broad way, between expenditure on goods and services for immediate consumption in the provision of services (i.e. current expenditure) and expenditures relating to benefits spread over a future period of years (capital expenditures). (Pp. 11–13.)

6. The period from 5 July 1948 (when the National Health Service came

into operation) to 31 March 1949 was in many respects a period of transition and development. We have therefore taken the financial year 1949/50 as the normal base year for the measurement of trends. (P. 23.)

7. The current cost of the National Health Service in productive resources was £371½ million in 1949/50. In subsequent years it rose by roughly £15 million each year, reaching £430½ million in 1953/4. (P. 26.)

8. The rise of £59 million in the current net cost of the Service over the four years was the combined result of a larger rise (£77 million) in gross costs, offset by a saving of £18 million arising from new or increased charges to beneficiaries. (P. 58.)

9. Expressed as a proportion of total national resources (the 'gross national product') the current net cost of the service fell from 3¾% in 1949/50 to 3¼% in 1953/4. (P. 60.)

10. During the period under review there was a considerable general rise in prices. We have tried to estimate the effect of price increases on the cost of the Service, recalculating expenditures at constant (1948/9) prices. The current net cost of the Service, expressed in 'real' terms in this way, was only £11 million greater in 1953/4 than in 1949/50. Thus, the net diversion of resources to the National Health Service since 1949/50 has been of relatively insignificant proportions. (P. 63.)

11. There was a rise of nearly 2% in population during the period under review. Allowing for this and for changes in the age structure of the population, the cost *per head* at constant prices was almost exactly the same in 1953/4 as in 1949/50. (P. 72.)

12. Trends of expenditure have been very different in different parts of the Service. Between 1949/50 and 1953/4 net current expenditure on the hospital services rose by £71 million, and that on local authority services by £11 million, while expenditure on executive council services fell by £24 million. The movement of total Health Service expenditure thus represented the combined result of these divergent trends, a fact which needs to be taken into account in considering possible future trends. (P. 27.)

13. A major part of the rise in hospital expenditure was attributable to rising prices (£41½ million of the £71 million increase from 1949/50 to 1953/4), but the rise in the real volume of goods and services purchased (£29½ million at 1948/9 prices) was also substantial. (P. 29.)

14. Throughout the period under review, revenue from charges has contributed only insignificant amounts towards the gross cost of the hospital service; little more than 1% in fact. (P. 27.)

15. Approximately 60% of the increase in resources purchased for the hospitals (£17½ million of the £29½ million) consisted of medical goods and services. (P. 30.)

16. In the hospital service, the cost of medical staff increased by £4 million between 1949/50 and 1953/4. This rise is attributable to a substantial increase in the number of staff employed, both part-time and whole-time; to the additional costs of more part-time (relative to whole-time) consultant work and to the growth of the domiciliary specialist service. (P. 128.)

17. The role of part-time service at the consultant grade has been increasing. This is particularly true if mental and mental deficiency hospitals are excluded.

There has probably been a net transfer of consultants from whole-time to part-time service. Service below the consultant grade is generally on a whole-time basis; this is becoming more frequent. (P. 121.)

18. The additional costs of part-time consultant work arise from the fact that on the average the part-time specialist is paid more than the whole-timer per notional unit of work. A special investigation in one region showed that this amounts to about 33 % on the average. In cases where specialists contribute only a few half-days to the hospital service part-time service can cost as much as 80 % more than whole-time service. When the maximum part-timer only does the number of hours for which he is paid, part-time service is still substantially more expensive. But when the maximum part-timer undertakes the same duties as a whole-timer there is little difference between the costs falling directly on the National Health Service. (Pp. 123–6.)

19. The domiciliary specialist service has expanded substantially. It may have cost £300,000 more in 1953 than in 1949. The use made of this service varies greatly in different areas. The reasons for this include the possibility that larger demands are made in areas with older populations, with greater proportions of the higher social classes, and with more part-time specialists available in such areas. (P. 126.)

20. The increase in labour services as a whole accounts for three-quarters of the increase in resources used in the hospital service at constant prices. The categories of staff which increased most were nurses and domestic staff. (P. 33.)

21. As a whole, hospital staffs were provided with board, accommodation and other services which cost at least £5 million more than the staff paid for them. (P. 111.)

22. In 1951, about 90,000 staff were resident. For all types of hospital, the proportion of resident staff to inmates was at least 22 % in that year. It varied from over 50 % for all teaching hospitals to 6 and 7 % for mental deficiency and mental hospitals respectively. It is suggested that this factor of resident staff may be as important in any consideration of hospital accommodation needs during the next decade or so as any likely changes in the national population or its age composition. (P. 104.)

23. Trading activities play a not inconsiderable role in hospital expenditures. In the South West Metropolitan Region farms and gardens roughly cover their cost. Canteens and shops are run at a profit. (Pp. 114–15.)

24. Current net expenditure on executive council services fell by £24 million between 1949/50 and 1953/4. Of this, £17 million represented a transfer of cost to beneficiaries by means of the charges introduced in 1951/2, but there was also a decline of £7 million in the *gross* cost of the services. (P. 35.)

25. The different executive council services show different trends in expenditure. While the pharmaceutical service and the general medical service each increased between 1949/50 and 1953/4 by £6 million, expenditure on the dental service fell by £24 million and that on the ophthalmic service by £13 million. (Pp. 35–6.)

26. The rise of £6 million over the four years in the cost of the general medical service was entirely due to a rise in 'price', i.e. to the increased cost

per patient-year resulting from the Danckwerts award to general practitioners. (Pp. 36–7.)

27. The rise of £6 million in the net cost of the pharmaceutical service resulted from a rise of £12 million in gross expenditure, offset by £6 million in revenue from charges. The rise in gross expenditure on pharmaceuticals is roughly attributable to the following factors: 35% to an increase in the amount prescribed, 35% to the substitution in prescriptions of proprietary for non-proprietary articles, a *decline* of 10% to lower rates of payment to pharmacists, and an increase of 40% to other factors (including the cost of ingredients). (Pp. 38–9.)

28. The decline of £24 million in the cost of the dental service over the four years was partly accounted for by £6 million revenue from the charges introduced in 1951 and 1952, but the major part (£18 million) resulted from a fall in gross expenditure. Of this figure, £13 million was the effect of the reductions in rates of payment to the dentists. The principal area of saving was in the cost of dentures which declined substantially. There is evidence that the decline in work done by the service was not simply due to the introduction of charges; demand was already falling before charges were introduced after the abnormal arrears of war-time needs had been at least partly dealt with. (Pp. 40–2.)

29. The fall of £13 million in the net cost of the ophthalmic service was partly accounted for by £4 million revenue from charges, but mainly by a decline in gross expenditure of £9 million. This decline was due almost entirely to a reduction in the amount of work done, chiefly in the supply of spectacles. From the evidence examined it would seem that some decline would have taken place even if charges had not been introduced. (Pp. 42–5.)

30. A major part of the rise in expenditure by local authorities (£7 million of the £11 million increase from 1949/50 to 1953/4) was the result of rising prices. The rise of £4 million in the real volume of goods and services purchased occurred principally in the ambulance, domestic help and home nursing services. (Pp. 45–7.)

31. The amount of capital expenditure by the National Health Service has been relatively small throughout the five years. This expenditure has two components, expenditure on building up stocks which has fluctuated between £4 million and minus £2 million in different years, and a fairly steady rate of about £12 million a year of capital expenditure on fixed assets. (Pp. 48–9.)

32. As prices of building work and other capital assets have risen substantially over the period, the rate of capital expenditure in real terms has progressively declined. As a proportion of national fixed capital formation, the fixed asset expenditure of the Health Service has been small and declining (from 0·8 to 0·5% in the four year period). (Pp. 49–50.)

33. Fixed capital expenditure is almost wholly attributable to hospital work. About 10% of expenditure has been for new hospitals and major extensions and a further 21% of expenditure has been for ward accommodation. Expenditure on accommodation for staff has accounted for 16% of the total. (P. 50.)

34. The rate of fixed capital expenditure on hospitals has averaged about one-third of the pre-war rate in real terms. At this rate it would take over

200 years to replace the present stock of hospitals. Approximately 45 % of all hospitals were originally erected before 1891; many are regarded by expert opinion as seriously in need of replacement. For this to be achieved in any measurable period the present rate of capital expenditure would have to be multiplied several times. (Pp. 51–4.)

35. There are considerable opportunities in the hospital service for the use of capital expenditure to save current expenditure. Evidence has been collected to illustrate the nature of these opportunities. (Pp. 133–6.)

36. An analysis of the hospital population on the census night 1951 has drawn attention to the importance of demographic and other social factors which influence the demand for hospital care. (P. 139.)

37. Compared with the demands made by single men and women (and, to a lesser extent, the widowed) the proportion of married men and women in hospital even at age 65 and over is extremely small. (P. 140.)

38. Among married men and women, the rise in the proportion in hospital with advancing age is not at all dramatic; it does not reach very high levels even after age 75. (P. 140.)

39. For all types of hospital and in relation to their numbers in the total adult population, the single, widowed and divorced make about double the demand on hospital accommodation compared with married people. (P. 140.)

40. About two-thirds of all the hospital beds in the country occupied by those aged over 65 are taken by the single, widowed and divorced. (P. 146.)

41. The bulk of the population of mental and 'chronic' hospitals are single people. Of the single and widowed men and women aged over 65 needing hospital care most are to be found in these two types of hospital. The married state appears to be a powerful safeguard against admission to hospitals in general and to mental and 'chronic' hospitals in particular. (P. 146.)

42. Among other factors of demand for hospital care which are outside the power of the National Health Service to control, accidents and injuries represent one of the more important elements in the total demand. (P. 148.)

43. In comparative terms, men aged 25–64 in social classes I, II and III appear to be making proportionately full use of National Health Service hospitals whereas semi-skilled and unskilled men of these ages in classes IV and V are making fewer demands than might have been expected from their relatively higher morbidity and mortality rates. (P. 149.)

44. We calculate that a higher proportion of the cost of the National Health Service is devoted to the medical care of the under 15 age groups (including confinements) than to the medical care of persons aged 65 and over. (P. 165.)

45. An analysis of the Government Actuary's estimates of the population of Great Britain in 1979 shows that among those who make by far the heaviest claims on hospital accommodation, the number of single women of pensionable ages will actually decline, while the number of single men of such ages will increase by only a negligible figure. (P. 147.)

46. At the request of the Guillebaud Committee we have estimated the order of magnitude of additional future costs to the Service arising *solely* as a result of projected population change taken as an independent, isolated

factor. Changes in age structure *by themselves* are calculated on a number of hazardous assumptions to increase the present current cost of the National Health Service by 3½% between 1951/2 and 1971/2. A further increase of 4½% is attributable to the projected rise in the total population of England and Wales (using the official projection figures). In total, therefore, population changes *by themselves* are not likely to exert an appreciable effect on the future cost of the National Health Service. (P. 164.)

INDEX

PUBLICATIONS OF THE NATIONAL INSTITUTE OF ECONOMIC AND SOCIAL RESEARCH

published by

THE CAMBRIDGE UNIVERSITY PRESS

None of the Institute's publications is sold direct by the Institute. They are available through the ordinary booksellers, and inquiry can be made of the Cambridge University Press, Bentley House, 200 Euston Road, London, N.W. 1.

ECONOMIC & SOCIAL STUDIES

*I *Studies in the National Income, 1924–1938*
Edited by A. L. BOWLEY. Reprinted with corrections, 1944. pp. 256. 15*s.* net.

*II *The Burden of British Taxation*
By G. FINDLAY SHIRRAS and L. ROSTAS. 1942. pp. 140. 15*s.* net.

*III *Trade Regulations and Commercial Policy of the United Kingdom*
By THE RESEARCH STAFF OF THE NATIONAL INSTITUTE OF ECONOMIC AND SOCIAL RESEARCH. 1943. pp. 275. 15*s.* net.

*IV *National Health Insurance: A Critical Study*
By HERMANN LEVY. 1944. pp. 356. 18*s.* net.

V *The Development of the Soviet Economic System: An Essay on the Experience o Planning in the U.S.S.R.*
By ALEXANDER BAYKOV. 1946. pp. 530. 37*s.* 6*d.* net.

VI *Studies in Financial Organization*
By T. A. BALOGH. 1948. pp. 328. 30*s.* net.

*VII *Investment, Location, and Size of Plant. A Realistic Inquiry into the Structure of British and American Industries*
By P. SARGANT FLORENCE, assisted by W. BALDAMUS. 1948. pp. 230. 18*s.* net.

VIII *A Statistical Analysis of Advertising Expenditure and of the Revenue of the Press*
By NICHOLAS KALDOR and RODNEY SILVERMAN. 1948. pp. 200. 18*s.* net.

IX *The Distribution of Consumer Goods*
By JAMES B. JEFFERYS, assisted by MARGARET MACCOLL and G. L. LEVETT. 1950. pp. 430. 40*s.* net.

X *Lessons of the British War Economy*
Edited by D. N. CHESTER. 1951. pp. 260. 25*s.* net.

XI *Colonial Social Accounting*
By PHYLLIS DEANE. 1953. pp. 360. 50*s.* net.

* The publications marked with an asterisk (*) are at present out of print.

XII *Migration and Economic Growth*
By BRINLEY THOMAS. 1954. pp. 384. 42*s*. net.

XIII *Retail Trading in Britain, 1850–1950*
By JAMES B. JEFFERYS. 1954. pp. 490. 50*s*. net.

XIV *British Economic Statistics*
By CHARLES CARTER and A. D. ROY. 1954. pp. 192. 21*s*. net.

OCCASIONAL PAPERS

*I *The New Population Statistics*
By R. R. KUCZYNSKI. 1942. pp. 31. 1*s*. 6*d*. net.

II *The Population of Bristol*
By H. A. SHANNON and E. GREBENIK. 1943. pp. 92. 12*s*. 6*d*. net.

*III *Standards of Local Expenditure*
By J. R. HICKS and U. K. HICKS. 1943. pp. 61. 4*s*. 6*d*. net.

IV *War-time Pattern of Saving and Spending*
By CHARLES MADGE. 1943. pp. 139. 10*s*. 6*d*. net.

*V *Standardized Accountancy in Germany*
By H. W. SINGER. Reprinted 1944. pp. 68. 6*s*. net.

VI *Ten Years of Controlled Trade in South-Eastern Europe*
By N. MOMTCHILOFF. 1944. pp. 90. 10*s*. 6*d*. net.

*VII *The Problem of Valuation for Rating*
By J. R. HICKS, U. K. HICKS and C. E. V. LESER. 1944. pp. 90. 7*s*. 6*d*. net.

VIII *The Incidence of Local Rates in Great Britain*
By J. R. HICKS and U. K. HICKS. 1945. pp. 64. 10*s*. 6*d*. net.

*IX *Contributions to the Study of Oscillatory Time-Series*
By M. G. KENDALL. 1946. pp. 76. 10*s*. 6*d*. net.

X *A System of National Book-keeping illustrated by the Experience of the Netherlands*
By J. B. D. DERKSEN. 1946. pp. 34. 8*s*. 6*d*. net.

XI *Productivity, Prices and Distribution in Selected British Industries*
By L. ROSTAS. 1948. pp. 199. 25*s*. net.

XII *The Measurement of Colonial National Incomes: An Experiment*
By PHYLLIS DEANE. 1948. pp. 173. 18*s*. net.

XIII *Comparative Productivity in British and American Industry*
By L. ROSTAS. 1948. pp. 263. 25*s*. net.

XIV *The Cost of Industrial Movement*
By W. F. LUTTRELL. 1952. pp. 104. 18*s*. net.

XV *Costs in Alternative Locations: The Clothing Industry*
By D. C. HAGUE and P. K. NEWMAN. 1952. pp. 73. 12*s*. 6*d*. net.

XVI *Social Accounts of Local Authorities*
By J. E. G. UTTING. 1953. pp. 81. 16*s*. net.

XVII *British Post-war Migration*
By JULIUS ISAAC. 1954. pp. 294. 30*s*. net.

STUDIES IN THE NATIONAL INCOME AND EXPENDITURE OF THE UNITED KINGDOM

Published under the joint auspices of the National Institute and the Department of Applied Economics, Cambridge.

1 *The Measurement of Consumers' Expenditure and Behaviour in the United Kingdom, 1920–1938*, Vol. 1
By RICHARD STONE, assisted by D. A. ROWE and by W. J. CORLETT, RENEE HURSTFIELD, MURIEL POTTER. 1954. pp. 448. £5. 5*s*. net.

3 *Consumers' Expenditure in the United Kingdom, 1900–1919*
By A. R. PREST, assisted by A. A. ADAMS. 1954. pp. 196. 42*s*. net.

5 *Wages and Salaries in the United Kingdom, 1920–1938*
By AGATHA CHAPMAN, assisted by ROSE KNIGHT. 1953. pp. 254. 55*s*. net.

Register of Research in the Social Sciences and *Directory of Institutions*

Editor: FEODORA STONE

No. 5.	1946/47.	pp. 104.	12*s*. 6*d*. net.
No. 6.	1948/49.	pp. 155.	15*s*. net.
No. 7.	1949/50.	pp. 175.	15*s*. net.
No. 8.	1950/51.	pp. 174.	15*s*. net.
No. 9.	1951/52.	pp. 188.	15*s*. net.
No. 10.	1952/53.	pp. 213.	25*s*. net.
No. 11.	1953/54.	pp. 168.	25*s*. net.

The annual issues of the *Register* are available directly from Cambridge University Press, Bentley House, 200 Euston Road, London, N.W. 1, or from the U.S.A. Branch, 32 East 57th Street, New York 22, N.Y.

Some Accounting Terms and Concepts—A Report of a Joint Exploratory Committee. 1951. pp. 46. 3*s*. net.

Published jointly for the Institute of Chartered Accountants and the National Institute of Economic and Social Research.

For EU product safety concerns, contact us at Calle de José Abascal, 56–1°, 28003 Madrid, Spain or eugpsr@cambridge.org.

www.ingramcontent.com/pod-product-compliance
Ingram Content Group UK Ltd.
Pitfield, Milton Keynes, MK11 3LW, UK
UKHW010049140625
459647UK00012BB/1707

* 9 7 8 1 3 1 6 6 0 6 8 8 9 *